PROMOTION

RONALD SERIES ON MARKETING MANAGEMENT

Series Editor: **FREDERICK E. WEBSTER, Jr.**
The Amos Tuck School
of Business Administration
Dartmouth College

Promotion

A Guide to Effective Promotional Planning, Strategies, and Executions

DAN AILLONI-CHARAS

A RONALD PRESS PUBLICATION

JOHN WILEY & SONS

New York • Chichester • Brisbane • Toronto • Singapore

Library of Congress Cataloging in Publication Data:

Ailloni-Charas, Dan.
   Promotion: a guide to effective promotional
planning, strategies, and executions.

(Ronald series on marketing management, ISSN 0275-875X)
   "A Ronald Press publication."
   Includes index.
   1. Marketing. 2. Sales promotion. I. Title.
II. Series.
HF5415.A36   1984   658.8′2   83-26017

ISBN 0-471-08060-8

Printed in the United States of America

10 9 8 7 6 5 4 3 2 1

*To the Promotion Marketing Association of America
and its quest for professionalism in Promotion*

Series Editor's Foreword

As business encounters the challenges of the 1980s, top management is increasingly looking to marketing for sharpened competitive effectiveness. The emphasis on strategy formulation and financial performance at the corporate level that characterized the previous decade is now evolving toward a broader concern for total strategic management. This sharpens the focus on marketing as the prime vehicle for implementing corporate and business strategies.

Marketing management is the most dynamic of the business functions. Marketing must respond to the everchanging marketplace and the constant evolution of customer preference and buying habits, technology, and competition. Marketing management continually grows in sophistication and complexity as developments in management science are applied to the work of the marketing manager.

The books in The Ronald Series on Marketing Management have been written for managers. They combine a concern for management application with an appreciation for the relevance of developments in such areas as behavioral science, financial analysis, and mathematical modeling, as well as the insights gained from analyzing successful experience in the marketplace. The Ronald Series on Marketing Management is thus intended to communicate the state-of-the-art in marketing to managers.

Both marketing practitioners and academic teacher/scholars have contributed to the works in this series which now includes coverage of advertising management, sales promotion, public relations, consumer research, industrial marketing, brand loyalty, financial analysis for marketing decisions, the impact of government regulation, selling and field sales management, new product development, and market planning for new industrial products. As new insights based on research and managerial practice in marketing management are brought forward, this series will continue to offer new entries that convey the state-of-the-art in a manner that permits managers to extend their own experience by using new analytical frameworks, and which acquaint students of marketing with the work of the professional marketing manager.

FREDERICK E. WEBSTER, JR.

Hanover, New Hampshire
September 1982

Preface

The practice of promotion as a distinct professional field of endeavor is slowly coming into its own. For too long, promotional expenditures have lacked a central focus requiring both overall, integrated strategic planning and total accountability for performance. Unlike advertising, which from the start enjoyed a clear functional identity that was further enhanced by the advent and growth of the advertising agency, promotional efforts were (and still are, to a large extent) fragmented between different departmental budgets.

The monies spent on promotion by consumer packaged goods companies and, increasingly, by all corporations (both consumer and industrially oriented) have been steadily outpacing expenditures on advertising. Few corporations to date have fully recognized this new reality by developing centralized promotion management and monitoring the various promotional efforts as part of an overall strategic plan. Adherence to the principle of "unity of command" insofar as the conduct of promotional efforts is concerned was, and generally remains, spotty.

Given this context, this book provides a theoretical and executional framework conducive to a better understanding of the role of "incentives" in influencing consumer and trade behavior in the marketplace. Further, it discusses their effective management in line with corporate strategic considerations.

The recent gathering of practitioners and academicians at Babson College under the joint aegis of the Marketing Science Institute and the Promotion Marketing Association of America was only one of the growing number of indications that both the study and the practice of promotion are gathering momentum. Hopefully, this book is but one of the first in a series devoted to the advancement of promotion as a part of business studies in our colleges, and the training of those entering the field at the corporate level.

I am greatly indebted to the several corporations which graciously searched their archives and contributed meaningful illustrations of their work to this book. Special thanks to General Foods, Procter & Gamble, Coca-Cola, Hunt-Wesson, General Mills, and Best Foods.

Also, for their encouragement and support, my personal thanks to Robert Wehling of Procter & Gamble, Daniel Haas of Coca-Cola USA, David Levi of General Mills, Steve Rothschild of Del Monte, Wesley Harju of Best Foods, Bill Shaw of General Foods, Dick Aycrigg of Nielsen Clearing House, Jim Comber of Hunt-Wesson, Russell Bowman of John Blair Marketing, Tony Lunt at the Association of National Advertisers, and Paul Pierce and Frank Dierson at the Promotion Marketing Association of America, and above all, to Yvonne Hoo Mook, my associate, who managed to survive through several drafts of this book before we acquired a word processor.

DAN AILLONI-CHARAS

Rye Brook, New York
March 1984

Contents

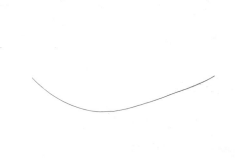

PROMOTION

PART ONE

PROMOTION: PERSPECTIVE AND PLANNING

ONE

Promotion: A Conceptual Overview

The post–World War II advent of the marketing concept has profoundly changed the way American enterprises in general and the consumer packaged-goods industries in particular conduct business. Cardinal to the marketing concept is its emphasis on consumer satisfaction, with the enterprise, in all its facets, geared to the achievement of consumer satisfaction by means of effective marketing strategy. Under this concept, positive consumer behavior in the marketplace is the overriding concern for all marketing endeavor, from the inception of the product or service to its ultimate distribution.

MARKETING AND THE EMERGENCE OF THE MARKETING CONCEPT

Paul Mazur, in the early 1950s, first suggested that the marketing raison d'être resides simply in delivering a standard of living to society.[1] This definition, which declared the centrality of the consumer in the marketing scheme, dovetails with the American Marketing Associations's definition of marketing advanced in the late 1940s, which identified marketing as "the performance of business activities that direct the flow of goods and services from producer to consumer or user."[2] The two definitions taken together

3

describe the direction and structure of the modern enterprise, whose primary functions, as noted by Peter Drucker, are marketing and innovation.[3] The modern corporation's adoption of the marketing philosophy has led to fundamental changes in the organization and the mandate given the enterprise in the second half of the 20th century.

Robert J. Keith illustrated such changes in his 1960 article that traced Pillsbury's transition to a marketing concept form of management.

> In today's economy the consumer, the man or woman who buys the product, is at the absolute center of the business universe. Companies revolve around the customer, not the other way around. Growing acceptance of this consumer concept has had, and will have, far-reaching implications for business, achieving a virtual revolution in economic thinking. As the concept gains even greater acceptance, marketing is emerging as the most important single function in business.[4]

J.B. McKitterick, at the time manager of Marketing Services Research Service at General Electric, defined the marketing function's main task in a management concept as "not so much to be skillful in making the customer do what suits the interest of the business as to be skillful in conceiving and then making the business do what suits the interest of the customer."[5] Frey and Dixon's 1952 study of the advertising industry and the marketing environment at the time led them to following conclusions.

> The marketing concept is variously defined but in general encompasses recognition of at least the following:
>
> 1. Marketing efficiency is basic to the success of an enterprise, and the marketing plan is the beginning of the total company planning effort.
>
> 2. The proper starting point for marketing is prospective customers.
>
> 3. Marketing includes all functions that help to stimulate and satisfy customer demand.
>
> 4. Prerequisite to optimum marketing efficiency is persistent thinking and action in terms of a properly proportioned and integrated mix of marketing components and elements.

5. The desired mix is spelled out quantitatively and qualitatively in a written program, with performance standards clearly expressed.

6. The organization for marketing must be such as to achieve efficient programming of the desired mix and satisfactory integration of the components in the execution of the program.[6]

Perhaps the most succinct definition of marketing under the marketing concept was suggested by Charles E. St. Thomas: "Marketing is a way of managing a business so that each critical business decision is made with a full and prior knowledge of the impact of that decision on the customer."[7]

MARKETING STRATEGY AND MARKETING MIX

The implementation of the marketing concept through the development and execution of appropriately managed plans of action focuses on the strategic aspects of the process itself. Marketing strategy, in Smith's words, "becomes the factor that integrates and coordinates the many and diverse tactics to be stipulated in the marketing plan itself."[8] Marketing management, in this context, is viewed as responsible for the decision-making process, whereby it "cooperates directly in the formulation of top level policies [designed to integrate] marketing with all the other functional activities of the business."[9]

Marketing strategy, whether short- or long-term, provides both direction and structure to the complex of elements involved in the marketing decision-making imperatives of the enterprise. It provides a central, logical construct to bring together operational objectives and the executional elements by which objectives may be attained. The term *marketing mix* was first used by Neil Borden who was apparently influenced in his choice of terms by James Culliton's earlier description of marketing managers as "mixers of ingredients," by virtue of their dealing with marketing "recipes" consisting of various action "ingredients" mixed together into targeted marketing plans.[10]

The definition of the several elements in the marketing mix varies. Oxenfeldt's definition in the early 1960s is perhaps the narrowest of the lot and the least acceptable in the 1980s.

> The "marketing mix" is composed of a large battery of devices which
> might by employed to induce customers to buy a particular product.
> The same devices are involved whether one is thinking of inducing
> altogether new buyers to purchase the product or of shifting
> customers from rival brands to one's own. These devices are here
> termed "sales promotion devices" and include a wide variety of
> instruments.[11]

The inclusion of all marketing mix elements under one "sales-
promotion devices" umbrella is simplistic—all elements of marketing action are designed to induce consumer and/or trade response to
marketing stimuli. The reason for a more careful separation of the
various elements into specific planning clusters is rooted in the
decision and action needs of the marketing plan.

A much broader classification of the elements in the marketing
mix is provided by Borden, who identifies 12 separate marketing-
planning variables: product planning; pricing; branding; channels of
distribution; personal selling; advertising; promotions; packaging;
display; servicing; physical handling; and fact-finding and analysis.[12]

A more popular definition of the marketing mix is advanced by
McCarthy, who has reduced it to four basic and broadly defined
variables all mnemnonically keyed to the letter *P*—*P*roduct, *P*lace,
*P*romotion, *P*rice. Says McCarthy:

> To limit the problem of choosing a marketing mix, without over-
> simplifying the problems, we settled on the four Ps—Product, Place,
> Promotion and Price—to identify the main decision areas of the
> marketing manager. The problem, in brief, is to satisfy our target
> customers with the *right* product, available in the *right* place,
> promoted in the *right* way, and available at the *right* price.[13]

MARKETING COMMUNICATIONS'
PROMOTION AND SALES PROMOTION

While all elements in the marketing mix could be conceived as parts
of a communication system designed to convey to consumers the
ultimate of satisfactions-in-use, the narrower and certainly the more
realistic view is to say that the marketing communications mix

actually consists of the subset of marketing tools that are primarily "communicational" in nature.[14]

The tools Kotler identifies as *promotools* are normally classified under promotion, one of McCarthy's four *P*s, and include, in broad strokes, advertising, personal selling, sales promotion, and publicity. Promotion is therefore defined as the complex of persuasive communications designed to inform and motivate people into the desired marketing behavior. The various promotools represent "complementary methods of communicating with consumers, [and] the marketing manager's job [is] to develop the most effective blend of these alternative methods.[15]

Pragmatically, however, and away from McCarthy's mnemnonics, we use the term *promotion* in a narrower context, identified by McCarthy, Kotler, and a host of other educators and some practitioners as *sales promotion*. Interestingly, throughout the years, both educators and practitioners have found it relatively simple to develop and work with definitions for *advertising* and *marketing*, but not for *sales promotion*. Much of the earlier, and to some extent continuing, confusion is illustrated by the definition of *sales promotion* that appeared in a popular marketing text in the early 1950s: "a term that is used in the business community with a wide variety of interpretations, there being no general agreement as to the exact number or type of specific activities included in its scope."[16]

Some professional groups, frustrated by definitions of promotion that seem too limited, have resorted to defining promotion as all marketing efforts other than advertising and personal selling. But in order to be useful for purposeful action, a definition must describe what a particular area of endeavor *is*, rather than what it *isn't*. Since we are dealing, in terms of promotional activities, with imperatives of action, the terminology we use must enable the specific planning of such activities into the strategic format prescribed by the marketing mix.

Alan Toop, a leading sales promotion practitioner in Great Britain, underlines some of the ambivalence still persisting to this day, in a book published in 1978:

> The origins of sales promotion are to be found in the concept of an incentive. The rationale was that if the target purchaser could not be

persuaded to buy your product or service by sales talk or advertising about the product's or service's own merits, then some additional incentive had to be offered. Perhaps a gift, or perhaps a discount, or perhaps a chance to win a big prize.

Implicit in this original concept of incentive was the idea that the product or service promoted could not sell itself on its own merits—that there was some inadequacy or failure that made it neceassary to assist sales by some extraneous means.

That the purchaser—having rejected the seller's attempt to persuade him or her to buy—needed forcing by means of the incentive. That the resulting purchase would be in some way against the buyer's better judgement. And that therefore nobody should be surprised if the purchase was not repeated once the incentive was no longer available.

From this original concept of "incentive" arose a number of bad and unfavorable opinions of sales promotion which have persisted among even some experienced and sophisticated marketing people until very recently, and which perhaps still underlie some continuing assumptions about the character of sales promotion compared and contrasted with media advertising.

For example: Sales promotion is short term and tactical in its effect; advertising is long term and strategic.

Sales promotion's effect can always be counteracted by an equal expenditure of sales promotional money by competitors. Whereas imaginative advertising can help define a personality for the advertised product/service which competitors will not be able to combat merely by matching advertising pound for advertising pound.

Sales promotion is liable to damage buyer's opinion of the product/ service that is unable to sell on its own merits. Advertising, in contrast, is designed specifically to improve opinions.

Sales promotion is a form of bribery, while advertising uses intellectual, emotional and moral persuasion to encourage free citizens to make a free choice. Honest advertising is thus a pillar of a free society, while sales promotion smacks of the graft and corruption of less perfectly organized societies.

Sales promotion is incentive; advertising is communication. Sales promotion can be managed competently by former street traders, fancy goods and novelty importers and reformed confidence tricksters. Advertising used to be for gentlemen, and is now for graduates of the Harvard Business School....

Indeed, the respects in which good advertising and good sales promotion come closest together is in their common and shared concern with communicating to the intended purchaser a favorable opinion of the product or service's personality.[17]

Even more recently, Kotler, in the 1980 edition of *Marketing Management,* suggests that "no single purpose can be advanced for sales promotion tools since they are so varied in form." However, he does identify three specific contributions made by sales promotion techniques to exchange relationships.

1. *Communication.*   They gain attention and usually provide information that may lead the consumer to the product.

2. *Incentive.*   They incorporate some concession, inducement, or contribution designed to represent value to the receiver.

3. *Invitation.*   They include a distinct invitation to engage in the transaction now.[18]

Frey and Dixon called sales promotion a "developing concept" in their study conducted for the Association of National Advertisers in the 1950s. Reviewing marketing trends in the previous 25 years, they concluded that

Sales promotion acquired a more specific identity although the term is still variously defined. The trend has been toward including in it certain activities, over and above those commonly associated with personal selling and advertising, that add to the impact of these two tools and increase the willingness and enthusiasm of sellers to sell and of buyers to buy.[19]

Frey's own definition of sales promotion comes closer to being actionable in 1980s terms:

Sales promotion is that component of the marketing mix that continually creates and applies materials and techniques provided by other components, *increases* the capacity and desire of salesmen, distributors and dealers to sell a company's product and makes consumers *eager* to buy it.[20]

Even under this definition, however, considerable vagueness remains about what such "materials and techniques" are. Much, one quickly finds out, depends on how a company views such techniques and who in the company, or outside it, executes action in this area. To some extent, promotion remains a matter of expediency in an organization rather than having a careful structure, which perhaps accounts for a great deal of the overall weakness of the promotional area.

A survey conducted by the Association of National Advertisers three times over the past 21 years identifies the assignment of responsibility for various promotional functions among different areas in the companies surveyed. The results of the latest survey still show no clear pattern, and very little agreement, among companies as to promotion techniques and assignment of planning and execution responsibilities. (Figures across do not add up to 100% because the tabulation covers internal departments only; companies' outside asssignments to advertising and promotion agencies and consultants are not included.)

Promotional Function	Responsibility by Internal Department				
	Advertising	Sales	Public Relations	Promotion	Other
Point-of-purchase displays	14%	11%	—	41%	4%
Consumer mailing	15	4	5	38	3
Trade mailings	8	41	—	27	3
A-M (Films, etc.)	25	35	15	8	
Co-op advertising	24	22	—	15	8
Consumer sweeps	13	7	—	47	2
Sampling	5	6	3	33	4
Couponing	10	7	—	40	4
Demonstration	8	18	2	24	1
Refunds/rebates	5	7	1	22	4
Trade promotion	11	41	1	22	4
Sales presentation	12	50	—	36	2
Product catalogs	7	43	—	20	5
Sales meetings/ conventions	13	76	—	20	4
Dealer sweeps	7	60	—	27	2
Premiums	14	12	—	47	1

The inclusion of promotion in the marketing mix as an integral part of the strategic plans drawn for either product or service runs into serious problems. It is clear that a better working understanding of promotion is required—one that brings together definition and implementation as well as a clear-cut determination of its position, in terms of both responsibility and accountability, within the corporate structure. With these goals in mind, we offer the following definition, which is representative of a number of recent attempts to reposition promotion within the marketing process.

> The study of promotion in marketing is the study of material inducements designed to accelerate selling and buying functions along the marketing process and to supplement the basic product/ service-in-use satisfactions anticipated by both ultimate and inter- mediate consumers.

An intriguing approach is presented by Beem and Shaffer, who view promotional inducements as a separate, unique mode of marketing. Breaking away from conventional theory, they suggest that

> Promotional inducements are not...just a special form of communi- cations. Indeed, promotional inducements are as distinct from communications as is the marketer's product or the marketer's price. They are a third mode or way in which marketers seek to manage the demand for their offers. The first mode is the basic offer, the way in which marketers shape their standard mix of substantive benefits to adapt as best they can to customer needs and wants. The second mode is persuasive communications, the way in which marketers shape messages to create or stimulate wants among target customers for their basic offer. The third mode, promotional inducements, is the way in which marketers trigger the actions they want from prospects by the offer of *extra* substantive benefits.[21]

The three modes reinforce each other, clearly functioning as a total process with bottom-line results obtained through the continuous interaction of all elements in the process.

> Each of the three modes plays a different role and has a different function for the marketer. To simplify: the basic offer meets customers' needs; persuasive communications create wants; and

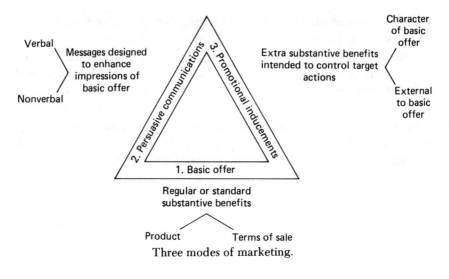

Verbal
Nonverbal

Messages designed to enhance impressions of basic offer

2. Persuasive communications

3. Promotional inducements

Extra substantive benefits intended to control target actions

Character of basic offer

External to basic offer

1. Basic offer

Regular or standard substantive benefits

Product   Terms of sale

Three modes of marketing.

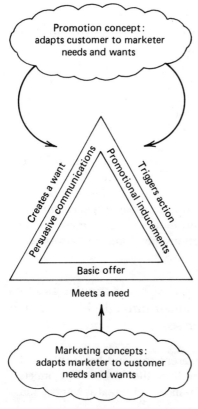

Promotion concept: adapts customer to marketer needs and wants

Creates a want

Persuasive communications

Promotional inducements

Triggers action

Basic offer

Meets a need

Marketing concepts: adapts marketer to customer needs and wants

Each mode plays a different role.

Each mode works through a different mechanism.

promotional inducement trigger particular customer actions. In general, a company strives to meet the needs or wants of potential customers better than substitutes that might be available. With the orientation to customers which we know as the *marketing concept*, the marketer adapts himself, shapes his basic offer to customer needs and wants. In contrast, a company uses persuasive communications and promotional inducements to adapt potential customers to its own needs and wants. We might call the persuasive communication and promotional inducement modes, working together, the *promotion concept*. Persuasive communications adapt customers to the marketer's needs by changing awareness, beliefs, or attitudes of the target customer toward the basic offer, so as to create a want for it. Promotional inducements motivate actions when, where, and in the manner which the marketer wants.[22]

What makes this approach to the positioning of promotional inducements particularly attractive is the current emphasis on trade-off analysis in the evaluation of consumer behavior in the marketplace. The utility inherent in the promotional offer, much as the utility provided by the product or service itself, can be viewed as a separate item of value whose presentation to the consumer is achieved and enhanced by means of persuasive communications.

Clearly an action-oriented competitive tool, promotion represents a critical strategic factor in the total marketing mix. Precisely for this reason, promotion can no longer be viewed and executed as a disjointed amalgam of separate events to be conducted primarily on the basis of immediate need, often downright panic, rather than on careful planning as part of the overall marketing plan. Eugene Mahany spotlighted this trend in a 1980 presentation to a Promotion Marketing Association of America (PMAA) seminar:

> It's always been part of the folklore that whereas advertising is strategic, promotion is always short-term and tactical. I'm reminded of the old story about the two workmen in the Middle Ages. Each was asked what his job was, and the one said, "I'm laying bricks," while the other one with the same job said, "I'm building a great catheral!" I think there is too much bricklaying and not enough cathedral building in the promotional field. [There is] a crying need for more strategic thinking, not just tactical executors. Too much *what* and *how*, not clearly enough *why*. "Management by objective" will be a discipline that will gradually appear in the lexicon of the promotional person.[23]

Conversely, in a more pragmatic, how-to vein, the following statement was adopted by the board of directors of PMAA at its meeting on March 18, 1981.

> Promotions should be considered one of several available marketing tools designed to build images and stimulate trial and/or continued use of products or services. Based on this definition, we believe that:
>
> 1. Promotions should offer the purchaser or user a meaningful value or an opportunity which he or she would not otherwise have.
>
> 2. Promotions should comply with the spirit as well as the letter of applicable laws. They should be in good taste and devoid of deceptive, misleading or ambiguous representations. They should be presented to the public in a straightforward, understandable manner.
>
> 3. Promotions, especially mail-in efforts, should provide a good balance between the quality and value of the offer versus the time and money involved to secure it.
>
> 4. Promotions involving premium or prize merchandise should ensure safety for all consumers, especially children, through premium

selection, appropriate quality control and inspection procedures, as well as through directions, advertising or other materials which may be necessary to illustrate proper use of the product.

5.   A good promotion should result in a positive experience for the consumer. Inadvertent errors or fulfillment problems should be promptly and vigorously corrected in each individual case.

Adds Ken Baumbusch, PMAA's president at that time, in the transmittal of the statement to PMAA members on April 10, 1981: "Promotion, as appropriately practiced, has come of age and deserves higher recognition and legitimacy than has been generally recognized."

ADVERTISING VERSUS PROMOTIONAL EXPENDITURES

A scan of the data on marketing expenditures in the 1970s quickly reveals a definite trend in relative spending levels for advertising and promotions. Corporate management has traditionally spent much of its time on those cost areas in the corporation subject to fastest increase, whether the increase is planned or not. Labor and energy stand out as prime illustrations of the common-sense emphasis in the 1970s. However, this rule has apparently not held true where advertising and promotion are concerned.

In 1974 the sales-promotion committee of the Association of National Advertisers (ANA) conducted a study designed to determine the relative levels of expenditure on advertising and promotion. The study was updated in 1975 and again in 1980 and yearly thereafter by Russel D. Bowman, currently vice president of John Blair Marketing.[24] The 1982 figures were published in *Marketing Communications*, a leading trade publication.

While expenditures for both advertising and promotion have continued to increase, more funds have been allocated to promotion than to advertising during the last few years, and the gap between the two is increasing. Promotion expenditures since 1975 have been growing at an annual rate of 12%, although advertising achieved only a 9% yearly growth rate. In terms of actual expenditures, about $65

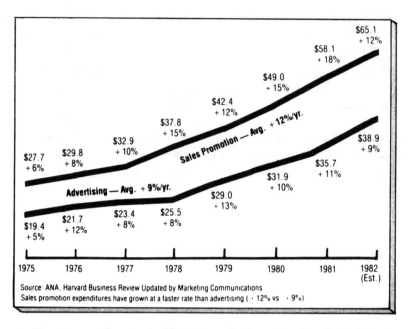

Year-to-year growth of advertising and sales promotion ($ in billions).

billion, representing about 60% of the combined advertising and promotion budget, was predicted to be the 1982 figure spent on promotion as against less than $40 billion (38% of combined budget) on advertising.[25] The increased emphasis on financial accountability of various company functions is helpful in determining how to position promotion, hence promotional efforts, within the proper strategic niche.

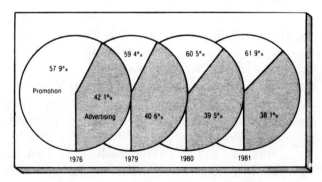

Split of advertising versus promotion budgets.

Clearly, whether supported by proper planning or not, promotional expenditures reflect the demand made on promotional efforts by realities in the marketplace. In terms of dollars and cents alone, the accelerated growth of such expenditures relative to advertising expenditures demonstrates that an increasingly larger burden for marketing action is being assumed by promotional programs motivated by the "new competition" that emerged in the early 1970s. The new competition is characterized by several vigorous trends.

1. *Increased Commoditization of Product Classes.* Earlier marketing writers stressed the "monopolistic competition" concept, whereby each product or service must enjoy a unique trait or group of traits that differentiates it from all other entries in the marketplace, which thereby allows the product or service to claim its own monopolistic space, however narrow. This concept eventually led to segmentation strategies, which are still widely observed, in form if not in substance. However, as product superiority claims narrowed, so did the available monopolistic advantages, to the point where most functional differentials ceased to have enough meaning to motivate the consumer to purchase. Through advertising, companies generally continue their attempts to substitute psychological claims for functional ones that are no longer sufficiently competitive, even though such efforts have little success. From the consumers' point of view, very few differences are perceived between products in many product classes. Certainly, there are no recognized differences in overall product performance within given price ranges. Consequently, many products are now regarded as commodities similar—if not totally identical—to many other products on the shelf in terms of anticipated product in-use satisfactions. With product classes thus commoditized and the resulting minimal difference in the product utility of individual entries, the burden in generating marketing action rests on other place, time, and price utilities.

2. *Rampant Me-Tooism.* The trends toward product commoditization have been further reinforced by the strategies of more and more manufacturers to tailor new products to approximate closely products already on the shelf. Such me-tooism is generally a more secure and less costly approach, but it forces advertising to carry the burden of creating distinct product identities in consumer

minds. As more and more similar products have taken their places on the shelf, all product distinctions have become blurred, which has led to a decline in brand loyalties, to the point where switching and substituting among products have become commonplace. Hence manufacturers' increasing reliance on material induce-ments—promotional tools—to bring the marketing process to fruition.

3. *Cluster Brands.*   An interesting outcome of me-tooism in the marketplace is the growth of the cluster brands phenomenon, whereby consumers "approve" the use of a number of brands within a given product class. On a given shopping trip, the consumer purchases the one brand that best fulfills, at that time, considerations other than product-in-use. The consumer's choice, may hinge on availability—of line, size, or type—or on some type of material inducements that tilts a consumer's selection to a particular brand. In such situations, ultimate purchase choices are increasingly influ-enced by promotional activites.

4. *Immediacy of Action.*   Under the new competition, the time available for effective marketing action is being increasingly telescoped within narrower spans of time. Since promotion as a marketing tool is more amenable to quick intervention in the marketplace than advertising, promotional activities have naturally grown faster than advertising.

Given these emerging trends, how corporate management views promotion within the marketing mix is critical, but it is questionable whether any meaningful shifts have occurred since a mid-1970 study conducted by Roger Strang. Among the more telling conclusions of that study, as reported by Alden G. Clayton, managing director of the Marketing Service Institute, were the following observations:

1.   Sales promotion is an orphan child of marketing. Both sales promotion *budgets* and sales promotion *objectives* are virtually ignored by senior management. Furthermore, evaluation of sales promotion *results* is seriously neglected. 17% of companies reported no budget at all for sales promotion research.

2.   Only about 1 in 5 companies uses corporate guidelines or senior management recommendations for allocating the *ratio* of advertising to sales promotion expenditures. In contrast, 4 out of 5 companies use

one or the other for determining *total* dollar expenditures for advertising and sales promotion.

3.   The impact of marketing factors which can influence decisions about advertising/sales promotion expenditures—and their relationship—varies enormously. In general, however, there seems to be a pattern which might be described as a "good news–bad news" response.[26]

Corporate management apparently has yet to recognize the major place of promotion as an area of marketing activity, requiring attention and encouragement as well as increased accountability.

PROMOTION AND PROFESSIONALISM
Keys to Growth

The following article is based upon a presentation at a recent Promotion Marketing Association of America "Promotion Update" by Robert L. Wehling, Division Manager, General Advertising, Procter & Gamble Company.

I want to spend a few minutes this morning talking to you about your role as a promotion marketing professional and about some of the challenges facing you as a promotion professional in the 1980's.

I will be trying to convince you of three fundamental points:

1. That you will do yourself, your company, and your industry a service by working harder than ever before to increase your knowledge, your sophistication, and your professional approach to the business.

2. That the most successful promoter in the future will be the principled promoter with a positive public image.

3. That the opportunities for all of us will be maximized if each of us commits himself to be an articulate spokesperson who effectively defends the promotion industry against unwarranted criticism and thus protects the right of principled marketers to use valid, ethical techniques to meet the needs and desires of their customers.

Now, let me expand on each of those points.

1

Increased Professionalism: In years past, I think it was possible for some people to be successful in the promotion business simply on the basis of their personality, their fast talking, or just having a good idea every now and then. I think I can illustrate this quickly by asking you what image first comes into your mind when I say the word "promoter"? Think about it. How many of you are picturing some kind of hustler who's ready to make you a good offer for a used car that was only driven on Sundays?

We, all of us in this room, are going to have to insure that when that same

Address given by Robert L. Wehling at the 1982 PMAA Promotion Update conference. (Reprinted with permission, *NCH Reporter*.)

*Bob Wehling
Division Manager,
General Advertising,
Procter & Gamble
Company*

question is asked in 1990, and let me remind you that's only eight years away. people will conjure up an image of a highly professional, very knowledgeable person who uses the latest technology to efficiently meet the needs of his or her customers. The speakers you will hear today and tomorrow will make it very clear why the promotion professionals with the most knowledge are the ones who will be the most successful in this new environment, but briefly, there are two reasons: technology and cost.

All of us need to learn how to take advantage of the tremendous opportunity represented by more sophisticated technology. The development of scanner data is a good example. Scanner systems provide extremely fine-tuned data. They make available weekly sales volume for a particular product. The effect of a coupon or other promotion doesn't get lost among all the other activity taking place during a Nielsen month — it stands out and can be measured versus the previous week and the post period.

Cable TV is another area of rapidly changing technology. As more and more American homes are equipped for cable, what opportunities arise for the professional promotion specialist? And what about the day when people not only own a personal computer, but a computer that is interactive with the television cable system and is used to order groceries from the regional food distribution center? Only the professional who has kept in the forefront of these developments will be able to use them to a business advantage and not become a victim of a more sophisticated marketplace.

When I talk about staying in the forefront of technological change, I'm not just talking about reading all the latest magazine articles and occasionally experimenting with a scanner market or cable effort. I mean a constant effort utilizing a variety of sources to develop **Actionable Learning** — learning which can translate into more efficient use of promotion dollars and better fulfill the desires of consumers.

You've all heard the statement in the past that more than 50% of our promotion dollars are wasted, but no one knows which dollars are productive. In today's economy, that's just not acceptable. Today's promotions must be cost effective and to accomplish that requires a detailed knowledge of your consumer, of the relative efficiencies of various promotion techniques, and an understanding of the packaging and delivery systems which can get your offer to your target customer at the lowest possible price. The tools exist to obtain this knowledge. Use them!

2

Principled Promotion: When you took your place this morning, you should have found a certificate which lists the Promotion Principles adopted by the PMAA Board of Directors last year (see page 4). Let's take a brief look at what these are:

— Promotions should offer the consumer a meaningful value or opportunity.
— Promotions should comply with the spirit and letter of applicable laws.
— Promotions should provide a good balance between the quality and value of the offer versus the time and money involved to get it.
— Promotions should ensure safety for all consumers.
— Good promotions should result in a positive experience for the consumer.

Said another way, principled promotions are those which are honest with the consumer as well as the trade. We need to ensure that, regardless of the

Address given by Robert L. Wehling (continued).

20

way in which we communicate our promotion offer, it is done so openly and honestly. Don't overstate or over-rate the offer. And this same honesty must be conveyed not only to our consumers, but to all we deal with — whether it be the trade, our sales force, jobbers, brokers, etc. Don't promise the trade that a promotion will do something it clearly won't. Remember, a good promotion will sell itself.

Our promotions must also be fair. Don't begrudge consumers a reward they're due by making unjustifiably high purchase requirements. Make sure your promotion offers are not dis-criminatory. And, above all else, make sure you always listen to what your consumers are telling you. If there are complaints about a promotion offer — follow up, find out what happened and help out. Rather than alienating this person, make him or her a loyal cus-tomer.

If you strive for honesty and fairness in all your promotion activities, you'll find that it equates to long-term benefits for you, your company and your in-dustry. Remember, the American con-sumer is smart, sophisticated and a darn good judge of value.

3

Promoting Promotion: Assuming that you are with me so far, and that you are committed to be a knowledgeable, professional and highly principled pro-motion marketer, the next task is to **promote promotion**.

What do I mean by promoting pro-motion? I mean that if we're to continue to be able to use the devices and tech-niques which have met the needs of our customers and built our business,

we're going to have to make sure that the consumer and the media have the correct facts about the value which these devices represent. We must be-come **advocates** of our profession. As you know, unwarranted attacks on various forms of promotion have been frequent over the past two years. Here are just a few examples:

— Retailers who suggest that coupon-ing is a form of discriminatory pricing which rewards the middle-class con-sumer at the expense of the poor.

— Retailers who resist price-off mer-chandise because it's too much trouble to handle.

— Economists who suggest that the elimination of all promotion would meaningfully reduce the cost of goods for all consumers.

— Legislators at the state and local level who place enough restrictions on some devices, such as sweepstakes and contests, so that it's not worth the time, effort and cost for many promoters to run an event which requires so many variations.

— Columnists, clubs and organizations which knowingly or unknowingly promote fraudulent coupon and refund practices.

I could go on, but I think these exam-ples collectively point out a variety of threats to the viability of basic promotion techniques. If we don't effectively re-spond to them, the list will grow and your freedom to provide your cus-tomers with promotions that work will be impaired.

So how do you respond? Let me suggest five specific steps.

1. First and foremost, accept, as of now, the personal responsibility to address any erroneous or unwarranted criti-cisms of promotion techniques and

Address given by Robert L. Wehling (continued).

the responsibility to challenge fraudulent practices wherever you see them. If there's an article in your local newspaper which attacks coupons or premiums, write a letter to the editor which presents a factual and persuasive response.

2. Secondly, ensure that all advertising, promotion and sales personnel in your company or agency are kept informed of both threats to the viability of promotion techniques **and** new facts which support the use of these techniques. Make sure, to the best of your ability, that they are equipped to respond to criticisms of promotion wherever they encounter them. Materials available through PMAA should be very helpful to you in this effort.

3. Third, work with and through the PMAA office in the effort to present the positive aspects of promotion to the public. Provide PMAA with reports of criticisms, attacks or potentially restrictive legislation. Provide PMAA with articles or facts that are helpful in rebutting these threats. Help us help you. The more data each of you share with the PMAA office, the more help the organization can give to other members.

4. You can be creative. Listen carefully and objectively to the attacks on promotion. Study the fraudulent practices. Examine the legislative restrictions. Then ask yourself how new techniques or innovative twists of old techniques can be used to effectively address these issues. You'll be doing yourself, your company and your industry a great favor.

5. Insure that your company or agency follows the code of ethics prepared by PMAA. Treat consumers fairly in **all** promotion activities, etc.

Let me repeat: You can't leave it up to someone else to ensure the viability of promotion devices and the freedom to promote in line with the desires of your customers. You have to take a personal responsibility to ensure a climate in which the use of creative promotions, which help all of our customers through changing and inflationary times, will prosper.

To sum up, I'm urging each of you to commit yourself to these actions:

1. First, to maximize your knowledge and skills. Become a top-notch promotion marketing professional.

2. Secondly, don't just take your copy of the PMAA promotion principles back to the office — put them to work. Infect your colleagues with the same sense of purpose. Use them in all your promotion planning and execution. Put them upon your wall to show everyone where you stand. Your business will benefit.

3. Finally, be an articulate and persuasive spokesperson on behalf of the promotion marketing industry. Commit yourself to "promote promotion." By so doing, you'll help to maximize the range of options open to you to meet the needs and desires of your customers.

Address given by Robert L. Wehling (continued).

PROMOTIONS IN THE THIRD MEDIUM[27]

Marketing is often viewed as a consumption process whereby anticipated satisfactions are met through the use of a product or service purchased in the marketplace—hence the marketing concept that the enterprise must optimize its efforts toward achieving effective marketing performance. Individual decisions to purchase a specific product or service, whether directly executed or through a purchasing agent, are expressions of purposeful behavior. Therefore, the key to a successful marketing strategy is a focus on the totality of the marketing process, which will help bring about behavioral expressions favorable to a product or service and also encourage the timely exercise of such behavior in the marketplace.

Within the marketing process, the critical position of communications is apparent, both as vehicles of information and as primary persuaders for the desired action, the consumer's purchase of a particular product. When marketing is viewed as a process and the marketing strategy centers on activities designed to culminate in repeated consumer usage through continued repurchasing, three information and persuasion stages can be identified:

Prepurchase stage

Purchase stage

Usage stage

In this context, consumer-oriented marketing communications consist primarily of advertising and promotion. While advertising concentrates, at least initially, on creating "sales in the mind," thus providing for "future demand" in the marketplace, promotions carry a certain urgency that require a more immediate response, in effect, bringing about "now" demand.

Advertising, which is central in the prepurchase stage, relies on a variety of broadcast and print media to:

Create awareness

Provide knowledge

Motivate use desires

through primary emphasis on product/service factors.

Promotion, however, exercises the stronger hold in the purchase stage. Operating mostly through the Third Medium, promotion

Amplifies the decision to buy and

Accelerates the execution of the buying decision

through primary emphasis on purchase factors.

Since the point of purchase is regarded as a full-fledged medium under Stratmar's Third Medium appellation, a review of its parameters is in order. The Third Medium is the medium to which millions of consumers are exposed everyday before they pass through check-out counters. The Third Medium is multidimensional; where the print media use a single dimension and the broadcast media two, at point of purchase, the consumer can try, touch, taste, smell, and ask questions about a product in the pursuit of custom-tailored answers about content and performance.

Importantly, the Third Medium is the arena for final decisions as to the purchase or nonpurchase of a product, where presell inclinations turn into buying realities. In addition to consumer readiness to buy in the Third Medium, as motivated by prepurchase advertising and accelerated by promotional efforts, product availability coupled with adequate trade support must also be present if the purchase decision is to be carried out successfully.

Finally, following the purchase stage, we reach the usage stage, where the product/service must prove its ability to provide the satisfaction anticipated from its use/consumption that was instrumental to its purchase. While the product-in-use performance is central at this stage, both advertising and promotion continue to play an important role in the build-up and maintenance of the desired consumer behavioral pattern—*advertising,* by reinforcing the initial use/purchase decision and *promotion* through aggressive follow-up activities designed to maintain the continuity of the consumer franchise.

Integrating all three stages in a single time continuum, a simple sequential schematic can effectivley represent the consumer buying process. Note that while advertising stresses the long-term, promotion, with its emphasis on immediacy, stresses the short-term. In the

Prepurchase stage Advertising	Purchase stage Promotion	Use stage Advertising and Promotion
Broadcast and print media	Point of purchase: the third medium	All media
Primarily product/service emphasis	Primarily purchase emphasis	Advertising
Creates awareness Provide knowledge Motivates use desires	Amplifies decision to buy Accelerates purchase	Reinforcement of use/purchase decision
		Promotion
	Product availability	Promotional follow—up to maintain continuity of franchise
	Purchase decision	Repurchase — Repurchase
	Trade support	
Future intent to buy	Now decision to buy	Decision to continue usage
Future demand Stress on long—term	Now demand Stress on short—term	Routinized purchases Inclusion in core group—brand loyalty

The three information and persuasion stages of marketing.

usage stage, however, both advertising and promotion emphasize continued usage through routinized purchasing to the point where such behavior can develop into long-term brand loyalty.

PUSH-PULL FUNCTIONS

The many changes since the end of World War II in the distribution stage of marketing have also increased the need for promotional efforts. Particularly critical are the changes which have taken place in the retailing structure in the Third Medium.

Both push and pull pressures are exercised on the point of purchase. The push function consists of all the activities required for proper pipelining to the retail floor. Obviously, the consumer cannot buy a product that is not in distribution on the retail shelf except through alternative channels of distribution, such as direct mail or door-to-door.

From the retailer's point of view, his most valuable contribution to the marketing process is the amount of shelf and floor space he makes available for the products he agrees to carry as a service to customers. Turnover per square foot of shelf or floor then becomes a yardstick by which the retailer can determine the profitability of any of the items stocked. Equally important are the mark-up levels the retailer can set on the merchandise bought from suppliers. While product turnover is directly related to consumer takeout, markup levels can be manipulated through push efforts. Though trade advertising plays a role in sensitizing the retailer to the products offered by various manufacturers, the bulk of push efforts are promotional in nature. Push efforts are discussed elsewhere in this book and include money and merchandise inducements designed to improve the retailer's bottom-line performance.

Pull efforts are totally directed toward consumer takeout. The higher the demand for a given product, the better the turnover experienced by the product at retail and the higher the likelihood that the product will be kept in distribution by the trade—hence on the shelf—for a longer period of time. While advertising is critical in motivating use desires on the part of consumers, promotion—effective in the Third Medium—amplifies the decision to buy and accelerates the carrying out of the actual purchase.

It should be noted though, that pull efforts, however strong, are often merchandised to the trade in order to obtain push results. Clearly, the efforts spent by a manufacturer against consumers in order to increase their takeout of particular products should be considered by a retailer when carrying that manufacturer's products. Such efforts will influence the retailer's depth of assortment as well as the shelf position–preferential or otherwise–assigned to the products.

Conversely, push efforts will influence pull results. Better and deeper assortment, better shelf position, price, and other featuring activities, all brought about through the award by manufacturers of special allowances and inducements will often result in their products being given an edge at retail over competing products and hence accelerate their sell-through. Obviously intertwined, both push and pull functions must be carefully considered in planning marketing action in the Third Medium.

Changes in the Retailing Outlet

Both self-service and self-selection by consumers in retail outlets came into their own in the late 1940s and early 1950s, and these changes were far-reaching. Without an intermediary—a floor salesperson—to assist in the selling and selection functions in most retail stores, manufacturers had to develop alternative ways to cause the consumer to reach out for and buy their products in preference to competing items.

Advertising, with its emphasis on generating "future demand" by concentrating on "sales in the mind," the "total" product appearance and appeal—including its packaging—and point-of-purchase promotional activities, all had to step into the gap in order to facilitate consumer buying activity in the retail store.

Branding realities further accelerated manufacturers' concerns with their ability to maintain a properly competitive stance on the retail floor. Retailer-controlled brands proliferated throughout the 1950s and 1960s into the 1970s and gained distribution at the expense of manufacturer brands. Generic brands are a more recent phenomenon, but they still manage to obtain considerable shelf space, particularly with items in product classes that have become at least semicommoditized while also being highly price-elastic. Since the emphasis in both cases is on perceived value-in-use and hence on retail prices, counteractions taken by manufacturers to secure their continued franchise are relying heavily on both money and merchandise inducements designed to improve the competitive value perceptions of consumers.

More recently, with the advent of cash-register scanners that read the universal product codes (UPC) at check-out and thus provide continuous movement and inventory levels for all items in distribution, manufacturers are faced with ever-increasing pressures to

PROMOTION MARKETING ASSOCIATION OF AMERICA

STATEMENT OF BASIC PROMOTION PRINCIPLES

Promotion should be considered one of several available marketing tools designed to stimulate trial and/or continued use of products or services.

Based on this definition, PMAA believes that:

1. Promotions should offer the purchaser or user a meaningful value or an opportunity which he or she would not otherwise have.

2. Promotions should comply with the spirit as well as the letter of applicable laws. They should be in good taste and devoid of deceptive, misleading or ambiguous representations. They should be presented to the public in a straightforward, understandable manner.

3. Promotions, especially mail-in efforts, should provide a good balance between the quality and value of the offer versus the time and money involved to secure it.

4. Promotions involving premium or prize merchandise should ensure safety for all consumers, especially children, through premium selection, appropriate quality control and inspection procedures, as well as through directions, advertising or other materials which may be necessary to illustrate proper use of the product.

5. A good promotion should result in a positive experience for the consumer. Inadvertent errors or fulfillment problems should be promptly and vigorously corrected in each individual case.

This statement was adopted by the Board of Directors of the PMAA on March 18, 1981.

PMAA's basic promotion principles. (Reprinted with permission.)

accelerate the movement of their products through the retail store if they wish to maintain their permanent home on the shelf. Obviously, the retailer is able to read quickly the performance of each of the items stocked, and since space on the retail floor is finite, products unable to meet minimum profitability criteria will be replaced by other products promising better turnover and markups. To safeguard their listings at retail, manufacturers will have to accelerate consumer takeout beyond the levels that were acceptable earlier. Promotional efforts in the Third Medium will be increasingly burdened by the survival demands of products. Were they to be delisted by a retailer they would be in imminent danger of being shut out of the market forever.

NOTES

1. Paul Mazur, *The Standards We Raise* (New York: Harper & Row, 1953).
2. Ralph S. Alexander (Chairman), "Report of the Definitions Committee," *Journal of Marketing*, October 1948, pp. 202–217.
3. Peter Drucker, *The Practice of Management* (New York: Harper & Row, 1954).
4. Robert J. Keith, "The Marketing Revolution," *Journal of Marketing*, January 1960, p. 35.
5. J.B. McKitterick, "What Is the Marketing Management Concept?" in *Marketing Management and Administrative Action*, edited by Stuart Henderson Britt and Harper W. Boyd Jr. (New York: McGraw-Hill, 1963), p. 18; originally published in *The Frontiers of Marketing Thought and Science*, edited by Frank M. Bass (Chicago: American Marketing Association, 1957).
6. Albert W. Frey and Kenneth R. Dixon, *The Advertising Industry* (New York: Association of National Advertisers, Inc., 1958), pp. 9–10.
7. Charles E. St. Thomas, "A Basic Guide to Marketing for the Smaller Company," *Industrial Marketing*, June 1959; condensed in *Modern Marketing Thought*, edited by J. Howard Westing and Gerald Albaum (New York: Macmillan, 1964), pp. 2–5.
8. Wendell Smith, "Factors That Shape the Organization," in *Concepts For Modern Marketing*, edited by Ralph L. Day (Scranton, PA: International Textbook Co., 1968), p. 21.
9. Robert Bartels, *The Development of Marketing Thought* (Homewood, IL: Richard D. Irwin, Inc. 1962), pp. 214–215.
10. Neil H. Borden, "The Concept of the Marketing Mix," *Journal of Advertising Research*, June 1964, pp. 2–7; James W. Culliton, *The Management of Marketing Costs* (Boston: Harvard University Graduate School of Business Administration, 1948).
11. Alfred R. Oxenfeldt, "The Formulation of a Market Strategy," in *Managerial Marketing: Perspectives and Viewpoints*, edited by William Lazer and Eugene J. Kelly (Homewood, IL: Richard D. Irwin, Inc., 1962), p. 40.

12. Borden, "Marketing Mix."

13. E. Jerome McCarthy, *Basic Marketing*, 5th ed. (Homewood, Ill.: Irwin, 1975).

14. Philip Kotler, *Marketing Management*, (Englewood Cliffs, NJ: Prentice-Hall, Inc., 1980, p. 467).

15. E. Jerome McCarthy, *Basic Marketing*, p. 77.

16. Theodore N. Beckman, Harold H. Maynard, and William R. Davidson, *Principles of Marketing*, 6th Edition (New York: Ronald Press, 1957), p. 434.

17. Alan Toop, *Only £3.95?!* (London: The Sales Machine, Ltd., 1978), pp. 9–11.

18. Kotler, p. 527. It is interesting to note that the subject of sales promotion received only passing mentions in earlier editions of Kotler's book.

19. Frey and Dixon, *Advertising Industry*, p. 7.

20. Albert W. Frey, *The Role of Sales Promotion*, (Hanover, NH: Dartmouth College, 1957), p. 3.

21. Eugene R. Beem and H. Jay Shaffer, *Triggers to Customer Action—Some Elements in a Theory of Promotional Inducement* (Cambridge, MA: Marketing Science Institutes, 1981), p. 3.

22. Beem and Shaffer, *Triggers to Customer Action*, pp. 7–8.

23. Eugene Mahany, written communication, 1980.

24. Russell D. Bowman, "The Changing Role of Sales Promotion (Paper delivered at the 65th ANA Annual Meeting, Hot Springs, Virginia, 1974); "Improving the Payout of the Advertising Promotion Mix" (Paper presented at the 66th ANA Annual Meeting, Palm Beach, Fla, 1975).

25. Russell D. Bowman, "Advertising and Promotion Expenditures: Third Annual Report," *Marketing Communications*, September 1982, p. 51.

26. Alden G. Clayton, "A New Look at Some Old Questions on Advertising vs. Promotion Expenditures" (Paper delivered at the Association of National Advertisers Advertising Research Workshop, New York, April 4, 1978), p. 5.

27. "The Third Medium" is a registered trademark owned by Stratmar Systems, Inc., New York, N.Y.

TWO

Planning Promotional Strategy

A successful promotional strategy is more than a series of promotional tactics joined end-to-end. Indeed, careful planning of promotional strategy is critical in order for the promotion manager to be able to integrate promotional efforts within the total marketing program. Both long- and short-term promotional planning is necessary, paralleling the efforts of the marketing director responsible for the total long- and short-term planning of the sequence of activities designed to enhance the marketing well-being of particular products or services.

CHECKLISTS

Earlier attempts to plan promotional events often consisted of single efforts aimed at limited, short-term objectives. Promotional activities were highly pragmatic and emphasized immediacy; they seldom touched on the broader implications of overall marketing strategies. Further refinements in promotion paralleled the growing sophistication brought about by the marketing concept and included the development of more elaborate checklists for systematic tactical planning of individual promotional events.

Still valuable and in wide use, such checklists must, however, be used in conjunction with considerations for the total marketing plan;

otherwise, marketing management cannot efficiently deploy resources in line with overall objectives.

Such a list was offered in 1962 by R.M. Prentice in a book published under the egis of the Association of National Advertisers.

1. Objectives (avoid generalities; use specific numbers for ease in measuring results)
2. Cost (budget considerations)
3. Flexibility
   a. By product
   b. By area
   c. By account
   d. To meet changing conditions
4. Selectivity—type of consumer to be reached
5. Timing (preparation or lead time needed)
6. Degree and kinds of advertising support needed
7. Acceptance and impact
   a. Consumer
   b. Trade
   c. Salespeople
8. Display opportunity and point-of-sale support
   a. Sell-displaying
   b. Special program involved
9. Compatibility with product image
10. Relationship to competitive activities
11. Feasibility of pretesting
12. List of specific advantages and disadvantages
13. Evaluation of results
    a. How will you measure results?
    b. What advance arrangements are required to obtain special measurements, reports, or research?

PROMOTIONAL AUDIENCES

In planning the promotional program, its desired impact on three audiences must be considered, namely, *sales force, trade,* and *ultimate consumers,* which collectively represent the conduit through which the marketing process is brought to fruition. Clearly, promotional efforts directed to all three audiences are necessary in order to motivate desired behavior patterns necessary for ultimate marketing success—internally, within a salesforce, and externally, across distribution channels and among consumer target groups.

The successful promotional strategy addresses all three audiences through vertically integrated programs while it interfaces with other marketing efforts included in the overall plans. We should recall here the push–pull concepts outlined in chapter 1. Promotional efforts directed to a salesforce become primarily a function of compensation; those to the trade fall on the push side of the promotional see-saw, while efforts aimed at consumers register on the pull side. All these efforts are important for keeping the process in motion, and the better all efforts are integrated, the better the promotional momentum.

THE PROMOTION PLAN

Most marketing plans are drawn up annually, then carefully monitored and revised at least quarterly. Logically then, the promotion plan should follow the same timetable. In effect, the promotion plan should be an integral part of the broader marketing plan, a written plan approved through the appropriate levels in marketing management. The plan can then serve both as a guide and a reference for the planning and execution of the specific activities required under the plan and further provides management with performance criteria.

In most companies the promotion plan is generally prepared by a sales promotion expert reporting to the marketing manager or group responsible for the particular brand or group of brands. Some companies are staffed internally with sales promotion professionals, others use outside sales promotion firms or consultants. A few companies seek such assistance from their advertising agencies.

It is critical that promotional plans be flexible enough so that changes can be quickly made in response to fast developing competitive and other similarly uncontrollable factors. The promotion plan, with variations for specific companies, should generally follow the format outlined here.

1. *Background.* The background section of the promotion plan is derived primarily from the overall marketing plan. It should include a full diagnostic review of current market conditions for a company's own brand or brands as well as competing entries. Each product's current positioning in the market, as well as relative measures of strength, should be carefully identified both in terms of consumer and trade franchises. A brief history of promotional programs conducted in the previous year is a useful addition to this preparative section of the plan.

2. *Objectives.* Clear and specific marketing objectives drawn from the overall marketing plan are the basis for objectives in the promotion plan. Essentially, such objectives are the projections of where the brand or brands should be at the end of the plan period. Beginning with the overall marketing objectives outlined by marketing management, promotion planners must frame the specific objectives assigned to the promotion function.

3. *Promotion Strategy.* An important section of the promotion plan are the strategic steps necessary to fulfill promotion objectives. Promotional efforts are targeted at specific areas designated under the promotion plan in line with the remainder of the marketing mix. Overall expenditure estimates and budgetary needs of the plan are clearly delineated. The relative position and emphasis in the promotion strategy regarding each of the three audiences—*salesforce, trade,* and *ultimate consumers*—are clearly identified. A number of strategic conditions may be reviewed at this point:

   a. *Short-Term versus Long-Term Strategies.* While promotional events, by their nature, center on immediate action, the strategic planning of promotions should consider both short-term and long-term marketing needs. For example, promotional efforts calling for short-term gains in distribution can also provide for a long-term buildup of assortments at retail. Different events may be necessary to achieve both short-term and long-term objectives, yet all these events must be viewed and planned as parts of a continuing process building upon itself from event to event.

   Two prime examples of successful long-term promotional strategies designed to expand and maintain a brand's consumer franchise over time are Procter & Gamble's continuous sampling of Pampers disposable diapers to new mothers in hospitals and General Mills' label-saving continuity promotion for several of its Betty Crocker products.

b. *Promotional Strategies and Product Life-Cycle Considerations.* Different promotional strategies are appropriate at different stages in the product life cycle. A new product requires promotional events that will speed up the adoption process among consumers while gaining the product initial distribution and placements at retail. Sampling, for example, will short-circuit the trial phase and accelerate the buildup of a consumer franchise— provided that the product enjoys demonstrable product-in-use advantages over competing entries. Special allowances to the trade, on the other hand, will get the product on the shelf quicker and in greater assortment, thus making it easier for the consumer to find and buy it.

Some of the same promotional efforts will continue through the growth stage as the product gathers momentum and both its consumer and trade franchises expand. For example, trial continues during this stage, although conversion levels, which were high among initial triers will somewhat decline as potential consumers come from secondary and tertiary groups. At this stage more efforts are directed to the trade in order to ensure full shelves and minimal out-of-stocks, increased facings at retail, and continuous featuring—all steps designed to support the growth momentum generated by the product.

Intensified trade promotions continue into the mature stage with activities in the Third Medium becoming increasingly critical. The promotion of a mature, established product, while still interested in obtaining new users if only to make up for those switching away, will concentrate on maintaining its existing franchise by motivating current users of the product to continue to purchase it and make sure that the product continues to be available at retail.

The promotion strategy during the mature stage may vary considerably, depending on three factors.

1. Whether the product category itself is growing or declining.

2. The degree of loyalty the product has attained and whether it enjoys a leadership position in the category. A lower level of loyalty, for instance, would recommend the use of promotional efforts designed to increase purchase frequency and product use. A laggard share in the category, on the other hand, may suggest that the product has topped at a questionable level of profitability that no longer justifies active marketing support. Or it may have settled in a narrow, specialized, and price-inelastic niche requiring minimal promotional support.

3. The nature, level, and frequency of anticipated competitive threats. For example, is a particular competitor likely to launch a major drive designed to make strong inroads among the product's users or will competitive activities concentrate on frequent, short-term, price-off promotions? Category promotional patterns should also be taken into consideration. The coffee category, for example, is subject to frequent couponing efforts after concentrating for years on label price-offs. Cereals, on the other hand, while frequent couponers, emphasize both in-pack and off-pack premiums, both free and self-liquidating.

A declining product must stay on the shelf as long as possible in order to maximize its profitability by "milking" its revenues. Little or no consumer advertising is used at this stage since the product is about to be phased out. However, promotional events will be used to slow down the decline and primarily to avoid a rapid loss of distribution. The longer the product remains on the shelf, the greater its "milking" potential.

c. *Offensive versus Defensive Promotional Strategies.* By and large, all promotions are meant to solve competitive situations. However, significant differences exist between promotions designed as offensive strategies and those planned and executed with defensive objectives in mind. In practice, *offensive promotions* reflect purposeful strategies that, if successful, will achieve specific gains. Such promotions are usually well organized and efficient because they have the advantage of proper lead time. *Defensive promotions,* on the other hand, are generally reactive in nature and seek to protect a product's turf against encroachment by competing products. Such efforts are usually limited in scope, since they represent mostly short-term responses to specific competitive challenges.

Ideally, an offensive promotion is built into the marketing mix as part of an overall marketing strategy; a defensive promotion often breaks the continuity of what a company should be doing for a given product or products and forces an unplanned and often haphazard event. In theory, at least, one could envision the development of several alternative strategies for various potential competitive situations which could be kept "on call" and put into action quickly, with only some fine tuning and last-minute adjustments. In this case, the promotion manager can start with an effort that has been planned—if only in broad strokes—budget estimated, and generally placed in the overall marketing strategy. In practice, however, few companies employ such an anticipatory approach to defensive promotions.

4. *Promotion Tactics.* Starting with the overall strategy as outlined above, one then plans separate promotional events along the promotional calendar covering the period under the plan. Although each event is separate, it must be viewed as part of a sequence of promotional efforts whose cumulative value should add up to more than the sum of its parts. Each promotional event should be carefully planned and detailed for execution. One useful approach to event planning follows a structured outline that elicits specific goals and parameters for a particular event.

WHY	Why is the promotional event needed?	OBJECTIVE
WHOM	To whom is the promotional event targeted? Salesforce, trade, ultimate consumers? Any or all of them? Any specific segment of any of these groups?	TARGET
WHAT	What rewards are we willing to offer in order to achieve the objective? What are the specifics of the offer(s) to be made?	REWARD
WHEN	What is the best timing for the promotional event? How does it fit in the overall marketing strategy, and how does it interface with the timing of other elements in the marketing mix? What seasonal considerations must be taken into account? When must the various elements be committed to? What lead times are we working with?	TIMING
WHERE	Where will the promotional event be presented to the target audience? What vehicle/medium will carry the promotion offer to the audience?	VEHICLE/MEDIUM
HOW MUCH	How much will the promotional event cost? What are the various elements of cost? Are alternatives available? What response rates and accrual liabilities must we provide for? If advertising support is required, how much	

do we budget for it in efforts
to the trade? To the consum-
er?   COST

Concerns in three additional areas might be relevant in considering a particular promotional event.

Legal Considerations.   Is the promotional event legally clear of liabilities? Is the promotional program or any of its parts in violation of any of federal, state, or local statutes or regulations? Have all applicable legal procedures—for example, the registration of chance promotions in certain states—been followed? The promotion manager must keep in mind that failure to give due consideration to the legal aspects of an event may result in costly unbudgeted liabilities.

Promotion Research.   Planning research is generally helpful in enabling the promotion manager to select the most promising of the several possible executions under consideration for each event.

Performance Measurements.   Evaluative research is highly desirable to determine whether the event has performed according to plan. Performance criteria must be established at the outset, in line with set objectives. Equally important in determining the parameters of the evaluative research required in the initial plan is the occasional need for prior, special arrangements with some of the factors involved in the program, i.e., the trade in order to obtain valid measurements.

Promotion Aura

The effects generated by a promotional effort may have an impact on a company well before the actual promotion is executed in the marketplace, and the effects of a promotion may last long after the promotion has come to an end. The span of time from the pre- through the postpromotion period comprises a *promotion aura,* a term coined by Carmine Iosue of Kimberly-Clark,[1] and its application to the planning of promotional events can materially enhance the overall benefits a company derives from such an event.

In planning a promotional event, one may specifically be concerned with moving incremental merchandise into trade channels and, through them, to ultimate cnsumers. Long before this takes place, however, the prudent manager anticipates merchandise needs and executes the specific production runs required to satisfy these needs. Taking this one step further, one may use promotional events to influence production planning. Through careful scheduling of promotions, for example, production peaks and valleys can be evened out, which, in many industries, would reduce waste and be more labor efficient. In-house group events can provide additional opportunities to manipulate production runs toward an optimal utilization of plant and equipment.

Nevertheless, at the trade end, the effects of a promotional event can last long after the promotion has run its course, a circumstance that must also be considered at the outset of planning the promotion. In the case of new products, a permanent home at retail—increased facings, distribution of additional sizes or types, distribution of line extensions, and so forth—can be strongly enhanced by specific promotional efforts. In a sense, the promotion aura concept again spotlights the need for careful, strategic planning of promotions as part of the overall marketing strategy.

In summary, the promotion aura is a scheduling concept which recognizes that primary sales, trade merchandising, and the consumer purchase impact of promotional events occur within a specific and consistent time frame starting before, and ending after, the execution date of an event.

To better integrate the promotion aura in the overall brand planning process, Iosue suggests the following annual promotional calendar principles:

Improve the predictability of results.

Achieve individual *brand* and *company* promotion *objectives within budget.*

Provide clear objectives and priorities with the agreement of sales management.

Gain efficiency while enhancing trade and consumer impact.

Enable capacity management or asset utilization by supporting increased sales during traditionally weak shipment months.

Acknowledge importance of the quarter and individual month. ("raise valleys and hold peaks.")

Increase size of orders—encourage larger, more profitable orders and shipments.

Discourage forward buying—mortgaging the business.

Encourage increased retail turns.

Acknowledge the *"promotion aura"* in timing and in setting up the annual promotion calendar.

Provide sufficient frequency of dates to provide *flexibility* to individual brands.

Acknowledge and incorporate any brand category *seasonality.*

Balance product mix during any one date (combination major and secondary brands).

Allow for regional marketing and promotion opportunities.

Take into account *best sales dates of quarter:* pay days, delivery of federal checks, major account drives, ad/rotos, and so on.

Spend according to importance of quarter and month—each date.

Promotion and commitment may not be equal by event.

Ensure variety of media vehicles to consumers (FSI/ROP, direct mail, women's magazines, etc.) and promotion devices (free offers, coupons, refunds, sweeps, samples, etc.).

Coordinate trade promotion calendar, selling cycles, and special packs.

Create a compelling "merchandising focus," maximizing trade support and *preempting competition.*

a. *Increase quality and frequency* of display and price feature activities on major brands.

b. *Encourage distribution and merchandising* support for *secondary brands.*

c. Stimulate incremental consumer take-aways and increased retailer turns.

The key purpose of the annual calendar is to *predictably achieve objectives within budget* as agreed to by marketing management.

A light-hearted yet effective way to convey to its clients some of

Ten Promotion Commandments

I. Thou shalt not plan promotion without first specifying objectives & budget.

II. Thou shalt select only the right promotion techniques to attain specific objectives.

III. Thou shalt direct thy promotions to thy target audience.

IV. Thou shalt not use confusing, complicated consumer copy.

V. Thou shalt not be greedy in consumer purchase requirements.

VI. Thou shalt support promotion with advertising when merited.

VII. Thou shalt test any major program in which there is no brand experience.

VIII. Thou shalt not wait 'til the last minute to plan.

IX. Thou shalt always honor the "kiss* philosophy."

X. Thou shalt always consult with promotion specialists when planning promotions.

CHAPTER I, VERSE 4
THE BOOK OF DFS

*Keep It Simple Stupid

Ten promotion commandments.

the planning imperatives of promotion was devised by a leading advertising agency, Dancer Fitzerald and Sample, with its "Ten Promotion Commandments."

NOTES

1. Carmine Iosue and Dan Ailloni-Charas, "The Promotion Aura" (paper delivered at Babson College, May 1983).

PART TWO

PROMOTIONAL METHODS

INTRODUCTION

Broadly defined, all promotions are designed to achieve one of two major objectives: to enhance and accelerate the development of a new franchise, or to defend, strengthen, and expand an existing franchise. Obviously, the achievement of these two objectives is not left to promotional devices alone; nevertheless, promotion plays a critical role in enabling marketing management to reach its bottom-line objectives in both areas.

Developing a New Franchise

The introduction of a new product or service follows a well-defined, sequential, adoption process. The process steps, as detailed in most basic marketing texts, are:

Awareness
Knowledge
Desire
Trial
Purchase
Repurchase

Each step on the way to the adoption of a product or service by the consumer is necessary, and the process does not come to fruition until and unless a repurchase pattern is established.

Awareness of the new product or service is initially needed before the consumer can even consider using it. *Knowledge* enables the consumer to identify potential in-use satisfactions, and *desire* represents the stage where the consumer decides to seek these anticipated satisfactions. Through *trial* or initial *purchase,* he or she actually experiences the product or service, and if the experience matches the buyer's level of anticipated satisfactions, *repurchase* follows in due course and continues over time until competing products or services intervene with superior satisfaction claims.

To complete the adoption of its product or service, a company must design an offensive strategy that will eventually lead a sufficiently large number of customers to repurchase routinely. All promotions are most effectively used in the last three stages of the adoption process, the stages where the product or service moves from the "cerebral" phase, where mental impressions of the product are formed, to the "physical" phase, where the consumer's actual experience with the product begins. Thus, promotions can enhance and accelerate the trial, purchase, and repurchase of the new product or service. Also critical to the adoption process by consumers are the sale and availability of the product or service in the pipeline leading to the point where consumers can purchase. Promotions directed both to the company's own salesforce and to the trade in general often provide the added motivation to accelerate the reach of "push" objectives.

Promoting the Existing Franchise

Even when a product or service shows signs of having reached a mature level, the astute marketing manager often finds ways to expand the product's franchise. Defensive promotions can help generate competitive preferences for a product or service on both the single-event and continuous bases while also supporting broader marketing strategies, such as the restaging, repositioning, or extension of a line.

Interestingly, it is during the declining stage of the product-service life cycle that a defensive promotion strategy is able to make its strongest contribution to bottom-line results. If the marketing manager recognizes the first signs of decline for a particular product, he or she can quickly move to curtail advertising expenditures, which may run as high as 35% of sales, while merchandising the product to trade and consumers through increased promotional activities. Thus, the product's distribution is efficiently prolonged, and profitability will increase significantly, even though such profitability from a "terminal" case is naturally short-term.

Classifying the Promotional Efforts

Overall, promotional efforts can be classified according to their audience or to the elements comprising each campaign. We have already indicated that promotions can be directed to many audiences. They may be designed to motivate behavior patterns among *ultimate consumers* across the distribution channels, to the *trade*, in efforts to achieve "push" results, and to the internal *sales organization*, direct or indirect, in order to provide motivation for enhanced sales efforts. Since most promotional tools are applicable to all three audiences, although perhaps in different configurations, a second classification—by type of incentive—may facilitate strategic considerations and action. Thus, incentives fall into two major categories: *merchandise/service* incentives and *money* incentives.

Merchandise/service promotions include all incentives that are not monetary. They may be either a product or service external to the product or service being sold but representing enough value to trigger the desired purchase action. Similarly, such promotions may rely on increased quantities of the product or service, at the same or reduced price, thus providing a powerful incentive to positive consumer behavior in the marketplace.

Premiums of all kinds belong to the group of incentives consisting of products or services with perceived value of their own apart from the value of the product or service being sold; bonus packs for example—that is, 2 ounces of coffee free with each 10-ounce jar purchased or one night free for each three paid nights in a resort hotel—fall into the second grouping of "more-of-the-same" incentives.

Money promotions, naturally, are strictly monetary in nature.

While all incentives trade off on the value perceived by customers for both product and incentive, money incentives key more closely on the specific value/use relationship for a particular product or service. Consciously or not, consumers sense how much a product or service is worth to them, and monetary inducements can alter that relationship and bring consumers closer to purchase. Off-label prices and coupons are very popular money incentives. The more elastic the product class is, the more successful the money incentive will be.

THREE

Merchandise/Service Promotions: Sampling

Merchandise/service promotions—programs not directly monetary in nature—can be classified in six broad groups.

1. *Sampling.* A trial device designed to accelerate the adoption process of a new product or service by short-circuiting the first-purchase requirement.

2. *Premiums.* Tangible rewards in the form of free merchandise or services in order to motivate potential customers to purchase a given product or service. Premiums have long been a fixture in the marketing game.

3. *Bonus Packs.* Primarily a defensive vehicle designed to stave off competitive inroads by enhancing the value/price relationship of the defending brand.

4. *Contests and Sweepstakes.* Among the most used promotional vehicles and perhaps the most liable among all promotional tools to constant and careful inquiry by legislative and enforcing authorities at all levels. They are listed under merchandise/service promotions, even though some contests and sweepstakes carry cash prizes or a combination of cash and merchandise/service incentives.

5. *Merchandise Trade Promotions.* Normally, a method of obtaining increased trade support for a particular promo-

49

tional effort by offering the trade incremental profit potentials in return for specific commitments for increased pipelining and featuring; parallels money promotions directed to
the trade for similar objectives.

SAMPLING

Sampling is perhaps the oldest marketing technique of any we are
using today. One finds mentions of sampling in ancient writings, and
we read in the chronicles of pioneer America how the country store
served as the treasure trove of new tastes, sensations, and product
ideas for rural shoppers eager for contact with the world of
manufactured and processed goods. Sampling long preceded mass
advertising as an effective tool in the adoption process and is
certainly ancient compared with the marketing concept.

Sampling enables the consumer to try out a product or service at
little or no risk before making a financial commitment to its
purchase. Since trial represents a necessary step in the adoption
process, before acceptance of a product or service for long-term
usage, sampling can short-circuit the process and lead to a much
swifter converson to full-revenue purchasing. Basically, the consumer remains the ultimate arbiter as to whether the sample product
or service measures up to the levels of satisfactions promised for it in
the first place. If it is affordable, sampling is the fastest way to
launch a good new product and to kill a bad one. To the extent that
the manufacturer creates more customers for products through
sampling, the retailer also achieves a higher sell-through of these
same products. Thus, the promise of higher consumer purchases
will generate increased trade-loading, which further provides for
support features, display activities, better shelf position, and so on,
to the enhancement of the product performance in the marketplace.
Importantly, by short-cutting the adoption process, sampling can
significantly accelerate adoption, hence, the movement of product
at retail.

A number of sampling techniques are popular now.

1. *In- or Near-Store Sampling.* Tied into the point-of-purchase, often leading to an immediate regular purchase of the product.

2. *Central-Location Sampling.* Often referred to as "high-traffic sampling," takes place in locations where large numbers of people can be reached efficiently over short periods of time.

3. *Sampling by Mail.* Samples mailed to potential product users.

4. *In-Home Sampling.* Often referred to as "door-to-door" sampling, product samples delivered to homes of potential product users.

5. *Institutional Sampling.* Sampling of prospective users through institutional channels.

6. *Sampling Parties.* One or more products sampled in the context of a group function, which involves aspects of peer dynamics.

Sampling Selectivity

In most cases, successful sampling programs are targeted at those persons most likely to respond favorably to the specific sampling experience. Proper selectivity of sample recipients can significantly enhance the productivity of the sampling effort.

Selectivity dimensions range from broad to narrow. Target groups can be identified through profiling by demographic criteria, either limited or detailed, and the sampling program is then directed at those who meet the specified criteria. Programs by mail, for example, can take advantage of the federal government's zip-code data, which have been variously refined by the many specialized electronic data processing (EDP) companies that have recently sprung up with the purpose of further qualifying these data with input overlays from other primary and secondary sources. On the other hand, personal, "in-hand" sampling, near a store or in a central location, can be selectively targeted by site, by visual identification, and by personal screening. The marketing planner thus enjoys a complete range of sampling options and can reach a specific and very narrowly defined group if desired, although cost factors, at some point, generally outweigh the benefits of more narrow targeting. In any case, selectivity considerations must be built into the initial marketing plan, with the intention of targeting marketing efforts to those persons most likely to buy.

IN- OR NEAR-STORE SAMPLING

Sampling should be viewed as a trial device designed to accelerate a product's adoption process, so marketing personnel must work in conjunction with the trade to insure that the product is stocked and available to those who positively respond to the sampling. Obviously, in obtaining clearances from the trade for sampling in or near

Stratmar in-store demonstrator sampling DelMonte Mexican foods salsas in Portland, Oregon.

their premises, the company sales force would also make sure that enough of the product is on hand to satisfy the consumer demand generated by sampling.

We pointed out earlier that good "pull" programs can also cause superior "push" results. Sampling within a given store or group of stores amply illustrates this relationship. Trade support for sampling includes increased pipelining to the retail floor, display activities, and product featuring. While such product support is essentially caused by the needs of a sampling program, it also constitutes long-term leverage on the franchise from the sampled product. In-or near-store sampling can be carried out in two ways, through immediate-experience sampling and hand-out sampling.

Immediate Experience Sampling. In immediate experience sampling, the shopper experiences the product at point-of-purchase, which thus allows for an immediate purchase predicated on the satisfaction value of the experience itself, together with any other incentives accompanying the sample, such as a special price feature

In-store sampling of "Sippin' pak," a new orange juice from Borden in an aseptic pack.

or a coupon. This type of sampling is common for a wide range of foods, toiletries and cosmetics.

The variant termed *wet sampling* refers to carbonated and noncarbonated beverages and even alcoholic beverages where such sampling is allowed by law. *Hot sampling* refers to the preparation of and presentation of food samples for immediate consumption, not all of which are actually hot foods. The sample can be a ready-to-eat snack or a frozen pizza that must be heated before serving, or a salad dressing that must be mixed with milk before use.

Sniff sampling and *touch sampling* are used with nonfood products. Counter testers are quite common in department stores so that shoppers can sample the scent of a cologne or experience the feel of a lotion on their skin. At times, demonstrators are assigned to specific stores in order to reinforce such sampling. Generally, they urge customers to sample the product while they verbalize a selling message that stresses product superiority points and answer questions.

Hand-Out Sampling.   Unlike immediate-experience sampling programs, hand-out samples are given to shoppers to take home and experience. This sampling vehicle is preferable to in-store immediate-experience sampling in a number of situations.

1.   If the shopper acts as a purchasing agent for others in the household who do the actual consuming—for an extreme example, samples of pet foods.

AN INTERCEPT® IN-STORE SAMPLING PROGRAM
A NEW BEVERAGE IN TWO MARKETS
(Sampled vs. Control Consumer Panels)

Albany/Schenectady/Troy	Percent Used in Past Month	Percent Using Brand Regularly
Sampled Panel	47.0	7.5
Control Panel	8.7	2.8
Charlotte		
Sampled Panel	41.0	10.0
Control Panel	Negligible*	Negligible*
*Less than 1%.		

Comparisons from an Intercept in-store sampling program.

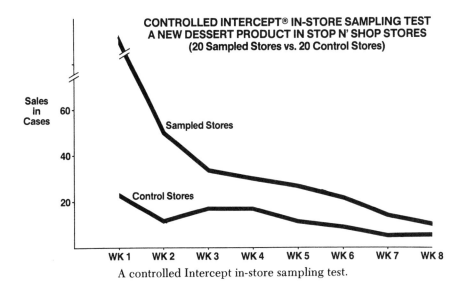

CONTROLLED INTERCEPT® IN-STORE SAMPLING TEST
A NEW DESSERT PRODUCT IN STOP N' SHOP STORES
(20 Sampled Stores vs. 20 Control Stores)

A controlled Intercept in-store sampling test.

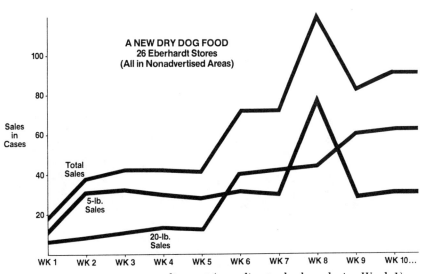

A NEW DRY DOG FOOD
26 Eberhardt Stores
(All in Nonadvertised Areas)

An Intercept near-store sampling test (sampling took place during Week 1).

55

2. If usage quantities beyond a mere taste are needed for a meaningful experience with the product—for instance, a week's supply of a cleansing lotion.

3. If a product must be used in a home in order for consumers to properly assess its performance—for example, a new scouring pad.

4. If a time span separates usage and results—for instance, analgesics and antacids.

5. If usage of a product is cyclical, such as feminine hygiene products.

6. If product usage is conditioned by outside factors, such as illness. To limit the lag time between sampling and usage of such products, programs are often rolled out on demand. For example, cough and cold remedy sampling is often conducted at the onset and during the winter season, when

About 10 million pounds of Ralston-Purina "Mainstay" were handed out near-store to dog owners throughout the country.

the incidence of colds and fevers can be expected to be relatively high.

Logistics.   While these sampling techniques seem relatively simple in concept, both immediate-experience and hand-out sampling often require complex logistics. A number of factors must be carefully considered.

Scheduling.   Since scheduling must take into account trade approvals and clearances, particularly for in-store programs, trade presentations must begin early enough to allow for proper planning time. Whether a program can be conducted over one week or more depends on the desired penetration levels, the number of accounts accepting and actively supporting the program (via additional activities at retail), as well as on limitations imposed by resources such as labor, equipment, warehousing space, trucking capabilities, and so forth. Scheduling must also give consideration to reaching consumers most efficiently, that is, when traffic is potentially at its highest. Normally, such programs are scheduled on Thursdays, Fridays, and Saturdays, which are known as the best-food days since they follow the major food weekly advertising, which usually appears on Wednesdays. Later hours on Thursdays and Fridays and earlier hours on Saturdays also generally offer higher shopper reach.

Equipment.   Equipment needs—primarily for in-store immediate experience sampling—range from small appliances to serving implements. Usage must be anticipated and sufficient equipment scheduled. Provisions must be made in the plan for the transportation of such equipment from sampling point to sampling point as needed.

Disposables.   Besides planning for reusable equipment, consideration must be given to the needs for disposable items, such as cups for sampling beverages and plates and napkins for food samples, which must be ordered in advance in sufficient quantities, preferably in bulk, and shipped to each sampling cluster.

Dress-Ups.   Supporting promotional aids range from sashes, buttons, or aprons, designed to identify and focus attention on the samplers to point-of-purchase materials such as shelf talkers, riser cards, and mounted ad tear sheets. Such items can greatly strengthen the presentation of the product sampled and the sampling program as a whole. It is important to create positive impressions with shoppers—potential buyers—and with trade personnel as well. This latter concern is often referred to as "showing the flag," and it works.

Product. Immediate-experience sampling often employs product obtained within the store. Stratmar's *credit-memo procedure*, for example, allows for the replacement of the used, or sampled, merchandise with new merchandise shipped in by the manufacturer. Thus, replacement is made on the basis of cost-of-goods rather than retail price, which naturally reflects retail mark-up. In certain cases, such replacement is either not possible or not acceptable to the trade, and the product to be sampled is either shipped directly to the store in special lots or is brought in personally by the sampler.

Coordination. Critical to any in- or near-store program is close coordination among the sampling organization, the manufacturer's sales organization (direct or indirect), and the trade. Unless everything, and everyone, works together as planned and scheduled, sampling programs are not likely to produce optional results.

Coupon Sampling. A variant of hand-out sampling, coupon sampling gives shoppers coupons that can be redeemed free at retail for a full-revenue unit, usually the smallest size in the line. This method has a number of serious shortcomings and is indicated only when the retail channels are overstocked to the point where delisting may be a distinct possibility. Although coupon sampling can quickly generate consumer take-out and thus impress the trade, at least short-term, with good product movement, such programs are usually defensive in nature and can be very costly.

1. Coupon sampling is expensive, since the program not only costs the company using it the factory dollars given up in the process of sampling but the trade mark-up as well.

2. Coupon sampling is potentially uncontrollable, particularly in areas where coupon misredemption practices are suspected.

3. A regular size of the product sampled, even at the lowest end of the line, may take consumers out of the market for too long a time, when repurchases among triers who like the product must be generated quickly in order to maintain the product's place on the retail shelf.

On- or In-Pack Sampling. Manufacturers often use one of their products as a carrier for a sample of another product, usually a new entry. Occasionally, agreements are made between noncompeting manufacturers for one to supply the carrier and the other the sample. Factory packs are usually flagged on the front panel, giving the carrier a promotional benefit while providing the sample with access to the carrier's regular users. The sample may be dropped in the pack or banded on the pack. This sampling approach is popular for a number of reasons. Costs can easily be controlled and fully budgeted up front, since they are limited to the production run of the carrier. Execution logistics are also simple for the sampling company, since little else needs to be done once the samples have been delivered to the factory door of the carrier's company. Potential drawbacks of such piggybacked sampling should, however, be carefully weighed for each promotion campaign.

1. Sampling is limited to those buying the carrier product, which may seriously curtail the reach of the samples, hence their ability to generate a sufficient trial base on which to build a usage franchise.
2. Depending on the production run of the product and on the month's supply levels stocked by the trade both at retail and in central warehouses, the sampling effort may not be fully completed for a long time. This approach will clearly fall short of optimum performance where the objectives call for rapid, widespread trial of the product.
3. The narrower the targeted market is, the more difficult it is to find a matching carrier, with a similar consumer profile. Consequently, such sampling programs produce considerable waste, with many samples reaching people outside their primary target groups.

4. The halo, or image, enjoyed by the carrier product will extend to the sample it carries. If the carrier's image is good, then everything is generally all right, even among those who do not use and hence do not buy the carrier product, but who are aware of the juxtaposition of the two products. If the carrier's halo is negative, or trends that way, the sampled product may suffer.

Specific Objectives Satisfied by In- or Near-Store Sampling Programs

1. Such sampling programs are conducive to immediate or short-term consumer action.

2. Given their immediate or almost immediate impact at retail, these promotions can gain trade support. As indicated earlier, while sampling programs qualify primarily as pull efforts, they can be effectively used for push purposes as well, since the trade will want to tie in with promotions that promise accelerated consumer take-out.

3. They can generate trial for products that cannot easily or inexpensively be sampled through other sampling media, such as mail.

4. Where they specifically involve a person-to-person contact, in- or near-store sampling includes a personal touch—a live selling message with each sample along with personalized answers to any consumer questions or objections.

5. Similarly, the person-to-person contact also permits pinpoint targeting of the product's potential users.

6. Such sampling is imperative if a product must first overcome negative consumer perceptions before positive attitudes can be exploited.

Summary—In- and Near-Store Sampling

Immediate-experience sampling is indicated where small-taste quantities may generate immediate purchase. This small-taste rationale applies to products other than food; sensory perceptions can be obtained from feeling a lotion, smelling a fragrance-containing product, and sensing a lack of wetness in a deodorant. Hand-out sampling in or near retail outlets, while potentially postponing actual purchases until a subsequent shopping trip, nevertheless carries some measure of purchase immediacy, which usually affects near-by stores. Similarly, coupon sampling and on/in pack sampling bring about trial after the sample product has been brought into the home and evaluated by family members who then decide for or against a full-revenue purchase. In any case, trade support should be obtained with all in- or near-store programs.

CENTRAL-LOCATION SAMPLING

The major application of central-location sampling hinges on its ability to sample large numbers of qualified consumers over short periods of time. Consumer qualifications refer to selective characteristics of a specific consumer target for a particular product. Even so, central-location sampling is generally indicated only when the usage incidence of the sampled product is high within the geographical boundaries of the central location to be used. The variants of this approach are limited only by the definition of central location.

Downtown Sampling

This application refers to sampling in any of the various commercial clusters that are generally well defined in most metropolitan areas. Such areas range from office strips or blocks, to railroad commuter stations and central squares. These mostly enjoy local traffic from passersby who, for the most part, live or work in the area. In some areas, traffic often skews to out-of-towners, which must be taken into consideration, particularly if the sampled product has a limited, test-market distribution. In such case, samples given to people coming from outside the test area will not help the marketing manager meet objectives. Downtown sampling may be restricted by local ordinances or accepted custom, and care must be taken in drawing the sampling plan to conform to such regulations or expectations.

Brightly clad Stratmar demonstrators serve a cab driver a cup of new ready-to-serve, 100% pure orange juice from Minute Maid.

Packets of Clairol's "Sea Breeze" were given out in high traffic midtown New York.

A major drawback of downtown sampling is the amount of litter they can generate, particularly where samples are handed out for immediate consumption—for example, a candy bar—or a printed sheet accompanies the sample. Care should be taken to police the immediate vicinity for any discarded materials. A second major drawback of downtown sampling is the potential for duplication if sampling stations are set too closely to one another. Some of the cigarette-sampling efforts place samplers at every corner of a limited cross-street area, which results in multiple-pack sampling for everyone who is willing to walk a little farther or cross the street a few extra times.

Careful attention must also be given to the problem of supplying sampling stations with additional samples as the day wears on. It is not desirable to leave unguarded samples stacked up next to the sampler. Pilferage of full cases can and does occur while the sampler is engaged in approaching and presenting samples to passersby. The more prudent course is to supply each sampler with just enough units to fill the tray or bag of samples. A good delivery system requires careful evaluation of traffic patterns. Routing of the resupply trucks must take into account traffic conditions at different times of the day as well as specific traffic regulations and traffic flows. Since vehicle standing is often limited in major downtown locations, each resupply truck should operate with a driver and a helper, so that the helper can deliver the new supply of samples while the driver remains at the wheel.

Van Sampling

A variant of downtown sampling, sampling out of vans is more costly than downtown sampling, but it offers several unique advantages while enjoying the high-traffic benefits of a central location.

The van is mobile and can shift location during the sampling period in order to take advantage of changes in traffic flows.

The use of a van extends the range of products that can be sampled. Since a van can be modified to include various types of equipment, samples can be refrigerated or kept hot, stored in bulk dispensers or in single units, and so forth.

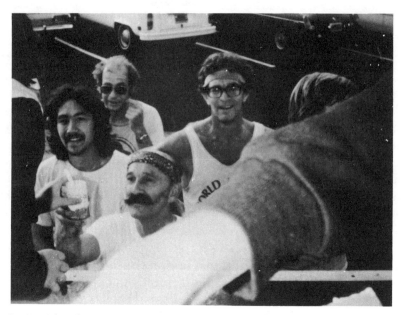

Yopläit sampling for participants in a sporting meet in Sacramento, from a specially outfitted mobile van.

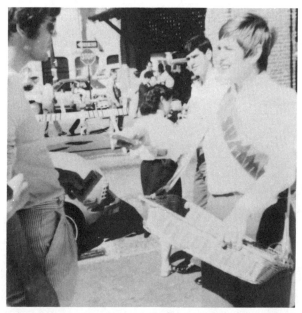

Mars' Summit sampler distributed in high traffic in Charleston, South Carolina.

64

Again due to its mobility, a van can improve a promotion's selective reach since it can be precisely placed near high-incidence clusters of people belonging to given target groups—on college campuses, at commuter stations, or at special events.

Clearly, in most cases a van can carry the sampling units required for a day's work. Only occasionally will a back-up supply truck be required, perhaps on weekends when the supplying warehouse is closed.

Fair Sampling

State, county, and local fairs are held throughout the country during the year and attract millions of visitors. Some fairs bring in only 20,000 to 30,00 people, while the state fairs of Texas and Ohio, the largest state fairs in the United States, attract millions of people over two weeks. Sampling at such events often represents a good promotional opportunity, although the fair visitor's profile is mostly skewed to rural America and consequently it does not always fit the description of the primary consumer of the products and services of much of corporate America. Participations at fairs by major manufacturers can become much more prevalent as fair visitors include a greater percentage of the targeted consumer group.

Shopping Center Sampling

At times, companies initiate sampling programs in shopping centers away from any specific store. Such a program may utilize vans—hence van sampling—or free-standing tables or booths in high-traffic mall areas. Clearances must be obtained from the shopping-center operator and substantial fees are often levied.

Specific Objectives Satisfied by Central-Location Sampling Programs

1. Such sampling programs are designed for concentrated reach over telescoped time periods.
2. Reasonable selectivity is possible in terms of location, sight, and verbal screening, the latter due to the fact that personal sample distribution facilitates dialog.

Yopläit booth at the Arizona State Fair where thousands sampled the product for the first time.

Sampling of Welch's White Grape Juice at the Chattanooga Mall.

3. Potential legal problems pertaining to in- or near-store sampling are avoided. Since central-location sampling is clearly directed to consumers in general traffic and do not favor, directly or by implication, one retail outlet over another, corporate legal departments more easily approve such programs.

4. By their nature, central-sampling programs enjoy broader exposure than other types of sampling. High visibility is gained for both the sampling company and the sampled product. Such possibilities for greater awareness and interest are captured in the fielding of a van-sampling program where the mobile unit, fully decked with the product's name and playing the appropriate theme music, was instructed always to take the longest way between two sampling points so that it would be viewed and heard by the largest possible number of potential customers.

Summary—Central-Location Sampling

Central-location sampling is one of the most popular forms of sampling. Combining personal touch with the benefits of mass efforts, such promotions are an important vehicle by which manufacturers generate accelerated consumer trial.

SAMPLING BY MAIL

Literally billions of samples have been mailed to ultimate consumer homes over the last decade. There are several reasons why using post-office channels and resources to deliver samples appeals to many companies seeking to reach potential new customers.

1. Mail programs are relatively easy to manage. All that has to be done, at least in theory, is to deliver the samples to the mailing house contracted for the job, the rest is handled by the supplier.

2. It is technically possible to reach every single address in the country, regardless of how remote and inaccessible, and at no extra cost beyond the basic delivery rate.

3. Since deliveries are zip coded, mailings can be narrowly keyed, using the wealth of demographic data available from government sources and supplemented by behavioral information collected and processed by specialized companies.

A number of caveats, however, also apply to mail promotions.

1. Unless first-class delivery is used, which is seldom, due to its cost, samples are sent out third-class, which is subject to the following limitations:

a. Delivery of samples will be made by the local post office as working loads permit and after other classes of mail have been processed. This kind of delay can create problems when the delivery of samples is scheduled to dovetail with other promotional and distribution efforts.

b. If the sample is addressed to a specific recipient who no longer resides at that address, the sample will be disposed of by the post office as undeliverable; the sample will not be returned to the mailing company unless a notice of nondelivery, which costs extra money, has been requested. This represents a major problem for mailers since mobility of households is high and a substantial lag often occurs before changes are posted. To circumvent this problem, companies often mark samples for the "occupant" or "resident" at a given address; such a sample will be left at the address no matter how many people have moved in and out over time. Still, mailing companies risk losing samples addressed for whole neighborhoods that have fallen in the way of redevelopment, or conversely, they may fail to reach new developments whose existence takes time to appear on the records.

2. At times, the management of sample-delivery-by-mail programs can be lax, especially with regard to deliveries to high-rise buildings. Partially beause of the limited size of individual mail boxes in high-rises, third-class mailing impersonally addressed to "occupant" or "resident" are often left together on a lobby table or bench. Obviously, the opportunity for mishandling under such

circumstances is ever present, and most mailings attempt to exclude deliveries in high-rise buildings.

3. Mailers also exercise other types of exclusions, not so much as a matter of selectivity, but of feasibility and policy. It is not uncommon for a mailing to exclude, for example, certain central city neighborhoods or homes owned by female heads of household. Obviously, the decision to use a particular mailing house or list must be informed as to the types of exclusions favored by that supplier.

4. The selectivity of mailings is often less than claimed. Better data and finer statistical analyses can always produce better skews of specific target groups within a given census tract, nevertheless, such refinements are seldom efficient. Even when an increased incidence of a certain type of consumer can be identified in an area and included in the sampling plan, a number of the samples mailed will still reach people who will not use them, for one reason or another, and thus will be wasted. Waste, in such cases, involves not only the cost of postage but the cost of the samples and their processing as well.

Sampling by mail involves both the mailing of samples on an unsolicited basis and the fulfillment of requests by consumers for samples in response to offers made by companies seeking to reach new triers for their products.

Unsolicited Sampling

Much of the broad-scale, deep-penetration sampling, often designed to reach as many as 25 million homes, is done on an unsolicited basis. Such penetration is desired by many major manufacturers whose products are widely used and whose new entries could conceivably reach homes with a usage incidence of 90% or more. Bars of soap, detergents, certain feminine hygiene products, and personal-care items such as shampoos and deodorants fall into this group. Mailings of unsolicited samples may be conducted on a *solo* basis or as part of a *cooperative* effort, which, besides samples, may involve coupons, direct-mail offers, and other items of literature.

Executing a sampling-by-mail program involves a number of steps:

1.   Determining one's strategy in terms of specific target reach, desired penetration, type and size of sample, timing of mailing—or mailings, if the program calls for a sequential roll-out by area in a number of waves—and estimated budgets.

2.   Selecting the mailing supplier that can best meet the strategic criteria decided on at the best price possible. Some suppliers own and maintain their own lists, others obtain them from list compilers. In evaluating mailing lists, particular attention should be given to the following questions:

    a.   How often is the mailing list updated, with the addition of new listings and purging of old? Given the high mobility levels of the past couple of decades, even broad-coverage lists based on census and other generally available data must be frequently updated to minimize sampling waste. More critical is the updating of specialized lists—such as a list of homes with new babies—whose applicable longevity is limited. Using an outdated list, a mailer may send a diaper sample to a home where the "baby" is about to enter kindergarten.

    b.   How well is the mailing list checked and maintained? Is research routinely done to ensure that listings continue to be valid? Are demographic breaks, when provided, also regularly validated?

3.   Equally important in selecting a specific mailer for the sampling program is to ascertain whether the supplier can meet the processing requirements apart from list validity. For example, will the supplier be able to process the whole mailing in-house or will parts of the processing be subcontracted? Although there is no innate difficulty with a supplier's subcontracting parts of the work, attention must be given to potential problems in the timing of the mailing.

4.   A sample that arrives damaged will most likely fail in its task of generating positive trial; it may actually turn off potential customers. Great care must therefore be taken to enclose the samples in mailers that will guarantee their arrival in good order. If such protection cannot be virtually assured the samples should not be sent by mail at all.

5.   A monitoring program must be set up at every stage of the process. Inspectors should be sent to the plant or plants where the mailing is being prepared to ascertain that all steps—from product insertion in suitable mailers to proper addressing—are done according to specifications. Inspectors should visit local post offices to confirm that the samples arrived from the mailing house on time and that their distribution to the proper addresses is proceeding without problems. A subsequent visit to a representative number of these post offices may reveal the percentage of "nixies"—that is, the number of samples that could not be distributed for one reason or another and were returned to the post office. Some companies will supplement a list with a number of addresses of their own workers or of persons specifically hired to monitor the receipt of samples.

6.   If a company chooses to participate in a cooperative unsolicited mailing, its choice of mailing partners is very important. On the positive side, everyone gains if all participations are complementary and the mailing achieves an overriding theme, such as back-to-school or spring cleaning. However, the participant in a cooperative venture must be wary that no other entries reflect negatively on its own products. Further, each company normally insists on product-class exclusivity—that is, the exclusion of competing samples, coupons, or other promotional materials.

Solicited Sampling

Many companies offer to fill requests for samples of their products through various channels. Solicitations may be made by mail—sending a coupon to a given address, most likely that of a fulfillment house—or by telephone—where an operator takes down the pertinent information and directs the mailing of the sample, again most likely through a contract-fulfillment house. Generally, such samples are free, although in some cases the company may request a small amount for postage and handling.

Obviously, the number of solicited samples mailed out represents a fraction of the samples that can be sent out on an unsolicited basis. Thus, such an approach is not recommended for either deep or fast penetration of the marketplace. On the other hand, there are some claims that solicitation sampling is far more productive on a unit-by-unit basis since responses to a sample offer tend to be self-selective. In other words, people who react to the offer and go to the trouble of requesting a sample are far more apt to use it. Further, if their experience with the product is generally positive, they will quickly convert to regular usage, in numbers far greater than people who receive the sample unsolicited.

Cost is a major factor in the decision to go the solicitation way. The higher the cost of the sample, the more likely it is that it will be confined to solicited sampling. Concerns about waste—about reaching people who will throw the sample away—increase in direct proportion with the cost of manufacturing the sample. Solicited samples are often mailed first-class, which further escalates the cost of the program. In choosing between the two sampling-by-mail methods, reaching fewer, but higher-potential, customers over an extended period of time must be weighed against a high-penetration "blitz" program across the board with a significantly smaller incidence of potential conversion to regular revenue purchasing. It must be noted that some states do not allow unsolicited sampling in certain product categories; samples of medicine must be requested and then personally addressed, which is meant to prevent such samples from falling into the hands of children.

Media Use in Offering Solicited Samples

Although samples could be offered through countless vehicles, from handbills to sky writing, four channels actually account for the bulk of such offers.

1.   Most offers are made in print, with coupons inserted in print ads or free-standing. Coupons include the address of the fulfillment center to which the coupon must be sent and space for the respondent's name and address. Occasionally, the form also includes additional questions designed to give the offering company a better fix on the people responding to its offer. In most cases, the coupon is coded to the carrying medium to enable the company to evaluate the relative pull of various media.

2.   The broadcast media—television and radio—are also used to offer samples. Listeners are given a local telephone number or an 800 number to call and request the sample. Telephone operators

note the request and process the sample mailing through a fulfillment center. Such efforts can be executed very quickly and have often been used by manufacturers of cough and cold remedies to elicit a fast response to their products at the onset of a flu epidemic.

3. Store take-one pads placed in the section carrying the new entry may offer small, one- or two-use samples as a way of introducing the product to nonusers. While not a popular means of generating sampling by mail, this approach has merit if the retail price of a full revenue unit is high. It is occasionally used by companies to sample their cosmetics or toiletries, particularly lines sold in mass outlets.

4. In/on pack offers are used by many companies that have products well-suited as carriers. This method obviously limits the promotion's reach to those persons who buy the carrier products, and the offers can be used only as fast as these products sell through. On the positive side, target profiles can be more closely matched by inserting the offers in packages of products that are bought and used by people falling in similar segments.

Eliminating Duplicates

Growing computer capabilities have given companies increasing success in eliminating duplicate requests for samples. Given the cost of samples and postage and the desire to reach as many people as possible within a certain budget, companies' concerns with and attempts to eliminate possible duplications are usually cost-justified.

Solicited Sampling through a Cooperative Effort

Recently, several promotion houses have begun offering a new sampling-by-mail program, whereby people receive product samples based on their responses to a self-administered questionnaire on their usage of products and product categories. Designed primarily as a competitive tool in lower-usage categories, this approach allows participating companies to send samples only to people currently using competitive products. Through such prescreening, companies heighten the potential response to the samples they send out while avoiding sampling to their own franchise. Costs are also lowered, since all samples from all participants are boxed and mailed in one unit. The number of companies participating in the program must be large enough to ensure that a reasonable number of samples will be mailed after the rigorous screening each questionnaire receives.

Such programs are included in the solicited-sampling category even though a person sending in the questionnaire does not know which of the samples will be sent and which will not. Nevertheless, the effort follows a solicitation pattern.

Specific Objectives Satisfied by Sampling-by-Mail Programs

1. Such programs are generally easy to administer.
2. They are very versatile, allowing for a wide range of strategic approaches.
3. They can be costed at the outset, with little likelihood of unanticipated overruns.
4. They permit many potential creative executions, in relation to the package and accompanying copy.

Summary—Sampling by Mail

Mailing samples has been a sampling workhorse for many major companies seeking quick and deep reach of households throughout the country. It has also served well companies that have limited their sampling to responding to those who solicit a sample after reading or hearing about the product. Escalating mailing costs in recent years have caused many of these companies to reassess their use of this sampling method, and it is likely that other sampling vehicles will gain at the expense of mail in the future.

IN-HOME SAMPLING

In-home sampling is another major form of sampling favored by some manufacturers who feel that the best way to introduce people to a product is by dropping samples on the doorsteps of potential users. A mass-reach method, in-home sampling is usually designed to blanket large areas, although some companies are becoming more concerned with selectivity. Unlike sampling by mail, which in a broad sense also delivers samples to a prospect's home, in-home sampling is carried out by special sampling crews supplied by service companies specializing in such efforts. Samples are delivered at the prospect's door—hence the term "door-to-door" often used to identify this type of sampling. Companies using in-home sampling claim certain advantages:

1.   Sampling directly to homes gives the sampling company total control over the completeness, timing, and selectivity patterns— where such are designed into the program—all the way through to the delivery of samples.

2.   Sampling of heavier items—a full-size liquid detergent bottle, for example—would be costly to deliver by mail; delivering such items through in-home sampling may hold a significant edge.

3.   Sampling of items that require expensive protective enclosures to maintain product integrity in the mail—for instance, certain snack items—could be done at considerably less cost when delivered to homes from bulk cartons.

Against these claims, however, one must balance certain potential pitfalls:

1.   Controls over execution are often illusory. Unless the manufacturer whose samples are being distributed is willing to invest heavily in fielding enough inspectors to follow up on the delivery crews, the controls exercised over home delivery are not any better and occasionally are worse than those potentially exercised over post-office personnel. Compounding the problem of control is the fact that private, in-home deliveries are denied legal access to the home mailbox. As a result, samples are usually hung on the front doorknob, usually in a small polyethylene bag supplied by the delivery contractor—and thus subject to mischief.

2.   In-home sampling is generally kept out of high-rise areas, concentrating on single-family and smaller multiple-dwelling homes. Apart from the fact that a growing number of households are falling beyond reach each year as urbanization increases, in-home sampling productivity is hampered by the distance between quali-

fying homes. Consequently, the savings claimed for in-home sampling over sampling-by-mail may simply not exist.

3. Certain products delivered in-home may still require strong child-proof packaging. Left unattended on a doorknob, the sample may be removed by children who could potentially harm themselves. Pilferage by adults, though less a concern from a safety point of view, can further increase waste in the sampling process.

Sampling in-home can be conducted in one of two ways:

1. *Ring and Leave.* The sample is left on the front doorknob or step; the sampler rings the doorbell before leaving, but goes away without waiting to see if someone is at home. This procedure allows the sampling crew to achieve the most productive delivery completions possible, although the program remains vulnerable to some of the pitfalls discussed earlier.

2. *Ring, Wait, and Give.* The sampler rings the doorbell and waits for someone to answer. The sample is handed over only if a person opens the door and is willing to accept it. This approach permits further screening, including as many selectivity criteria as desired and eliminates many problems connected with most in-home programs. But this approach is far more costly to execute than the ring-and-leave approach. One must factor in refusals and not-at-homes as well as the longer time spent at the door. Still, the opportunity to hand-deliver a sample together with a message has merit in some situations. However, cost and return must be measured against these factors for similar deliveries of samples in or near stores or in central locations.

Specific Objectives Satisfied by In-Home Sampling Programs

1. They provide for the delivery of samples to their ultimate usage point—in-home—thus accelerating the trial process.
2. They permit versatility of coverage and scheduling, in line with other strategic considerations.
3. If cost is not a factor, in-home sampling programs have the greatest potential of the sampling programs for selectivity and thoroughness of coverage.

Summary—In-Home Sampling

Wide usage of in-home sampling suggests that many manufacturers find this method of sampling desirable for their promotional needs. Care must be taken, however, to recognize fully the advantages and disadvantages of in-home sampling and properly account for them in the sampling plan.

INSTITUTIONAL SAMPLING

Sampling through institutional channels attracts both cooperative and solo efforts to reach potential consumers who are in these channels for varying lengths of time.

A number of cooperative sampling programs are directed to new mothers, who generally receive sample packs upon their discharge from the hospital. The "new mother" qualification is broad, since it includes all mothers who have given birth at the time the sample pack is distributed, whether they have other children or not. When a baby-oriented product cannot get into such a pack because of exclusivity limitations—the category having already been pre-empted by a similar entry—the product must establish its own solo-sampling system. Such was the task for the manufacturer of Johnson's Baby Diapers, which had to organize its own hospital distribution channel covering some 5,000 hospitals throughout the country.

Similar programs are directed to schools, primarily colleges, where samples or sample packs are distributed to students, often through the campus bookstore.

Doctors and dentists often distribute to their patients various samples they receive from manufacturers' representatives. Such samples are for the personal consumption of the patient receiving them under 'professional sponsorship' and are directly related to the medical problem they are meant to alleviate.

Overall, sampling through institutional channels benefits from two specific advantages:

1. It can reach certain types of people, in large numbers, at a time when the need for the type of product sampled may be most pronounced.

2. It generally benefits from the sponsorship of the channel itself, which will accelerate the sample use and help overcome some resistance to certain new products. This is particularly true in the distribution of a new medicine, where the involvement of a physician in the transmittal of the sample carries with it an implied endorsement of the product. Tylenol, a pain reliever manufactured by McNeil Laboratories is a classic example of a proprietary medicine that achieved widespread success through sampling via medical channels long before its marketing strategy included mass advertising and mass merchandising.

SAMPLING PARTIES

Certain products can benefit from being sampled and talked about in a group context. Apart from being able to reach larger numbers of people at the same time—people who share a commonality of need or interest in line with the product's marketing objectives—sampling at an organized group function can accelerate positive reactions to the product through peer-group acceptance. The group setting also encourages the interchange between those attending a sampling party and sample presenters who are usually knowledgeable and persuasive about the products sampled.

Sampling parties for a specific product or product line can be quite expensive if conducted on behalf of a single participating manufacturer. There are a couple of services, however, which design such parties around samples from several principals who then share costs proportionately. Besides their high costs, sampling parties are not used more widely or beyond specific product categories because of their limited reach. Most sampling programs are meant to reach potential users widely, en masse, over telescoped periods of time. A new product requires mass support quickly in order to build a viable consumer franchise that will keep the product in distribution and provide a reasonable payout for the manufacturer's investment. Sampling parties cannot gain such mass support; they can help build a franchise, slowly, over time. Parties for mass products are primarily designed with the objective of building a long-term corporate image—almost purely a public-relations objective—and not toward achieving immediate market gains. Sampling parties can be used in many different situations, but three types of parties prevail.

Wine-Tasting Parties

Wine-tasting parties are often sponsored by a winery seeking to introduce its products or by an importer desirous of presenting its products to a particular market area. Normally, the wine-tasting aspect of the function is just part of a social event on behalf of some worthy cause. Wine-tasting parties are commonly used for fund-raising purposes, at conventions, for a new theatrical group, for an artist, and so on. The sponsoring group is responsible for scheduling the party and distributing invitations, as well as for publicizing the event. The wine producer or importer provides the product and necessary implements together with enough personnel to set up the program and intelligently present and discuss the wines to be sampled. Written materials are often handed out with the samples. At times the wine purveyor teams up with a cheese manufacturer, thus creating a wine-and-cheese event whose costs can be shared to some degree of mutual benefit.

Cosmetic Parties

Cosmetic parties, conducted by specific manufacturers, are intended as much to sell as to sample their products. Often arranged in conjunction with and on the premises of a major retailer, such parties usually require payment of a participation fee, which is generally returned to the participants in the form of free samples. The appeal of such parties is in their show-and-do aspects. Trained cosmeticians work with each participant, using the sampled product to teach her how to enhance her appearance through judicious use of cosmetics. Orders are taken for the sampled products at the conclusion of the party, which are immediately filled from the store's inventory. Overall, in the late 1970s orders at cosmetic parties averaged $50 to $60 per participant, which means that such parties— with an average per-session attendance of 25 to 30 persons—are very attractive to host stores. Although such parties seldom are designed to bring in revenue for a manufacturer directly, they serve to extend the use of cosmetic products through sampling to new potential customers. Given the high gross-profit levels of these products, cosmetic parties are obviously advantageous to the cosmetic manufacturers.

Meal Parties

Food-sampling parties are usually luncheons prepared with sampled products and served by service companies to organized groups, either on their premises—for instance, a church social room—or in a convenient central location. Although the goal of a reasonably balanced meal may require that the service company add purchased items to the free items being sampled, the participation is usually broad enough to make supplementation unnecessary. This sampling approach has the advantage of introducing new food items prepared under test-kitchen conditions, which presumably gives potential consumers their first taste of the product under ideal conditions. Such ideal conditions are more likely in a fixed central location where facilities are standardized and fully maintained than in locations that change from day to day and may range from excellent to barely satisfactory. During the meal, a "master of ceremonies" introduces each item sampled and boosts it, according to a script provided by the manufacturer. Questions and answers can be built into the script according to time limitations set by the number of items sampled. More recently, take-away nonfood samples have been included at these parties in order to help defray increasing costs. Such samples also qualify for a certain amount of "billing," with the same master of ceremonies discussing their attributes and urging trial. Participations at these parties are booked in advance, and the service organization usually provides the group booking the function with a set number of tickets at a required total fee. In turn, the group resells the tickets to its members at a price that will return some profit to the group, usually for a particular fund-raising need.

SOME FINAL COMMENTS ON SAMPLING

Despite certain real advantages, promotion through sampling should be undertaken after certain caveats are considered.

1. Sampling serves to accelerate the adoption of a new product by facilitating its trial, risk-free. Sampling is an important tool in the establishment of a new franchise—especially critical in certain product categories—since it intrudes on established buying and usage patterns.

2. Sampling a product that fails to meet competitive criteria is the surest and fastest way to kill it.

3. Sampling may not be indicated in mostly commoditized product classes that are highly elastic.

4. Sampling primarily fits, primarily, an offensive strategy.

5. Sampling quantities must be carefully gauged in the case of products with long purchase cycles so that people will not be kept out of the market when the goal is to turn them into full-revenue purchasers as quickly as possible.

6. Sampling alone will not achieve all that is expected from a successful strategy. Sampling must be supported during and after sample distribution, by other means available to marketing managers. In this sense, sampling must be planned from the start as part and parcel of a total marketing strategy.

7. Sampling programs must be merchandised to the trade much as they are directed to consumers. Sampling is recognized as powerful leverage in generating new customers, and as such it can be used to obtain good in-store distribution, good shelf positioning, and introductory support of the product including featuring and other retail floor activities. However, the primary objective of sampling is to generate as much of a trial base as is affordable. Thus, salable samples, usually prepacked 96 units to a shipper, limit trial to fewer than 100 people per store; assuming that all samples are sold at only one sample per customer, such an effort does not qualify as a sampling program. More often than not, salable samples are meant to placate the trade with increased profits through the sale of samples obtained free from the manufacturer.

FOUR

Merchandise/Service Promoting: Premiums, Sweepstakes, and Contests

The two meanings that Webster lists for *premium* are (1) a reward or recompense for a particular act, and (2) something given free or at a reduced price with the purchase of a product or service. The Promotion Marketing Association of America (PMAA) discussed the definition of premiums in a 1975 publication:

> Probably the best definition is "an article of merchandise offered as an incentive for the performance of a specified action—a reward for performance." A consumer premium may be defined thus: "an item offered free, or at a nominal cost, as an incentive to buy a product or service." In the main, the object of the premium is to attract attention to the advertised product and give the consumer a reason for buying the product or service now. It also gives the seller an opportunity to produce an immediate increase in sales. It leaves the consumer with a direct tangible benefit.[1]

These definitions for *premium*—all relating to merchandise or service items given buyers in order to induce them to act in the marketplace as desired by those who offer such incentives—tie in with the definition of all promotional efforts provided in an earlier chapter. In that instance, we qualified promotions as "material

83

inducements designed to accelerate selling and buying functions along the marketing process and to supplement the basic product/service-in-use satisfactions anticipated by both ultimate and intermediate consumers."

HISTORY OF PREMIUMS

The first recorded premium program in the United States occurred in the mid-19th century. Seeking to differentiate his laundry soap from others on the market, Benjamin Talbott Babitt decided to sell it in wrappers bearing his name. The custom at the time had grocers cutting pieces off a long bulk bar for sale to customers. Reactions to Babitt's departure from custom was lukewarm—until Babitt decided to make the wrapper itself valuable by offering to redeem 25 wrappers for a full-color lithograph. Babitt not only made his soap successful, he also pointed the way how promotional ideas can contribute to product success. Soon after Babitt's venture, other soap manufacturers started offering picture cards packed in paper-wrapped soap cakes. The premium era in the marketing of consumer packaged goods was launched. As more manufacturers offered in-pack picture cards as a way to stimulate sales of soap, coffee, baking powder, tobacco products, and many other items, they also inadvertently fueled a collecting mania still in evidence today and the cornerstone of many continuity programs.

Within a decade after Babitt's premium offer, merchandise offers of more substance than picture cards were made to consumers who saved proofs-of-purchase to redeem for various goods. These goods were first described in premium lists, which later developed into full-fledged catalogs. Known as coupon plans, these promotions spread rapidly, used by about a hundred companies in some 12 product categories. Among early premium users were American Tobacco, Wisconsin Milk, Colgate, and American Cereal. Many companies still use premium catalogs, but General Mills for its Betty Crocker line and Brown & Williamson for Raleigh cigarettes are the only two major manufacturers using premium plans.

Thomas Sperry's introduction of trading stamps at the turn of the century was a natural outgrowth of the coupon plans offered by individual companies. Trading-stamp plans allowed the objectives of premiums to be met on a cooperative basis and gave retailers a promotional vehicle comparable to that used by manufacturers to push their own products.

Liquidating premiums made their entrance shortly thereafter. To counter customer reluctance to wait through many "use cycles" in order to save enough premiums for high-ticket items, manufacturers began to offer combination plans. Customers could accelerate the redemption process by paying some cash together with fewer coupons. In what appears to be one of the first such liquidating premiums in the United States, Davis Milling Company in 1912 offered buyers of Aunt Jemima pancake flour an Aunt Jemima rag doll by mail for a coupon and 10¢.

Basically, most types of merchandise/service promotion vehicles now used had been introduced by the start of World War II. As outlined by Meredith and Fried in *Incentives in Marketing:*

> Young though it may be in acceptance and stature as a modern marketing force, incentive (or premium) promotion actually is well over a century old. Development through the period from 1951 has been in four roughly defined cycles:
>
> 1. The age of picture cards, from 1851 until about 1900.
>
> 2. The period of the coupon plan, which began about 1900—though there were numerous active users somewhat earlier—and continued until about 1930.
>
> 3. The era of the self-liquidator. This cycle began in the early thirties and extended to the late forties.
>
> 4. The next stage in the development of the field, which might be called "the age of balance," began in the 1950s and is identified by a maturity of approach to incentive and a more selective use of the many ways they can relate to sales and profits when applied to specific marketing needs.[2]

DEVELOPING THE PREMIUM STRATEGY

As with all promotions, premium programs must be strategically placed in line with all other marketing efforts. Strategic direction can then lead to a clear set of objectives. Every program must be

THE IVORY SOAP
WATCH CHARMS.

A miniature fac-simile of a cake of Ivory Soap, with a gold-plated ring to attach it to the watch chain, or may be tied to the button-hole with a piece of ribbon, and used as a badge for a club, society, etc., etc.

HOW TO GET ONE FOR NOTHING

Save the outside wrappers of Ivory Soap, and when you have twelve, cut out the center piece of each wrapper and send them to us (as per directions below), and we will send you, by mail, one of the Watch Charms. If you are not now using Ivory Soap, buy twelve cakes, and you will get full value for your money in soap, and the watch charm for nothing.

FOLLOW THESE DIRECTIONS.

Cut out the center piece of each wrapper and put them in the envelope with your letter, saying what you want, and give your address in full. *No attention will be paid to requests for Watch Charms unless the twelve (12) center pieces are in the envelope with the request.*

PROCTER & GAMBLE, CINCINNATI, OHIO.

(Please mention this paper.)

An 1888 premium offer for Ivory Soap. (Reprinted with permission.)

planned, themed, timed, implemented, and ultimately evaluated against objectives.

Objectives

To a large extent, the objectives to be built into a strategic blueprint for a premium program—or any other promotional program—must be in response to specific marketing needs, actually themselves

WHILE THEY LAST {A WONDERFUL OFFER FOR TEXANS!

The captive Santa Anna is brought before General Sam Houston April 22, 1836, the day after the great Texas victory at San Jacinto.

NINE DRAMATIC PICTURES, SOUVENIRS OF THE TEXAS CENTENNIAL . . . FOR ONE GRAPE-NUTS FLAKES TOP, AND A DIME!

IN connection with the great Texas Centennial, General Foods recently commissioned Norman Price, the famous artist, to make nine commemorative drawings, depicting the most dramatic events in the history of the Lone Star State.

Handsome monogravure reproductions have been made of these nine historical subjects. They measure 9 by 12 inches, and are printed on a fine, heavy paper. Free of all advertising, they are ready for framing, and make up a series that every Texas patriot will be proud to own.

The supply is limited but while it lasts, all nine pictures will be mailed you postpaid, in return for one red and white Grape-Nuts Flakes package top and 10c in stamps. Don't wait . . . send for yours today!

THE SUBJECTS OF THESE NINE ILLUSTRATIONS ARE:

1. *Colonel William B. Travis at the Alamo.*
2. *Remember Goliad.*
3. *Coronado visits Texas.*
4. *Recruiting for the Republic of Texas Navy.*
5. *Awarding land grants to Texas settlers.*
6. *The Texas Republic celebrates Independence Day.*
7. *Gen. Santa Anna surrenders to Gen. Sam Houston.*
8. *Early Texas Rangers fighting outlaws.*
9. *Texas joins the Union.*

TRY A REAL CEREAL SURPRISE . . . GRAPE-NUTS FLAKES

Are they good? Just fill up your bowl with these curly, golden flakes—and the world's grandest breakfast is ahead of you!

Crispy as popcorn! Crunchy and nut-sweet! Full of that glorious Grape-Nuts flavor. Grape-Nuts Flakes are a dish for a king!

And they're one *flake cereal* that gives real nourishment, too. Served with fruit and milk or cream, they pack more varied nourishment than many a hearty meal. Get a package at your grocer's today.

Grape-Nuts Flakes

Your breakfast favorite in a new package

General Foods, Battle Creek, Mich. H-8-36

Please send me . . . sets of the nine Norman Price pictures depicting great events in Texas history. I enclose 1 Grape-Nuts Flakes package top and 10c in stamps for *each set* I am ordering.

Name_____

Street_____

City_____State_____

(Offer good in U.S.A. only)

A POST CEREAL—MADE BY GENERAL FOODS

A 1936 premium offer from Grape-Nuts Flakes. POST, GRAPE-NUTS, TOASTIES and SWANS DOWN are registered trademarks of General Foods Corporation. Advertisements reproduced with the permission of General Foods Corporation, White Plains, New York.

A 1936 premium offer from Post Toasties Corn Flakes. POST, GRAPE-NUTS, TOASTIES and SWANS DOWN are registered trademarks of General Foods Corporation. Advertisements reproduced with the permission of General Foods Corporation, White Plains, New York.

A mid-30's premium offer for Bisquick. (Reprinted with permission.)

The earliest premium produced by The Coca-Cola Company in 1896, a porcelain fountain syrup dispenser offered as a premium to druggists who bought and dispensed as much as 100 gallons of syrup annually. Since early sales of Coca-Cola were centered around the soda fountain, most of the premiums offered at the time were directed to this outlet. The dispensers, while rewarding druggists for their performance, also served as promotional units at point of sale.

representing at least part of the solution. In the following list, the marketing objective introduces the premium strategy.

To maintain the current franchise at both retail and ultimate consumers: Use a premium program to reward current product users and to promote the continuing of consumer takeout at retail.

To counteract a competitive strategy: Add to the perceived value of the defending product/service; offer the consumer reason to buy it over competitive entries.

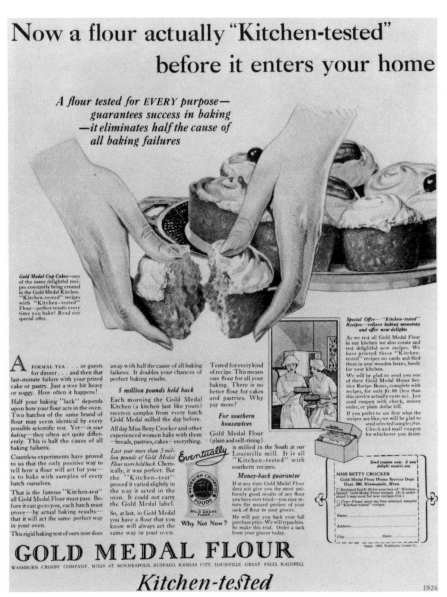

An early premium offer for Gold Medal Flour. (Reprinted with permission.)

Trays, calendars, and other novelty items were used extensively by The Coca-Cola Company since the turn of the century. Many have become part of the "collectibles" trend and are quite valuable today. These metal serving trays were given out (in order shown) in 1903, 1910, and 1909.

To accelerate consumer takeout and increase usage among current users: Use premiums to generate quicker repeats and multiple purchases and to promote trade-up to larger sizes.

To support line extensions: Extend the brand image and capitalize on its creative positioning.

To generate trade support: Focus on the sell-through capability of a premium program and elicit trade support at retail by means of increased pipelining, display activities, and featuring.

To enhance the readership of advertising for the product/service: Offer premiums that involve the consumer with the offer-bearing advertising.

From a tactical point of view, the strategy statement of specific objectives must take into account certain related factors:

1. The target consumer of the trade account to be motivated
2. Seasonality and/or relevant timing
3. Geographical area of the program

4. Media vehicles and types of communications to be used
5. Potential for trade support, particularly at point of purchase —for example, store displays
6. Relationships to competitive activities

Planning the Premium Program

Once objectives have been determined and a premium program is on the drawing board, the next step is planning its execution, best done through disciplined, team effort. If the participation and expertise of all persons ultimately to be involved in the program are solicited from the beginning, problems can be anticipated better and their solutions are easier. The planning team should include representatives from departments and organizations involved in the promotion.

Sponsor of brand, product, or service

Promotion planner/strategist

Advertising agency

Premium supplier

Fulfillment house

Market Research Department (MRD)—both market analysts and sales statisticians could be useful

Working together, this group can

Discuss and agree on specific objectives for the program

Establish criteria for premium selection

Estimate projected redemptions based on recommended media support and/or other offer circulation figures

Select and/or develop the appropriate materials to support the program at point of purchase as well as materials to communicate the offer to the trade

Determine a working budget

Arrive at a practical timetable for implementation. The timetable should include enough time for research, which, at minimum, may gather recommendations about the premium most likely to deliver the desired results among several submissions, or at most, may be running a full-fledged test market.

Establish clear-cut evaluation criteria and a program for monitoring performance in order to determine if the program meets objectives.

Criteria for Premium Selection

As indicated earlier, part of the planning process includes setting the criteria for premium selection, which will vary by program. The following guidelines, however, should be helpful across the board.

1. The premium(s) must be carefully matched to the target audience, so knowledge of this audience is very important. Both demographic and psychographic information should be solicited from MRD. Obviously, the better that planners understand the targeted consumers—their lifestyle and anticipated behavior in the marketplace—the more successful the premium selection will be.

2. Select the premium(s) that relate(s) best to the advertising/promotion theme in one of three ways:

   a. *Directly*—the item selected should be related either to the product/service or to its usage.

   b. *Thematically*—the item should be tied to the advertising or promotion theme.

   c. *Indirectly*—the brand logo or product/service name can be used in conjunction with the selected premium in order to register and/or reinforce the registration of the logo or product/service name in the consumer's mind. The ever-popular T-shirt, for example, is increasingly used as a walking billboard by sponsors.

3. Consider name-brand items or name manufacturers for the premium selected. In most cases, consumers have had media exposure to name brands that will aid in the impact of the premium.

4. The premium itself must have good perceived value, otherwise its incentive performance will be poor. It should be negotiated for the lowest possible price, with assurances that it cannot be obtained for less in discount stores.

5. If possible, the exclusive use of the premium during the promotion period should be contracted.

6. Check a proposed premium's availability and reorder lead time; this is particularly critical for items produced overseas.

7. The premium offer must be kept simple, with its elements clearly communicated. An otherwise good offer can fail if it is based on confusing requirements or directions. Consumers respond best to offers requiring least effort.

8. The less available the offered item is in general commerce, the stronger its appeal as an exclusive, desirable premium. Since most premium programs are used by manufacturers of packaged consumer goods, it is also important to use premiums that do not compete with products regularly distributed and profitably sold in mass outlets—supermarkets, drug stores, or mass merchandisers.

9. Any premium to be advertised on television should lend itself to easy dramatization and demonstration. Under such circumstances, primary consideration should be given to action-oriented items.

10. If the premium is to be fulfilled by mail, the ease and cost of packaging and processing must be taken into consideration. By definition, bulky, heavy items—particularly where response may be heavy—are less desirable. The ideal premium weighs less than 16 ounces—packaging included—to qualify its fulfillment for the more cost-efficient third-class bulk rate.

11. Careful legal review of all premium programs is a must. Apart from various federal requirements, attention must be given to local regulations in all the jurisdictions where the offer will be made. Failure to anticipate and comply with legalities may entangle the

premium offerer in legal problems and a great deal of negative publicity.

Types of Premium Offers

A number of premium vehicles, or modes, are available, depending on the objectives set under the promotional plan. Premiums can be classified in four main types:

1. *Factory Packs.* Package-related premiums, often called *direct* premiums since the consumer receives them at the time of the purchase, usually at no cost. The term *factory pack* indicates that these premiums are usually assembled in or on the package in the manufacturer's own plant and then shipped through distribution channels to retailers and/or wholesalers.

2. *Send-Away Premiums.* Premiums the consumer must send away for to a designated fulfillment center with or without additional payment.

3. *Continuity Promotions.* Premiums used by both manufacturers and retailers in continuity programs designed to promote the continued usage of a given product or line of products or the patronage of a given retailing store or stores. Mostly used as long-term programs.

4. *Traffic Builders.* Premium programs specifically designed to increase the level of consumer patronage in participating stores. Usually effective over the short-term.

FACTORY PACKS

Factory packs, or direct premiums, are designed to obtain on-the-spot impact at point-of-purchase by causing the immediate purchase of the products they promote. The premium must quickly convey to the in-store shopper the additional value to be gained by purchasing the special pack and therefore cause immediate action (that is, purchase). A number of different kinds of factory packs are popular.

In/On Pack Premium Promotions

Basically, in- or on-pack premiums are either attached to or packed in the product package at the factory. They are usually promoted with special on-package copy that spotlights the offer and is designed to draw attention to the package on the shelf under normal store lighting conditions. Shipment to retailers through the normal distribution channels is made in specially marked or coded cases. Often, the products come in prepacked display shippers, which facilitate their display on the retail floor. Normally, in- or on-pack premiums are offered free with purchase. Seldom, if ever, is the package marked up to compensate for the premium. Usually, free in- or on-pack premium promotions are offered for set periods of time and are limited by the production run planned for the promotion. Notable exceptions are premiums packed in children's cereals and the traditional free surprises inside Cracker Jack boxes. Even in such cases, the production run for a specific premium is still limited, though much longer than normal.

Specific Objectives Satisfied by
In- or On-Pack Premium Promotions

1. They represent a tangible, action-oriented incentive providing immediate satisfaction and hence encourage immediate purchase.
2. Since they are designed to increase consumer takeout, they also encourage retail off-shelf display and increased pipelining during the promotional period.
3. Good in-packs and on-packs can greatly encourage consumer trial in certain product categories, since the perceived value of the premium will lessen the risks assumed by the purchase of the new product.

For only $5.00 and two proofs of purchase Borden will send you a Lake Placid Winter Olympic Sweatshirt and contribute 50¢ to the U.S. Winter Olympic Team. (Proof of purchase is the ingredient list from any Borden Ice Cream package.)

Winter Olympic Sweatshirts imprinted with the Lake Placid Olympic Symbol are of excellent quality, made of 50% cotton and 50% polyester.

SIZE CHART	SMALL	MEDIUM	LARGE	X LARGE
YOUTH SIZES	6 - 8	10 - 12	14 - 16	
ADULT SIZES	34 - 36	38 - 40	42 - 44	46

To order: On a 3 x 5 piece of paper—specify size (Youth or Adult). For each Sweatshirt include check or money order for $5.00 payable to Borden Sweatshirt Offer along with two lists of ingredients clipped from any Borden Ice Cream package.

Include your name, address and zip code.

Send to: **BORDEN SWEATSHIRT OFFER**
P.O. BOX 8510
BRIDGEPORT, CT. 06602

Allow 4 to 6 weeks for delivery. Offer good in Continental U.S.A. Void where taxed, restricted or prohibited by law. Offer ends December 31, 1980.

BORDEN. Golden Butter Fudge Swirl ICE CREAM

Made With Golden Vanilla Flavored Ice Cream
ARTIFICIAL FLAVOR ADDED

Very Big on Flavor

Official Ice Cream Winter Olympics
SWEATSHIRT OFFER ON SIDE

HALF GALLON

Borden on-pack premium offer tied in to the 1980 U.S. Olympic team.

4. Certain in-packs or on-packs can encourage and promote the repeat purchase of the product they promote if the premium relates to the product's usage—for example, a food bowl in a bag of dry dog food or a recipe book in a box of cake flour.

Summary—In/On Pack Premium Promotions

A good in-pack or on-pack premium will draw attention to the product it promotes and away from competing products. To do so, the premium must be clearly identified on the package, if it cannot actually be seen attached to the product. However, the packaging must be secure enough to prevent pilferage, which not only loses the premium, but also may leave a product package unfit for sale. Both in-packs and on-packs may require special packaging equipment as well as special-size packages. Obviously, the more effort and cost required to work out such a promotion, the more carefully its potential advantages must be weighed. While in-packs using small, flat items are relatively easy to use, as they may lend themselves to normal production line handling, elaborate on-packs demand careful assessment of their potential contribution before such a promotion is implemented.

Bonus Packs

A premium promotion similar to in- or on-pack promotions is the bonus pack, whereby the consumer receives an increased quantity of the product without an increase in the normal retail price. The incentive here is more-of-the-same for an advantageous price, rather than an incentive external to the product itself. Given additional product quantity "free," the consumer is encouraged to see a different price/value relationship that justifies immediate purchase of the product. Such promotions are particularly useful in highly price-elastic categories such as coffee.

As in the case of in- and on-pack promotions, bonus packs are limited to specific production runs. Apart from the "fatigue" that may cause any promotion to lose its effectiveness over time, an extended use of bonus packs for a particular product may lead to claims that the "regular" price of the product is indeed the one represented by the bonus-pack quantities, forcing a manufacturer to lower the price on regular packs.

Bonus-pack promotions can be classified as follows:

1. *On-Pack "Add-Ons"*—ranging from heavier fills to special pockets constructed as part of the package to contain additional merchandise.

2. *Multipacks*—several packs banded together and sold at a reduced price, with the effect that one or two units are given "free" with the purchase of the remaining units. Soap bars are a frequent example of banding promotion, with, for instance, four units banded together and sold at the price

Sunlite card and neck tag for a bonus-pack promotion on Hunt-Wesson's Sunlite Sunflower Seed Oil. (Reprinted with permission.)

normally charged for three units. Such promotions are easily identified by some variant of the slogan: "Buy two, get one free."

3. *1¢ Sales*—a variation on multipacks, offering the purchaser of one unit of a product at the regular price the opportunity to buy a second unit for only 1¢, or at half price, and so on. Vitamin manufacturers, for example, have for many years used 1¢-sale promotions to accelerate consumer takeout of certain brands.

Specific Objectives Satisfied by Bonus-Pack Promotions

1. They represent a powerful promotional tool for moving large quantities of merchandise to ultimate consumers over short periods of time and therefore can gain considerable position over the competition at retail.
2. Defensively, they serve to take one's customers out of the market over longer periods of time, away from competitive new entries.
3. They encourage heavier and multiple usage in the home.
4. They sell through rather quickly, clearing the way for further promotional activities.

Summary—Bonus-Pack Promotions

Bonus packs, on the whole, provide the opportunity for marketing efforts that combine both "push" and "pull" elements. They are relatively easy to execute, since only marginal demands are made on factory equipment and efforts. Their incremental costs must naturally be taken in consideration when making evaluations of performance, but most important, bonus-pack promotions must be used sparsely to avoid debasing the consumer-perceived base price of the product.

Container Promotions

The container in which the product is packaged can itself become an important incentive. An attractive, reusable container, properly flagged to attract shopper attention, can have considerable immediate draw value, if the price-cum-package continues to show a good price/value relationship. Special-pack containers assume added value either in their functional reuse with the product, or in some cases, in their decorative or other use away from the product. Reusable pitchers packed with powdered drinks and storage jars containing coffee will be continued in similar uses. Some fast-food chains have promoted drinks sold in specially decorated glasses to be taken home after use, although in most cases, the price of the drink has been adjusted upward so that the glass is not totally free.

Specific Objectives Satisfied by Container Promotions

1. They represent a strong point-of-purchase promotion with potential for strong pipelining at retail.
2. They are conducive to special display and off-shelf activities, as well as other trade support such as featuring and mentions in best-foods ads.
3. They give the product's price/value relationship an advantage over competitive products at retail.
4. They motivate users to trade up to larger sizes.
5. They provide a change of pace for products using in- or on-packs on a frequent basis.

Summary—Container Promotions

Container promotions are indicated if the container itself represents real value and can be so perceived by shoppers. Often, containers extend into the collectible range, whereby shoppers are encouraged to purchase the product repeatedly in order to obtain all the items in the collection. A notable example was the series run by Log Cabin in 1976, and since repeated, of a collectible series of authentic reproductions of early American flasks. The program was very successful and well adapted to both broadcast and print media support. However, cost factors may inhibit broad-scale use of container promotions since special container runs can be expensive. Nevertheless, if the dollars-and-cents evaluation of incremental sales and other benefits versus incremental costs can be satisfied, such programs can be highly successful.

Near-Pack Premium Promotions

Near-pack premiums are usually displayed next to the promoted product, together with appropriate point-of-sale copy urging the shopper to purchase the product and hence be entitled to receive the premium free or at nominal cost. Often, the near-pack premiums are shipped as part of a display prepack; at times they are shipped in separate cartons.

Specific Objectives Satisfied by Near-Pack Premium Promotions

1. Near-pack premium promotions are mostly used as a means of generating off-shelf display activities.
2. They are also used to gain trial of new products or renewed purchase of reformulated or repositioned products.

Summary—Near-Pack Premium Promotions

As with all factory-pack premium promotions, near-packs are meant to provide immediate satisfaction to buyers of the promoted product. However, near-packs are not very frequently used, even though they "stand out" on the retail floor and can gain manufacturers considerable shopper attention. Coordinating the arrival of promoted products and near-pack premiums at the retail outlets often falls short of objective. Such problems, together with the fact that free items displayed separately are more susceptible to theft and harder to check for shopper compliance, have held down the enthusiasm of retailers for this type of premium promotion.

SEND-AWAY PREMIUMS

Consumers are constantly exposed to merchandise incentive offers in various magazines, in store announcements, and occasionally in broadcast media. These offers are all designed to motivate consumers to send away for various items of merchandise proposed as inducements for their acting in the marketplace in a manner consistent with the corporate or brand objectives of the offerer. In short, in return for buying a given product or service, the consumer can obtain certain merchandise of value, at a reduced cost or free.

Free Premiums

These premiums are sent free to consumers who comply with the offer, which usually requires one or more submissions of proofs-of-purchase of the promoted product. At times, the offerer may require postage and handling fees even though the incentive merchandise is identified as free. Such charges are on the decline, however, as companies seek to avoid the perceptual conflict of asking for money on an item advertised to be "free."

Self-Liquidators

Valuable merchandise, often at a substantial discount from normal retail, is offered as an incentive to persons who submit a specified number of proofs-of-purchase together with an order for the merchandise. The sponsoring company does not usually commit money for the merchandise beyond advertising the promotion itself; instead, the manufacturer uses its or its agent's buying power to obtain a discount from the supplier of the merchandise and then proceeds to offer the discounted merchandise to its customers. Companies may choose to include fulfillment charges in the price quoted to consumers, or they may decide to absorb such costs into the total cost of the promotion.

Partial Liquidators

Neither free nor fully liquidated, partial liquidators fall between the two. Essentially, the offerer contributes to the cost of the premium merchandise which makes the promotion attractive to consumers.

Combination Programs

Some promotional programs involving send-away premiums give consumers alternatives ranging from obtaining the incentive merchandise free to its being fully liquidated. The amount of money necessary usually depends on the number of proofs-of-purchase the consumer is ready to send in, and to some extent, on the degree of patience on the part of the consumer. If the premium is attractive and the number of proofs required to obtain it free is high, consumers may prefer to send in some money and fewer proofs. Such programs are more appropriate for group promotions— involving more than one line of products—with items that have short consumption cycles and are therefore prone to more frequent purchasing. A recent illustration of such a program is the 1982 Yumkins promotion from Del Monte.

Specific Objectives Satisfied by Send-Away Premiums

1. As with all premiums, send-aways provide a visualization of "real value," and to the extent that the premium meets either an immediate or latent consumer want, send-aways generate incremental purchases. Even stronger impact is obtained when the premium is unique, not normally found in retailing outlets, or when it is an item that a consumer may not normally buy, often for lack of discretionary funds, but which is an attractive reward for buying specific brands in categories in which products are routinely purchased.

2. Self-liquidators normally require no liability, immediate or accrued, unless minimum quantity commitments are necessary for favorable discounts.

3. Some premiums can be personalized with corporate or brand logos, so that their continued personal or household use can provide continued awareness for the product involved.

4.   A send-away premium program can be limited to a bud-
     geted number of units if a clear notation is made on the offer
     that the amount of incentive merchandise is limited and
     available on a first-come, first-served basis.

5.   A send-away premium program can be further contained by
     setting up specific periods during which the promotion is
     valid and submissions for merchandise will be accepted.
     Technically, the post-office box assigned to a promotion can
     be closed on the exact date of promotion expiration, with
     later submissions being automatically returned to senders.
     In fact, most companies tend to keep boxes open several
     weeks beyond the promotion period in order to allow all
     mail already in the pipeline to reach its destination. Besides
     avoiding bad feelings among customers, this practice also
     reduces consumer complaints.

6.   Where self-liquidators are concerned, policing the exact
     number of proofs submitted is really unimportant. In such
     programs, the objective is to maximize consumer response;
     since the promotion does not entail any assumed liabilities,
     the tendency is toward requiring a minimum number of
     proofs and often supplying the premium even if no proofs
     are submitted.

Summary—Send-Away Premium Promotions

Send-away premium programs give marketers a flexible incentive
vehicle that can be used selectively to shore up existing brands as
well as to accelerate the takeout of new entries. Such promotions,
however, do require particular cautions:

1.   Enough time must be allowed for the fulfillment process
     and this must be clearly indicated on the offer. Given the
     slowness with which bulk mail is usually handled, the offer
     should note that 8 to 10 weeks may elapse before the
     premium is received. According to current United States
     postal regulations, delay cards must be sent out if the
     merchandise will be delayed more than 30 days beyond the
     last date of delivery promised.

2. Securing reliable sources of supply is important for all premiums but particularly so for send-aways. Even good pretesting may fail to forecast the response a premium generates, and running short on merchandise that cannot be quickly and reliably replenished can result in complex and costly problems.

3. All possible delivery problems should be anticipated, with the objective of eliminating consumer complaints in this category.

    Packaging must be sturdy enough to ensure that the merchandise arrives in good condition.

    Bulk deliveries to multiple-dwelling locations, that is, high-risers, where the premium does not fit in standard mail-boxes, is vulnerable to theft, hence consumer complaints of nonreceipt and requests for substitute shipments.

    Disappearance of merchandise in transit is becoming more widespread; the sender must be prepared to generate substitute shipments.

4. In the case of promotions in which consumers are asked to pay for the premium—either on a full or partial liquidator basis—some requesters may want to return the premium for their money back. While such returns may not be mentioned in the offer, few companies will refuse these requests and should be prepared with both repayment and refurbishing procedures. The latter allows for the premium to be returned to stock and reshipped as other requests come in. Also, premiums may arrive damaged or inoperative and be shipped back with requests for refunds or replacements. The higher the ticket on the item, the more demanding consumers will be.

CONTINUITY PROMOTIONS

Continuity merchandise-premium programs are designed to promote a continuity of franchise for a product, a product line, or several lines in the context of wider corporate efforts. Consumers responding to offers made as part of continuity promotions are given the opportunity to obtain related merchandise—for instance, cooking sets—or to collect enough points over time to obtain free or at nominal cost high-ticket items—for instance, cameras and stereos. Some of the earliest promotions, at the turn of the century, were designed on a continuity basis and offered a limited number of collectibles—for instance, painting reproductions or posters. Baseball cards in gum packs and the long-running Betty Crocker merchandise program are current examples of continuity promotions. Over the years, similar programs were implemented for a number of cigarette brands.

In some cases, the premium merchandise is packed in with the product being promoted, which qualifies such a continuity effort as an in-pack promotion. Mostly, however, the product package carries a stamp or a coupon worth a certain number of points redeemable against merchandise. Merchandise catalogs are available to collectors on request. In turn, the catalogs motivate consumers to become more determined collectors—and hence, repeat purchasers of the product involved—by attractive, visual layouts of the premiums obtainable.

Attempts have been made to develop cooperative continuity programs, whereby products from different companies participate in a joint effort, on an exclusive, per-category basis. Mostly for logistic reasons, these programs, exemplified by the Bonus Gifts stamp promotion which got off to a quick start in the early 1960s, eventually failed.

Specific Objectives Satisfied by Continuity Promotions

Continuity-merchandise programs are primarily aimed at maintaining the consumer's franchise for the product or products promoted over the longer haul. At times, the limited need to shore up a franchise results in a mini-continuity program extending over a specific number of purchase cycles. In other cases, continuity programs run for years and are, in a sense, open-ended.

Summary—Continuity Promotions

While continuity-merchandise programs have never been overly popular—perhaps because they require long-term planning and commitment from a marketing management environment that emphasizes short-term thinking—they have maintained a respectable place among the merchandise promotion vehicles in use today.

TRAFFIC BUILDERS

As their name indicates, traffic builders are designed to increase consumer patronage levels at participating stores. Two forms are possible:

1.   Specially priced merchandise is obtainable in the store upon the presentation of store check-out tapes or receipts for a minimum amount of purchases or multiples thereof. The promotional merchandise usually comes in the form of sets—for instance, a table serving or encyclopaedia set—and each week a different piece in the set is offered at a greatly reduced price to customers shopping in the store. For those who want to complete their sets at a faster rate than one-piece-a-week, the remainder of the items can be purchased at higher, though still advantageous, prices. Also, when the sets are large, more than one piece per week may be offered at the promotional price. Overall, such promotions seldom run for periods of more than 12 weeks.

2.   Trading stamps given to shoppers in proportion to the amount of their purchases can be collected over time and redeemed for merchandise, usually by mail or at special merchandise centers maintained by the trading stamp company. Strictly a patronage-builder and maintenance promotional vehicle, trading stamps have known periods of great popularity as well as long periods of general trade neglect. During their last heyday, in the 1960s, some trading-stamp plan was offered by most food and many other retailers. It quickly became obvious, however, that only the first and perhaps the second account adopting such a plan in a given market stood to benefit by it. As soon as most food retailers, as well as some drug stores and mass merchandisers, joined in with their own plans, the motivation for a consumer to switch patronage from one store to another declined rapidly, which left all accounts with increased incremental costs of doing business.

Given the long-term commitments inherent in the adoption of

trading stamps, few retailers that are not already offering stamps would readily consider them of interest today. The emphasis for generating patronage has turned to short-term efforts and primarily to money promotions.

Specific Objectives Satisfied by Traffic Builders

1. Traffic builders provide a viable vehicle for retailers to increase and maintain consumer patronage over time.
2. Traffic builders can be used both short- and long-term, depending on the objectives of the store or account using them.

Summary—Traffic Builders

Retailers' merchandise promotions are as important to them as such promotions are to companies that use them to support their products or services. Overall, their objectives are similar: Retailers and manufacturers both wish to affect consumer buying behavior— retailers, by directing such buying to their own stores, and companies, by offering incentives to cause incremental consumer take-out of a product or service.

SWEEPSTAKES AND CONTESTS

In line with increases in all facets of sales promotion, significant growth has occurred in recent years in the area broadly defined as chance promotions—even when skill is involved—including sweepstakes, contests, merchandise giveaways, and so on. Participants in such promotional efforts may be rewarded by either merchandise/ services or cash. Since about 70% of the awards consist of merchandise or some form of service such as travel, such promotions are discussed in this chapter.

Chance Versus Skill

By and large, contest promotions usually involve an offer of participation (entry blank) representing a chance to win a prize in the form of merchandise or service, with an alternative in cash. Awards are determined by a drawing or similar device in which the process of naming a winner is beyond the will or control of the participant or sponsor. Skill contests are legally distinguished from chance promotions in that winners are rewarded on the basis of skill or merit rather than chance; but if chance is also present, the legal rules governing chance equally apply to contests of skill.[3]

Both sweepstakes and contests involve customers in the "promotional event" beyond the level of involvement possible with most other promotional tools. They are often used to heighten the awareness of a user or potential user about a product or service as much as to accelerate purchase. Although contests are used routinely by many companies, it is the promise of substantial winnings, beyond the small premium or cents-off coupon given in other promotions that has made sweepstakes and contests popular and kept them attracting large numbers of entries.

Sweepstakes Versus Contests

Sweepstakes are built entirely on chance, but chance may be missing either partially or totally from contests, with skill taking its place. Sweepstakes require participants only to send in their entries in order to be registered in the drawing for the winners. Participation in a contest requires participants to do some work—for example, writing a jingle or completing a statement about the promoted product. Obviously, sweepstakes usually elicit a larger response than contests precisely because contests require more effort.

Why Companies Use Sweepstakes and Contests

As with all promotions, sweepstakes and contests are meant to accelerate purchase actions for one's product or service by consumers who use or may be induced to use the product or service. These promotions are generally easy to execute and effective; from a financial point of view, liability can be contained and planned into the budget from the start with little fear of surprises. On the other hand, sweepstakes and contests are subject to many legal restric-

Skill Contest Versus Chance Promotion-

Federal and State Legal Precedents

Copyright © 1982
Promotion Marketing Association of America, Inc.,
New York, N.Y.

**SKILL CONTEST
VERSUS CHANCE PROMOTION –**

Federal and State Legal Precedents

INTRODUCTION

It is a general rule of Federal and State law that a genuine skill contest is not subject to the lottery law, for that law defines a lottery violation as requiring three essential elements – prize, *chance* and consideration. A contest of skill, as such, does not involve the element of chance. Therefore it does not constitute a lottery violation if participation is conditioned upon a purchase, payment or a substantial expenditure of time or effort by the participant.

If a skill contest also involves an element of chance it may violate the Federal and State lottery laws if consideration is required for entry. A 1909 amendment extended Federal lottery law coverage to promotions which offer "prizes dependent *in whole or in part* upon lot or chance." (18USC 1301) This language would cover, for example, a skill contest in which a tie is broken by a drawing, and a lottery violation would result if entry is conditioned upon a purchase. Similar language was inserted in the Federal law against mailing lottery materials (18 USC 1302 and 39 USC 3005), and against broadcasting lottery information (18 USC 1304).

The following legal precedents deal with the distinction between a chance promotion and a skill contest; the former violates the lottery law if entry is conditioned upon a purchase or payment.

FEDERAL PRECEDENTS

Essay Contest: A manufacturer's newspaper advertisement offered prizes for the "best" essay on the name of a certain breakfast food, the essay to be judged by three competent persons named, and each essay to be submitted with three labels from the food product advertised. **Held:** The promotion is not a lottery but a skill contest where the offer is made in good faith, the prize is awarded on merit rather than chance, and the advertisement contains a sufficiently definite statement of what the word "best" means in order to advise competitors of the standards of comparison to be applied

PMAA's special legal bulletin on skill versus chance promotions. (Reprinted with permission.)

by the judges, e.g., literary merit for advertising purposes. *Brooklyn Daily Eagle v. Voorhies* (1910) 181 Fed. 579.

Easy to Win Contest: A 1958 release by the U.S. Department of Justice reported that all U.S. Attorneys had been instructed by the Attorney General to prosecute certain promotional schemes victimizing the public, including the following:

"Easy To Win Contests. The general format of these contests usually consists of an open invitation to the public to win a 'prize' by the performance of a relatively simple task. For example, an advertisement shows a woman attired in a polka dot dress; a cash prize is to be awarded to the person who correctly counts the number of polka dots, a feat requiring no more than a mastery of elementary arithmetic. All entrants, of course, are winners and are told to call for their prizes at the business address of the advertiser. The winner then learns that his 'cash prize' can be obtained only as a credit against the purchase of merchandise sold by the advertiser. * * *"

Contest versus Drawing: "I note that you refer to your proposal as a 'contest.' Strictly speaking, a 'contest' involves a procedure whereby the winner is selected not on the basis of chance, but rather on the basis of some exhibited talent, skill or personal quality. Thus, your plan to draw a winner at random is not a 'contest.' " (FTC Staff Opinion, 1976.)

Win-a-House Contest: FTC Advisory Opinion No. 266 of July 17, 1968 reads as follows: (a) The Federal Trade Commission rendered an advisory opinion advising a magazine publisher that there would be no objection to a proposal to give purchasers or readers the opportunity to participate in a contest to win a house if implemented in the manner outlined below. (b) The plan as presented was to give the reader, whether a purchaser or not, the opportunity to participate in a competitive contest to win a house. The contestant was to send in a numbered coupon clipped from the magazine with a written answer of 50 words or less to a question as, for example, "Why do I believe in democracy?" The answer was to be judged by an independent panel, with the best essay being declared the winner. The contest was to take place every 3 months, at a prefixed date, in a public community event. The purpose of the number was to identify the contestant, with the judges knowing only the numbers of the participants and not their names. (16 CFR 15.266.)

Useful Idea Contest: The Federal Trade Commission found no objection to a proposed "Most useful and beneficial idea" contest in conjunction with a proposed nationwide membership campaign by an educational organization. Participation in the contest was conditioned upon application for membership in the organization. "Under the laws administered by the Commission no objection would be made to promotions involving a competitive contest fairly administered, so long as their material terms and conditions are clearly and adequately disclosed and complied with." However, the Commission reserved the right to proceed against any misrepresentation of the nature of a contest, the rules governing it, or the chances of winning a prize; and also against any promotion in which winners are not determined strictly according to the published rules. (Informal FTC Staff Comment, 1977.)

Skill Contest Requirements: A 1976 FTC Consent Order involved a manufacturer and its promotional agency. The Order defined " 'Skill Contest' as one in which the prize award is determined on the basis of the winning answers submitted by participants through the exercise of a substantial degree of skill . . ." For purposes of this Order the promotional agency was directed to base future skill contests solely on matters of established, provable fact, such facts to be readily available from reference materials. The contest must disclose that skill is involved, must identify the reference works upon which the answers are based, and must file the questions and answers with an independent organization prior to the promotion. Answers and a list of winners must be available to participants 60 days after judging the contest. The original complaint was based, not on lottery violation, but on failure to disclose certain conditions necessary to win a prize. (Coca-Cola Co.; Glendinning Cos., Docket 8824.)

Puzzle Contest Order: In a 1972 Consent Order the Federal Trade Commission required a conductor of puzzle contests to cease misrepresentations and to make disclosure of material facts. Adver-

PMAA's special legal bulletin (continued).

tisements for the contest were enclosed in egg cartons, and also appeared in newspapers and in mailings. The offer failed to disclose, among other things, that the contest was free only if contestants wished to play for the prizes initially announced. Payment of fees was required to become eligible for substantially larger cash prizes announced during subsequent tie-breaker puzzles. The FTC complaint did not charge a lottery violation as did a 1976 Florida complaint against the same promotion. (Lee Rogers, American Holiday Association, FTC Docket C-2312.)

Best Letter Contest: A 1957 Post Office Department statement on "Elements of a Lottery" contained the following paragraphs:

"A highly popular form of contest is the so-called 'best letter' contest wherein the prizes are given for the best essays or statements on a given subject, frequently having to do with the product of the plan's sponsor. These plans fall within that class of enterprizes in which the awards are made upon a basis of skill, assuming that the comparative skill of the contestants determines the outcome and the winning entry is not selected by some method of chance. Therefore, in this and other contests of skill, the plan does not become a lottery by the insertion of a requirement that the entrant purchase an article of merchandise or furnish some other consideration.

"However, although skill is involved, yet if a tie is possible, such as in 'best name' or 'best slogan' competitions, and a consideration is required to be furnished, it is necessary to include a rule that a prize identical with the one tied for will be awarded each tying contestant. This goes back to the question of chance in the amount of the prize, as already referred to."

Skill Contest or Lottery: A 1961 Interpretation was proposed but not formally adopted by the Post Office Department (or by the successor U.S. Postal Service), but the statement contains instructive reasoning on the lottery aspects of skill contests. A pertinent excerpt follows:

The element of chance will be deemed present:

(1) In any contest where the winning depends upon submitting the greatest number of box tops, labels, coupons or other proof of purchase.

(2) In any contest in which winners will be selected according to their choice of a name for a baby, animal, or other object, unless the nature of the thing to be named is such as to provide a genuine opportunity for the exercise of skill in creating a descriptive name with special appropriateness to design or purpose (such as the naming of a medical research organization) or unless the contestant is offered an opportunity to explain the basis for his name selection, and the winner is selected according to the merits of his explanation.

(3) In any contest calling for the submission of last lines for a limerick, or jingle, where the subject of the limerick or jingle, or the line to be supplied, is such as to provide no genuine opportunity for the exercise of creative skill in composition, and there is no genuine opportunity for the judges to discriminate among the contestants according to their demonstrated skill, the selection resolving itself into an arbitrary choice by the judges.

(4) In any contest where contestants are to complete a sentence, or to submit a whole sentence or sentences, in less than forty words, so that the writing provides no genuine basis upon which the contest judges may make a slection according to the comparative literary or other merit of the entries.

(5) In any contest where a demonstration of skill or diligence is required by contestants and (i) no rules are announced for judging the entries; or (ii) the rules are inadequate to describe and define the standards for judging or are inappropriate to the subject; or (iii) in selecting winners, the judges give weight to factors not disclosed in the announced rules (e.g., mentioning sponsor's name) or give to announced factors inordinate or predominant weight not disclosed in the rules (e.g., equating a standard of originality to that of uniqueness).

PMAA's special legal bulletin (continued).

Examples of acceptable statement of standards:

	Maximun value (points)
Appropriateness (specific reference to attributes of the subject)	20
Freshness (interest, creativeness, "sparkle")	30
Clarity (suitable and effective use of words)	35
Sincerity (believabiilty)	15

STATE PRECEDENTS

California: The 1974 Puzzle Contest Law is a unique regulatory statute (Business & Professions Code, Sec. 17539). It applies only to puzzle contests which require the payment of money for entry, and it requires disclosure of specified information about the game, the prizes, and the conditions for participation.

Florida: A 1971 Lottery Memorandum applied the gambling law prohibition (Stats., Sec. 849.14) to a game of skill in which contestants were required to pay consideration for entry; this, on the theory that participants would be making a bet on the result of the contest. This rule is not being applied to a genuine skill contest where entry is conditioned merely upon a purchase. However, it has been judicially held that a word puzzle game, with a registration fee requirement, constituted unlawful gambling where guesswork instead of skill determined winners. The Court also ruled that the value of prizes won was really determined by the amount of fee paid by each contestant. The game was illegal because it appealed to gambling instincts by allowing additional consideration or wagering as contestants became more and more involved in the several levels of each game. *Florida v. Lee Rogers, American Holiday Association* (1976) 329 So. 2d 257.

Indiana: A merchant offered a prize to the purchaser who came closest to determining the number of beans in a jar on display. **Held**: The promotion is an illegal lottery. "An expert mathematician might more nearly fix the number of beans in the globe than persons of less judgment; yet the exact number would be a mere matter of guessing. That any one should guess the correct number would be a matter of the merest chance . . ." *Hudelson v. State* (1884) 94 Ind. 426.

Nebraska: Excerpt from pamphlet by Deputy Attorney General C.A. Meyer, entitled "Lottery Analysis of Business Promotions in Nebraska" —

The English rule is that a lottery does not exist unless pure chance is used to determine the winner; that is, under the English rule such schemes as guessing the number of beans in a jar, or the total vote which will be cast at a forthcoming election, would presumably not be deemed to be lotteries. The American rule is set forth by the Nebraska Court in *Baedaro v. Caldwell* (1953) 156 Neb. 489, 56 N.W. 2d 706: "The test of the character of the game is not whether it contains an element of chance or an element of skill, but which of these is the dominating element that determines the result of the game." The same case contains this test for determining the presence or absence of chance: "A game of chance is one in which the result as to success or failure depends less on the skill and experience of the player than on purely fortuitous or accidental circumstances incidental to the game or the manner of playing it or the device or apparatus with which it is played, but not under the control of the player."

Texas: If the conduct of a contest and the answers given to a set of questions are dependent primarily upon skill and knowledge rather than upon mere chance, the contest is lawful, even if conditioned upon a purchase by the participant. Opinion of Attorney General, V-1483 (July 18, 1952).

Wisconsin: Excerpt from advisory letter by Assistant Attorney General W. W. Wilker, March 18, 1980:

PMAA's special legal bulletin (continued).

Chance is present in a contest when a person does not know and cannot learn whether he/she will win. Factors considered in determining if the outcome of a contest is determined by skill or ability rather than by chance are: (1) Participants are apprised as to the exact nature of the skill required of them (e.g., in a writing contest, participants must be informed of what type of writing skill is sought, and not just that the "best" entry will win), (2) the contest is actually judged by competent judges on the basis of that skill, (3) each participant is allowed equal opportunity to win based on the quality of his/her performance, and (4) duplicate prizes are awarded in case of tying entries. It should be remembered, however, that a contest is a lottery if the outcome is determined essentially by chance, "even though accompanied by some skill." Sec. 945.01 (2) (a), Stats.

November 1982 (FTD)

PMAA's special legal bulletin (continued).

tions and require expert legal advice before being offered to the public. They are slower than other forms of promotion to generate results, and since they generally do not require any proof of purchase—an illegal requirement for any sweepstakes or contest containing chance elements—the direct link between promotion and actual purchase is weak.

This last legal consideration is critical and deserves elaboration. Chance promotions that require any form of "consideration" on the part of participants in the promotion—that is, the purchase of a specific product—qualify as "lotteries" and are subject to lottery laws. On the other hand, a contest of "skill" is not subject to the lottery laws unless it contains elements of prize, chance, and consideration. The element of chance may be introduced into a skill contest if the promotion contains undisclosed rules, if it fails to apply and to describe appropriate standards for judging winners, if winners are determined arbitrarily or without due regard for rules, or if a tie-breaking procedure involves a drawing.[4] Adds Barton Freedman, Marketing Counsel of Brown & Williamson Tobacco Corporation:

Fill in this card correctly...

YOU COULD WIN
$1000, $500 or $100!

ENTER THE
"IT PAYS TO KNOW ORVILLE REDENBACHER'S" CONTEST

ALL YOU DO IS...

Study the following ORVILLE REDENBACHER'S® GOURMET® Popping Corn Fact List. Not only will you gain an appreciation for America's favorite, most profitable popping corn but you can pick up some nice cash as well! Just answer the easy questions on the Business Reply Card (or a facsimile) and mail. You can be a winner in the big prize drawing!

ORVILLE REDENBACHER'S Fact List
DID YOU KNOW THAT...

(1) ORVILLE REDENBACHER'S is the leading national brand in this snack category and has held the position for the past 3 years.

(2) ORVILLE REDENBACHER'S is the most heavily supported brand in the category — by far. In the last 12 months it outspent the next major competitor 4 to 1 in advertising. Plus, over 85 million coupons will be delivered in upcoming months.

(3) ORVILLE REDENBACHER'S is the best popping corn available! Research proves:
- ORVILLE REDENBACHER'S is the best known brand of popcorn.
- ORVILLE REDENBACHER'S is rated highest in quality over the other leading brands.
- ORVILLE REDENBACHER'S consistently pops up bigger and fluffier, making it more satisfying.

(4) ORVILLE REDENBACHER'S is largely responsible for category volume and profit growth the past 5 years:
- The market has increased an average of +8% per year in cases and +17% in dollar volume.
- Almost a third of U.S. homes serve popcorn once a week or more often.
- Category profitability runs high — in the 25% to 40% range — with Orville especially lucrative to retailers.

(5) ORVILLE REDENBACHER'S continues to grow. Consumers increasingly appreciate the low calories, natural qualities and low-cost-per-serving of popcorn. It's fun to make and eat, and that's why ORVILLE REDENBACHER'S is the brand they think of first, including ORVILLE REDENBACHER'S® GOURMET® BUTTERY FLAVOR® Popping Oil.

(6) There's no faster way to disappoint your customers (and your banker) than being out-of-stock on ORVILLE REDENBACHER'S products. Order sufficient inventory for display to prevent this from happening.

No Postage Stamp Necessary If Mailed in The United States

BUSINESS REPLY CARD

First Class Permit No. (2631), St. Paul, Minn. U.S.A.

Orville Redenbacher's Contest

P.O. Box 82065

St. Paul, Minnesota 58182

Instructions for entering a trade-oriented Orville Redenbacher contest. (Reprinted with permission.)

HOW TO ENTER

Refer to ORVILLE REDENBACHER'S Fact List before answering the questions. You must answer all 6 <u>correctly</u> to qualify for the prize drawing. All entries must be received by <u>November 15, 1982</u>.

CONTEST RULES

Entries should be submitted on the official mail-in Business Reply Card, or a facsimile. No purchase is required. If you wish to use a facsimile, you may still enter by mailing a postcard to: "Orville Redenbacher's Contest," P.O. Box 82065, St. Paul, MN 58182. List the questions A through F, and the correct answers — 1, 2, or 3 — next to each letter, and include your return address. Any resident of the U.S. is eligible to enter except employees of Hunt-Wesson Foods, Inc., and its agencies. One entry per person, please. All entries must be received by <u>November 15, 1982</u>. Winners will be determined from entries containing correct answers. Winners will be notified by mail. Odds of winning a prize are dependent on the number of entries. Any tax liability is the responsibility of the prize winner. No substitutes for prizes; prizes are transferable to approved recipients. Offer void where prohibited.

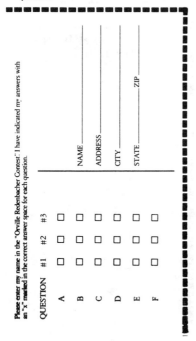

QUESTIONS (NOTE: While many of the answers below may seem appropriate, the "correct" answers are based on the accompanying Fact List. Choose only one answer per question. Mark an "X" in the correct answer box on the attached entry card or facsimile.)

(A) ORVILLE REDENBACHER'S ™ GOURMET® Popping Corn is...
1. Named after a World War I flying ace.
2. The nation's leading popping corn brand for the past 3 years.
3. The official popcorn of the 1982 International Snackers convention.

(B) ORVILLE REDENBACHER'S combined advertising and promotion support is...
1. The heaviest in the category.
2. Growing by an average 8% a year.
3. Known by most consumers.

(C) ORVILLE REDENBACHER'S is the best popcorn because...
1. It is the only popcorn with each kernel individually inspected.
2. It costs 25% to 40% less per serving than other snack foods.
3. Consumer research indicates its quality to be the highest.

(D) ORVILLE REDENBACHER'S means <u>profit</u> for you because...
1. It has lucrative profit margins as the leading brand in a growing category.
2. Almost a third of U.S. homes buy ORVILLE REDENBACHER'S once a week or more often.
3. Along with each jar sold, you move more oil, salt, napkins, beverages and party goods.

(E) ORVILLE REDENBACHER'S continues to grow because...
1. Scientists are finding ways to increase popcorn yield per acre.
2. More homes are buying poppers.
3. It's the snack that's right for today's more nutrition and economy-minded consumer.

(F) Out-of-stocks on ORVILLE REDEN-BACHER'S are...
1. A loss of sales and profit.
2. Preventable with sufficient inventory and display.
3. Both of the above.

©1982 Hunt-Wesson Foods Inc. 2823-G

Instructions for entering a trade-oriented Orville Redenbacher contest (continued).

118

The whole essence of a sweepstakes promotion is to creatively find ways to avoid the "consideration" element of a lottery without hurting the marketing objectives too much. If anybody can enter your sweepstakes, at any time, and nobody makes a purchase, you may end up running the biggest charity organization around. So the challenge with a sweepstakes is: How do I make my consideration element disappear, but still let me sell some product? That is the big technicality in sweepstakes games.... Generally speaking, as a broad overview, as long as you have "no purchase required," and as long as you give the consumer the ability to enter by alternate means other than purchase, sweepstakes are pretty safe today.[5]

Beware of the Consumer

Stories abound in the media about consumers who allegedly fail to receive their due as they participate in one promotion or another. While many such promotions may be suspect, and warnings against them proper, the likelihood that a major visible corporation will purposefully mislead consumers is at best remote. Being "too clever," however, in structuring and communicating the sweepstakes or contest may lead to trouble. In Freedman's words, "the consumer will catch you, and make a fool out of you."[6]

Virtually all corporations who have used, and are using, sweepstakes and contests as part of their promotional efforts have experienced consumer claims—often pursued through the legal system—based on technicalities that have little in common with the intent of the offer.

Freedman illustrates some of the problems that can develop in this area:

> Brown & Williamson, about a year and a half ago, ran a "Win an Island" sweepstakes. Some of you may remember. We gave away an island with house in Florida worth close to $400,000. We thought we were doing a great thing for this lucky prize winner. As reported in the newspapers from time to time, our prizewinner was very unhappy with her prize. The roof leaked, the plumbing backed up. If someone gave me a $400,000 island tomorrow, I wouldn't care if I had to go outside to use the plumbing. According to the *New York Times*, she's also blaming us for her marital problems.

One practical rule to learn from this is: Never award a prize that can stick like glue. Always find a prize concerning which you can say, "Goodbye. Take it. Take your trip to Pago Pago, and enjoy yourself." Don't give away houses. They don't seem to go away.

Here's another story. You've all seen the rules about employees of the sponsor and their families, being ineligible to win. There are now some states that are trying to pass legislation defining what "family" is.

This resulted from an actual lawsuit that was brought by a second prize winner who discovered that the first prize winner was the brother-in-law, or something like that, of some minor functionary at the sweepstakes advertiser's ad agency, a very remote connection. The second prize winner brought a suit to have the sweepstakes voided, and have the first prize awarded to the second prize winner.

And then there's the all-time classic that I leave you with, to show you how sometimes your friend the consumer can figure out ways to get you. A soft-drink bottler in Maryland was running a bottle-cap sweepstakes and offered several alternative ways to get facsimile bottle caps.

The plaintiff went out and purchased about twenty or thirty eight packs of the given beverage, and won about $7 in bottle-cap prizes, and then sued under the state lottery statute for a couple of thousand dollars' punitive damages on a theory that, since *he* won *his* prizes without getting facsimiles, he bought the bottles, and so to him the promotion was a lottery.[7]

Planning Sweepstakes and Contest Promotions and Drafting Participation Rules

Perhaps it is axiomatic to stress that any sweepstakes or contest offer must state clearly, fully and accurately the terms and conditions of participation. Besides the need to avoid the potential for misunderstandings and negative consumer reactions, there are obvious legal implications in any misrepresentation, whether intended or not. The following considerations come from Frank Dierson, currently general counsel of the Promotion Marketing Association of America (PMAA), and probably the most knowledgeable authority in this field.

1. *The Entry Blank.* Common to such offers is the instruction to the participant to write name and address on the official entry form or on a reasonable facsimile (a card or piece of paper on which the participant has drawn a replica of the entry blank or of the designated elements of the sponsor's product or service).

2. *Facsimile.* If the promotion involves chance elements, lottery violations can be avoided if a facsimile is accepted in lieu of a proof-of-purchase. The rules, however, must be very explicit as to what the facsimile is to state or reproduce.

3. *Burdensome Requirements.* Facsimile requirements should be simple. If they are so burdensome that they inhibit free participation, the facsimile may be ineffective as a substitute for a proof-of-purchase requirement. Should that happen, the promotion may be interpreted as a lottery. Generally, "consideration" is deemed to be an element in a chance promotion if a considerable amount of time and effort must be furnished by the participant.

4. *Eligibility.* It is critical that full details on eligibility are included in the offer. Are there any age limits placed on participation? Is the promotion open to employees and families of the sponsor, its advertising or promotion agencies, and its suppliers? Is the promotion restricted to residents of certain states and void in others?

5. *Multiple Entries.* Is the promotion limited to one entry per participant? Per family? If multiple entries from one individual are acceptable, should individual mailings for each entry be stipulated?

6. *Random Drawing.* In chance promotions, where skill is not a factor, the rules often indicate that winners will be randomly drawn and that the drawing itself will be conducted by an independent organization.

7. *No Purchase Required.* The "no purchase required" notation is now common on all chance promotions because it clearly signals the absence of consideration requirements. Care must be

taken not to qualify this notation, by offering to sweeten the winnings of those who may have nevertheless purchased the sponsor's products. Such a statement would turn the promotion into a lottery.

8. *Description of Prizes.* The nature and number of prizes should be clearly spelled out in the promotional material. Any values assigned to the items of merchandise or service offered should be stated at regular retail, not at the (discounted) price paid by the sponsor.

9. *Restrictions on Awards.* Any restrictions applying to prizes must be stated in the offer. The promotion may limit a family to one prize or set a time limit for exercising a service prize.

10. *Amount and Guarantee of Prizes Awarded.* Sponsors should not make claims for prizes to be awarded, merchandise or cash, in excess of the amounts to be actually disbursed. Nowadays, many sponsors deposit the promised amount in trust with an outside agency—that is, a bank—to ensure credibility with the public.

11. *Consistency of Representations.* All promotional and advertised claims for the offer must be consistent with the terms stated in the rules. Discrepancies between the two could lead to liabilities costing far more than the amount budgeted for the promotion.

12. *Notification of Winners.* In most cases, the rules provide for mail notification of winners. In some instances, however, the rules state that notification will be accomplished through the same medium initially used to publicize the offer.

13. *Odds of Winning.* Where chance is involved, the odds of winning should be stated in the offer. The offer should employ practical winning odds and avoid predicting prize winnings in amounts that have only a remote possibility of being awarded.

14. *Requirements for Additional Expenditure.* If an award requires the winner to incur personal expense as a condition to being able to enjoy the prize won, a full disclosure of the condition must be included in the offer to avoid any claims of deception. Such may be the case, for example, if the winner of a vacation lodging award has to provide his or her own transportation to the place of lodging.

15. *List of Winners.* If a list of winners will be available after the sweepstakes or contest has been concluded, the offer usually

carries a notation to that effect: "For a list of winners, send a stamped, self-addressed envelope to the address given below."

16. *Voiding Clauses.* Since the laws of certain states may include restrictions that are not acceptable to the sponsor, and since some offers—particularly those inserted in national or regional media—may still circulate in those states, it is prudent to include in the rules a disclaimer stating that the "offer is void where prohibited." Sometimes the disclaimer may refer to a particular jurisdiction, for instance, "this offer is void in Wisconsin."

17. *Publicity Rights.* At times, a sponsor may want to use the prizewinner's name and/or picture in follow-up publicity plans. Warning of such an intention should be given in the offer and a statement that a formal release to this effect will be required from winners and is a condition of participation.

18. *Income-Tax Liability.* The rules should stipulate that winners will be responsible for any federal and state income-tax liability arising from their winnings, unless the sponsor states an assumption of such liability.

19. *Sales-Tax Liability.* The sponsor is considered the ultimate user of the prizes purchased for the promotion and hence is liable for applicable sales taxes.

20. *Return Address.* All entry blanks should carry clear instructions for mailing, particularly when the address given for mailing entries is different from the address of the sponsor's main place of business.

21. *Purchase Orders.* When a sweepstakes or contest entry is made available in conjunction with an order form for the sponsor's products or services, great care must be taken to differentiate clearly between the two, by format and by instructions, so that participants will not inadvertently sign the purchase order.

22. *Affidavit of Compliance.* If prizewinners are required to sign a sworn statement that they have complied with the rules of the chance promotion, the initial promotion must clearly communicate this condition.

23. *Avoiding Ambiguity in Describing Awards.* It is obviously important that all prizes be carefully and fully described in order to avoid demands by prizewinners that may exceed the intent of the

sponsor. Both language descriptions and pictorial representations of prizes must be accurate. Experience has shown that legal adjudications of ambiguity in the rules have generally gone against the sponsor/drafter of the rules and in favor of the winning participants.

24. *Tie-Breaking.* The problem of ties usually arises in a promotion that includes both skill and chance elements. If several entries qualify for a single prize, the rules should clearly state the procedure to be used in breaking the tie, perhaps a random drawing among the several entries to determine a single winner.

25. *Dealer Participation.* The sponsor often wants to involve the trade more closely in a sweepstakes or contest promotion. As a way of enlisting such cooperation, the sponsor may designate an additional or duplicate prize to be made to the dealer providing a winning entry blank or having some other connection to a winning participant. Where such is the intent of the sponsor, the participant will be asked to identify the dealer on the entry blank.

26. *Deadline for Entries.* Obviously, all sweepstakes and contests run for a finite time period. The rules must therefore specify the last date for submissions to the sweepstakes or contest. Such dates are usually expressed as dated postmarks. More recently, however, the proliferation of postage machines has caused some sponsors to honor submissions by date of receipt as well.

27. *Submission of Final Reports.* In states requiring contest registration and an announced termination date, the sponsor should consider the period of time needed to determine the winners and complete the awarding of prizes after the submission deadline and thus determine the promotion's termination date, 30 days after which a final report must be filed with the registration agency.

Executing the Sweepstakes/Contest Promotion

Legal compliance in the execution of contests and/or sweepstakes clearly is of constant concern to the promotion or marketing manager conducting the event, particularly one that includes elements of chance. Both federal and state laws and regulations must be consulted before the execution of such a promotion. Some states require advance registration of promotions that include

---

CHECK LIST FOR PREPARING THE RULES

"No Purchase Necessary" — Conspicuous declaration

Facsimile entry alternative

Random drawing reference

Voiding clause, where necessary

Disclosure of odds of winning

Prize description; cash substitute option

Notification of winners by mail

Mutilated or illegible entries disqualified

Mass entries and reproductions disqualified

No limit on mail entries, but only one per envelope

Eligibility provisions; sponsor-related parties; minors

Minors; certain prizes delivered only to parent or guardian

Affidavit of eligibility and compliance with rules

Addresses: for entries; for winner list requests; for free entry

Reservation of publicity rights; use of name and photograph of winner

Deadline for receipt of entries; for postmark

Termination date of promotion

Disclaimer of liability

. . . For taxes on prizes

. . . For lost or stolen entries

. . . For prize merchandise of independent supplier

Checklist for preparing the rules for chance promotions.

chance elements; all such requirements must be identified and satisfied in a timely fashion. In the conduct of a promotional program containing chance elements, several points of legal concern are worth special mention.

1. *Fairness.* Proper supervision of a promotion includes seeing to it that all participants have a fair opportunity to win a prize. Provisions must guarantee sufficient time to enter the event on the part of all those wishing to do so and ensure that all prizes will be awarded to winners among the entrants.

2. *Deception.* The rules and the materials involved in a chance promotion may be held deceptive if any of the statements or pictorial presentations are judged to be false, deceptive, or misleading. Also, a sponsor may be penalized as misrepresenting chance, if the promotion gives the appearance of making awards by chance, but in effect, chance plays little or no part in the actual selection of winners.

3. *Use of the Word "Free".* The use of the word "free," frequently used to describe the offer itself or the prizes to be awarded, is permissible, but subject to special regulations prescribing disclosure of terms, limitations on frequency and duration of the promotion, as well as the type size to be used for the word "free."

4. *Disqualification.* Participants who submit entries that do not conform to the rules of the promotional offer may be disqualified. It is critical, however, that careful records be kept of such disqualification for use in potential legal action.

5. *Fraud.* If submissions of winning entries appear to be fraudulent, prize delivery may be postponed until each suspected case has been investigated. Here, too, careful records must be made and kept of the procedures followed and actions taken.

6. *Availability of Sufficient Prize Merchandise.* The supply of prizes offered in the promotion must be firmly secured beforehand, so that delivery delays cannot lead to official and consumer complaints.

7. *Changing the Rules.* The prudent manager tries to avoid tampering with or changing the rules of a chance promotion after they have been printed and disseminated. But if such a course of action is truly unavoidable, timely notice should be given of any change in any term or condition involved in the promotion.

8. *Product Safety.* The Federal Consumer Product Safety Act and related legislation apply to product prizes intended for children. Obviously, product safety should guide the selection of such prizes; age limitations may be included in the rules for certain types of prizes unsuitable or unsafe for children.

9. *Rejection of Void Entries.* Given the broad circulation of media containing a chance promotion, voiding clauses should be appended that exclude from the offer residents of specific states

where, by state law, the promotion is either restricted or prohibited. By rejecting or disqualifying entries from those states, the sponsor can avoid violations of specific state laws.

The points just discussed by no means exhaust all the complications one must consider in order to be in full compliance with all possible legal requirements. Legal counsel is highly recommended, both in the planning and execution of such promotions. However, few companies have resident legal personnel specifically expert in the field of promotion, and in-house legal departments called on to review such promotions are further hampered by the need to continually update their legal files in this area. The legal bulletins prepared by Frank Dierson under the egis of the PMAA help fill this need rather well but they are available only to PMAA member companies.

The Fulfillment Function

Fulfillment, as detailed by the PMAA, "embraces all the physical operations necessary to move premium merchandise into recipients' hands; shipment from manufacturer to the staging area, order processing, repackaging, and actual individual shipment."[8] Fulfillment is an essential function in merchandise promotions where the incentive is delivered by mail and the services of either an in-house or a contract fulfillment supplier are required.

The Fulfillment House. A large number of fulfillment houses have sprung up throughout the country as the need for their services grew. Some houses developed as extensions of mail-order operations; many have gone beyond the handling of premiums to deal also with cash refunds and coupon redemptions.

While price competition is increasingly fierce, woe to the marketing manager who accepts the lowest bid as the sole criterion for selecting a fulfillment supplier. Some fulfillment houses have grown into full-fledged marketing-support organizations, able to help develop and plan the promotional program using expertise gained over time from many other programs and marketing strategies. Some fulfillment houses specialize in the handling of

Mr. John Jones
ABC Corporation (client)
1234 Main Street
Anywhere, U.S.A. 00000

Dear Mr. Jones:

We submit our quotation for handling your_____premium offer on_____ (product)_____,
as you have described it to us.

Following are the labor operations we will perform in connection with this program:
1. Allot a post office box for your use in receiving consumer requests.
2. Pick up mail at the post office daily for the duration of the program.
3. Face, count and slit mail.
4. Remove contents and qualify for correct money and proof-of-purchase.
5. Address mailing labels.
6. Sort labels geographically according to postal or UPS regulations.
7. Affix labels to pre-packaged premium item.
8. Bundle, tie, and bag according to postal/UPS regulations.
9. Deliver to United States Post Office or United Parcel Service.
10. Submit periodic cash, production, and inventory reports.

_____ (fulfillment house) _____will perform the above operations at the rate of $____per M units processed. This
does not include the cost of mailing. If we are able to use bulk rate mail (which requires 50 lbs. or 200 pieces of
identical mail per mailing) and assuming a mailing weight of____ounces, postage will be $____per M pieces
mailed. If we are not able to use bulk rate, we will ship via regular third class mail/UPS, which at____ounces will
cost $____per M pieces mailed. UPS charges are estimated basis 5th zone average; you will be billed for actual
costs incurred.

Additional charges are as follows·

Monthly Minimum Charge	$_____
Post Office Box Rental	$_____, semi-annually
Printed Mailing Labels (basis __M)	$_____per M
Endorse & Deposit Checks	$_____per M
Bulk Mailing Permit	$_____per calendar year
Business & Grief Mail	$_____each, plus postage

Telephone orders from the client are charged at $____per shipment.

Postage/UPS and supplies costs are at the present rates. Should rates change, these changes will be passed on
to the client.

Should you require media or geographic sorts of requests received, this service is charged at $____per M for the
first two sorts, plus $____per M for each additional sort.

Postage due on incoming mail and merchandise is the responsibility of the client.

N.S.F. and other uncollected checks are the responsibility of the client and are deducted at face value plus bank
charges incurred.

Fire and extended coverage insurance on all merchandise consigned to our warehouse is the sole responsibility
of the consignor.

Consumer requests will be held for 60 days and then destroyed unless otherwise specified.

Storage charges are at $___per month per skid on all merchandise which remains in our warehouse over 30 days.

If our proposal meets with your approval, please sign one copy and return to us for our files. Thank you for this
opportunity and we look forward to working with you.

Sincerely,

Fulfillment House

by:_____

Approved by:_____ (client company) _____

Name:_____

Title:_____

Date:_____

Sample agreement between a fulfillment house and a client. (Reprinted from
PMAA's *Fulfilling Your Orders* book.)

ACE FULFILLMENT HOUSE

PRODUCT_____   Lot No._____

Report To_____   Report No._____

Offer_____   Date_____

Orders Received	THIS WEEK		CUMULATIVE	
	Orders	Amount	Orders	Amount
Correct Requirements (Consumer Orders)				
TOTAL				

Merchandise Mailed

	This Week	Cumulative

Orders Mailed_____

Replacements Mailed_____

Miscellaneous (Sales, Samples, Etc.)_____

TOTAL MERCHANDISE MAILED_____

Form Letters Sent_____

Material Inventory Units

    Previously Received_____

    Received This Week_____

    TOTAL Receipts_____

    Previously Mailed_____

    Mailed This Week_____

    TOTAL Mailed_____

    Balance on Hand_____

Sample fulfillment house activities report. Reprinted from PMAA's *Fulfilling Your Orders* book.

sweepstakes and contests, and their involvement in such a program can almost guarantee success.

Working with Fulfillment Suppliers. The results obtained from working with a fulfillment house can be greatly improved if the relationship of supplier and sponsor is carefully structured and backed up by a carefully delineated range of fulfillment executions. The following checklist provided by the PMAA provides helpful guidelines for this partnership.[9]

1. Discuss the program with more than one fulfillment house
   a. Check credit and company references
   b. Inspect premises
2. Prepare contracts with fulfillment house
3. Consult fulfillment house on
   a. Item or alternatives
   b. Packaging
   c. Pricing offer
   d. Advertising and point-of-sale activity
   e. Coupon form, size, and copy
   f. Estimating returns
   g. Costs
   h. Order rate to supplier of premium
   i. Back-up inventory
   j. Parcel-delivery costs
   k. "Grief" handling methods
   l. Out-of-country shipments
   m. "Keying" the offer
   n. Money handling
   o. Credit cards
4. Design reports to come from fulfillment house and decide their frequency
   a. Proofs-of-purchase

    b.   Names and addresses

    c.   Money control

    d.   "Bad checks"

    e.   Inventory control

    f.   Order procedure

5.   Design internal records

    a.   Advertising schedules

    b.   Sales reports

    c.   Coordination with reports from fulfillment house

    d.   Budget comparisons

    e.   Cash flow

NOTES

1. *Marketing with Premiums* (New York: Promotion Marketing Association of America, 1975).

2. George Meredith and Robert P. Fried, *Incentives in Marketing* (Union, N.J.: National Premium Sales Executives Education Fund, 1977), pp. 10–11.

3. Frank T. Dierson, *Planning for Chance Promotions* (New York: Premium Advertising Association of America, 1976), p. 1. (Premium Advertising Association is now Promotion Marketing Association of America.)

4. Dierson, *Planning for Chance Promotions*, p. 14.

5. Barton H. Freedman, "Legal Aspects of Promotion" (Paper presented at the ANA Workshop *Reaching Today's Changing Consumers with Promotions*, 1982, pp. 12–13).

6. Freedman, "Legal Aspects of Promotion," p. 7.

7. Ibid., pp. 13–45.

8. *Fulfilling Your Orders* (New York: Promotion Marketing Association of America, 1979), p. 4.

9. *Fulfilling Your Orders*, pp. 14–15.

FIVE

Money Promotions: Coupon Programs

As an incentive for bringing about a certain type of marketing action, money has always scored high. Clearly, if each product or service is perceived by the user to hold a certain value relative to its cost to the user, it follows that the lower the product's effective cost, the higher the value-in-use it represents. Precisely because of the simplicity of this relationship, money offers, of one kind or another, have grown so popular over the years.

Money offers hold strong sway over both aspects of promotional efforts—they help disturb existing behavioral consumption patterns by motivating purchase and usage of new products or services and they help maintain existing patterns by causing repurchase and continuing usage of products or services. In both instances, buyer/consumer perceptions of the value/cost relationship inherent in such products or services are manipulated. It is important to note, however, that money incentives are earned only after a purchase has been made, either at point-of-purchase—through coupons—or by subsequent fulfillment of claims—that is, refunds. It is this direct and often accelerated relationship between most money promotions and the purchases they generate that makes money promotions, in many forms, so attractive to sponsors.

TYPES OF MONEY PROMOTIONS

1. *Money Promotions as Price Cuts.* Discounting through price cuts has been a way of life in this country for so long that it is hard to imagine a time when shoppers had little choice but to pay the full retail price on most of their purchases. Beginning with increased competition of "mass" dimensions and the increased credibility of manufacturer brands, price discounting has spread from consumer package goods across the whole spectrum of consumer goods and services.

2. *Money Promotions as Paper Redeemable for Cash.* The number of coupons and purchase certificates offered to shoppers continues to grow by leaps and bounds. The ease and flexibility of launching and executing such promotions have sustained their popularity with manufacturers and trade factors, despite some serious drawbacks.

3. *Cash Refunds and Rebates.* Increasingly, companies are rewarding buyers of their products with cash incentives, available upon the submission of the prescribed proof(s) of purchase. While there is little real difference between refunds and rebates, refunds are usually offered in conjunction with the general run of consumer packaged goods, while rebates are more often used on higher-ticket items, for instance, appliances and cars.

4. *Cash Giveaways.* Money giveaway primarily are promotions that offer prize money as a reward for specific actions on the part of the consumer in the marketplace. Usually, a "monitor" determines whether the consumers approached by the monitor on a random basis are qualified to receive a prize, and often, if the qualification is positive, the monitor makes the award on the spot.

PRICE-CUT PROMOTIONS

Most price cuts fall in one of two categories:

Manufacturer-controlled and funded incentives designed to accelerate immediate consumer takeout at point-of-purchase.

Retailer-generated price reductions resulting, at least in part, from special allowances and/or free goods obtained by the retailer from the manufacturers.

While, in effect, both types of price cuts appear as reductions at retail, they represent distinctly different incentive routes to increased consumer takeout. In the first case, shoppers normally associate the price cut with a manufacturer that wants to increase product sales over competitive entries; the latter type of price cut is often seen as part of a retailer's effort to increase customer patronage.

This incentive difference has particular meaning during the introduction of new products. Although it is important for a manufacturer to use money incentives in the form of price cuts at retail in order to speed up adoption of the new product, the better price-cut avenue is via retailer-sponsored and -executed price reductions. The reason is simple. For a price reduction to be perceived as desirable, customers must have a clear idea of what the nonreduced price is. They can thus appreciate and respond positively to the value/price enhancement offered through the price cut. On the other hand, since retailer-generated price cuts are expected by shoppers as a regular part of patronage incentives, they are understood as "bargains" and such prices will not have a negative effect on the "regular" price a manufacturer will seek to establish for a product. Price cuts at point-of-purchase take several forms.

Off-Label Pricing (Price-Packs)

Off-label pricing represents the largest area of manufacturer-structured, -executed, and -funded direct-price incentives. Price-pack promotions consist of specially marked packages sold to the trade as reduced-price "specials" and delivered to the retail floor during a specified period. Each package—can, jar, or box—must clearly state the cost saving to be achieved by the consumer. In effect, the package states that the "price marked is X¢ off regular retail price—you pay only...." Specific FTC guidelines govern such promotions and how they are billed to the buyer.

A variant of off-label pricing promotions are manufacturer "pass-on" drives, which represent specially authorized—and funded—price reductions applying to a complete line or certain items in a line. Such drives are usually designed around higher-ticket items such as appliances, offered for a finite period of time, and identified and advertised to consumers as "manufacturer authorized" or "factory authorized" price promotions. In contrast, off-label priced consumer packaged goods find their way to the shelf, or the retail floors, with a minimum of advertising fanfare, and the promotion lasts until all the labeled packages sell through. By and large, manufacturer pass-on drives have lost much ground to the spread of discounting and the decline in the observance of retail price maintenance.

Specific Objectives Satisfied by Price-Pack Promotions

1. To accelerate consumer takeout at retail by giving the brand(s) involved a value/price edge over competitive entries.
2. To give the trade reason to buy heavily against the promotion and follow it up with off-shelf and special displays on the retail floor.
3. To stimulate impulse switching within the product category.
4. To reward current users and keep them in the franchise for the brand(s).
5. To fend off potential share losses to competitive product introductions by causing a higher takeout of customers from the market during the promotional period for the competitive product(s).

Potential Problem with Price-Pack Promotions.   Off-label pricing promotions are not without potential problems, which should be carefully examined before the inclusion of price packs in a marketing plan. Perhaps the strongest argument against such promotions stem from the growing automation of physical handling functions in the trade. Central warehousing, store deliveries, and inventory controls at retail continue to benefit from increased applications of data processing. Consequently, any intrusion on established accounting and inventory routines is frowned on, particularly when the departure from norm is temporary. The price-pack promotion is temporary—the duration of the promotion is by definition limited—but since the promoted product carries a different price, it requires a new Standard Counting Unit (SKU) listing. Not surprisingly, trade acceptance of such promotions has fallen to 50% and the decline will probably continue.

Continued or frequent use of such promotions will cause confusion in the minds of consumers and might negatively affect their perceptions of the value/price relationship for the brand(s) involved.

FTC Regulations Guiding the Use of Off-Label Pricing. The use of off-label pricing—price packs—comes under specific FTC regulations designed to prevent potential abuse. Broadly, these regulations mandate the following stipulations:

1. No more than 50% of a brand's volume over a 12-month period can be price-packed, that is, carry off-label pricing.
2. Only three price-pack promotions per year are permitted on any one brand/item, and a period of at least 30 days during which regularly priced packs are sold must separate two price-pack promotions.
3. Price packs must be accompanied by display material clearly stating the following information: brand name, regular price, cash savings, and new price.

Summary—Price-Pack Promotions. Price-pack promotions can play a particularly important role in highly price-elastic categories, where even slight changes in price can strongly impact consumer value/price perceptions toward the brand(s) promoted and cause significant and immediate switching from competitive products. Often used in conjunction with a "trade-loading" objective, price-pack promotions must be considered in terms of their potential, long-term impact on the promoted brand franchise, separately from whatever short-term benefits may derive. Finally, alternative point-of-purchase efforts may have to be developed and used side-by-side with the price-pack promotion if only half or fewer of the trade factors in the marketplace are willing to accept the promotion.

Retail Price Featuring

Weekly price features, advertised or unadvertised, are now an accepted way of life for all classes of trade retailing consumer packaged goods to ultimate consumers. Basically, a retailer price feature refers to a price reduction planned, executed, funded, and above all controlled by the retailer on one or more items in a line or lines, with the purpose of bringing more shoppers to the store(s). Known in earlier days as a "loss-leader" strategy, whereby the retailer offered a few items on the shopper's frequent purchase list at "below-cost" prices in order to encourage patronage, price featuring mushroomed to where bargain prices—not usually below cost except for closeouts—are offered for products in most if not all of the high usage categories.

Price features are usually advertised to consumers—unadvertised point-of-purchase specials are also common—through a variety of mostly local broadcast and print media. From the consumer's vantage point, much of this advertising has been conveniently routinized. Wednesday is generally the "best food day" in local newspapers, which carry most of the food trade advertising for the week, including incentive offers from retailers and manufacturers.

Objectives Satisfied by Retail Price Featuring. Retail price featuring helps a retailer:

1. To attract more customers to the store.
2. To direct shopper interest to specific items and lines whose accelerated take-out may improve the retailer's profit performance. Conversely, price featuring may also help in "flushing through" items that are being discontinued by the retailer, but whose perceived value may be such that price featuring can attract potential shoppers to the store.
3. To work together with manufacturers and/or suppliers in featuring items of mutual interest and thus being able also to earn certain monetary allowances from manufacturers and/or suppliers.

Summary—Retail Price Featuring.   An often-used promotion technique, retail price featuring is strategically controlled by the offering retailer. It is up to the retailer to determine the size of the price reduction, the period it will be offered, and the way it will be communicated to customers, including the prominence a particular price feature receives relative to similar features for other products in store advertising, flyers, hand-bills, point-of-purchase cards, on and off shelf, and any other media used by the retailer.

MONEY AS REDEEMABLE PAPER FOR CASH: COUPONING PROGRAMS

The opportunity given shoppers to obtain instant price discounts at the cash register has caused coupon use to soar. Distribution of manufacturer's coupons, through all media, exceeded 100 billion in 1981, double the rate of six years earlier. According to a 1977 U.S.

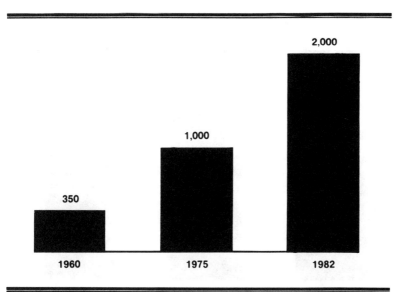

Source: A.C. Nielsen Co.

Growth of couponing companies since 1960. (Reprinted with permission.)

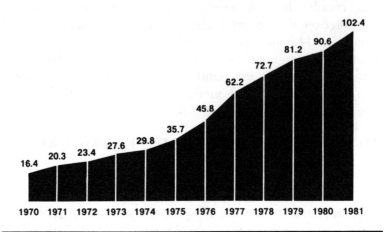

Source: A.C. Nielsen Co.

Coupon distribution trend since 1970 (in billions of coupons). (Reprinted with permission.)

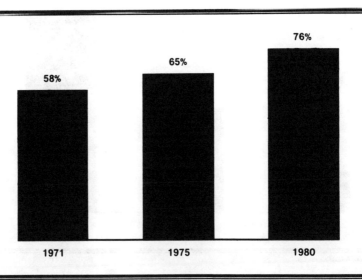

Source: A.C. Nielsen Co.

Increasing coupon use since 1971—percentage of households using coupons. (Reprinted with permission.)

140

Department of Agriculture survey, at that time four out of five households had used coupons.

Clearly, coupons have become a potent promotional tool and an important factor in the strategic considerations of most manufacturers, of consumer packaged goods as well as an increasing number of other companies supplying products and services to consumers.

HISTORY OF COUPONING

It was inevitable that the "something extra" given by retailers to encourage customer patronage at the turn of the century would eventually translate to offering price inducements against future purchases. The wooden nickels given out by some of the early country stores may have been the first money incentives in this country redeemable at point-of-purchase against purchases, although the wooden nickel possibly was offered in lieu of legitimate but scarce change. According to Russell Bowman, the first documented coupon was offered by C.W. Post in 1895 in support of the introduction of Post's new health cereal, Grape Nuts. The coupon, a one-cent certificate, could be presented to any grocery store carrying the product for a penny price reduction.[1]

Since these early days, couponing grew slowly and was generally limited to a few large companies. Broader interest in couponing occurred in the 1950s, and distributions of coupons reached 5 billion a year by the beginning of the 1960s, tripled to over 16 billion by 1970, and exploded to 91 billion in 1980. Whether this growth pattern will extend throughout the 1980s and beyond remains to be seen. Most likely, the growth will continue but at a more moderate pace. It should be noted that these figures include coupons issued by manufacturers only. Retailer (in-ad) coupons are not included, since the data on their distribution are scarce. However, retailer coupons seem to be on the decline since the mid-1970s.

Growth Factors in the Use of Coupons

Coupons are increasingly popular, from the points of view of consumer, retailer, and manufacturer.

Early 'coupons' in the form of metal tokens. (Reprinted with permission.)

From the consumer's point of view:

1. Coupons are easy to use. They require little effort beyond clipping—if they are in print media—and organizing.

2. Coupons are widely accepted by retailers of consumer packaged goods, which is in keeping with the trend toward intensive distribution as such goods become increasingly commoditized. Obviously, wide coupon acceptance gives the consumer considerable freedom of choice about which retail outlets to patronize.

3. Coupons are immediately actionable at point of purchase; they are the next thing to money.

4. Coupons can save shoppers considerable money, particularly where manufacturer coupon values are doubled and occasionally

Coupon Users	100%
Actively Look For Coupons	57%
Use Coupons If They Happen To See Them	41%
Both Ways	2%

Source: A.C. Nielsen Co.

Coupon-user behavior. (Reprinted with permission.)

even tripled by the trade. Coupons further provide a form of "time utility," since consumers can keep the coupons over time—within expiration limits—and use them as needed.

5. A certain amount of fun has become attached to couponing, as indicated by the recent emergence of shoppers' clubs and newsletters throughout the country. Members and subscribers trade with each other over the whole range of "paper-redeemable-for-cash" incentives.

From the retailer's viewpoint:

1. Although coupons accelerate sales on the retailer's floor, it is the manufacturer, in most cases, who assumes the liability for their redemption.

2. The handling of coupons demands no special processing within the retailer's organization. Additional work is involved, but the retailer is paid a special coupon-handling fee, which is currently about 7¢ per coupon. Part of this fee is also meant to reimburse the retailer for the cost of money advanced to the consumer—in effect, the discount value of the coupon—until the retailer is reimbursed by a coupon clearinghouse.

From the manufacturer's view:

1. Couponing enables the manufacturer to reach consumers directly with a promotional effort positioned right against product price. Manufacturers cannot dictate retail prices and have no assurance that various allowances given retailers are passed on to consumers through product price featuring, so coupons are often manufacturers' only sure influence on retail pricing.

2. Couponing programs are easy to handle, both in terms of planning and execution. Although, because of the very ease of working with couponing programs, most manufacturers have used such efforts tactically—often on a panic basis—rather than strategically. There are indications, however, that more and more manufacturers are starting to include such programs in their strategic plans.

3. Couponing programs are highly flexible, enabling manufacturers to achieve a high degree of pinpointed targeting. Depending on the couponing vehicle used, a manufacturer can achieve substantial selectivity using a wide spectrum of demographic and socioeconomic criteria.

4. Couponing programs are easy to communicate to internal sales organizations and can be used to generate trade support through increased loading at retail for the couponing "event." The potential impact of such events has been greatly weakened, however, as the number of couponing programs presented to the trade has escalated.

5. Couponing programs provide manufacturers with considerable "push" strength precisely because they foster direct consumer takeout. Retailers must take a product in distribution and place it on the shelf, however reluctantly, if the product is backed up by a strong couponing program that will generate meaningful shopper demand at point-of-purchase. In effect, then, couponing serves to enhance the position of the manufacturer vis-à-vis the retailer, a position that has otherwise been eroding as leading chains have grown bigger and more powerful. Furthermore, smaller or regional manufacturers whose clout with retailers is even weaker can use couponing programs to attain periods of greater receptivity and support from retailers.

6.   On the negative side for manufacturers is the fact that coupon liability is open-ended. Improved forecasting techniques have enabled manufacturers to refine anticipated redemption estimates, but redemption liabilities continue to accrue, year-to-year, as the "floating" life of coupons becomes longer. The problem is further aggravated as the level of misredemptions appears to be rising.

7.   In times of wide price fluctuations, manufacturers can at least keep their regular retail prices on an even keel by tactically using coupons, either broad scale or during temporary downturns. Thus, consumers are able to buy the product at a price they are willing to pay while the manufacturer can prevent undue volatility in pricing structure. A case in point: Several years ago, soft-drink manufacturers raised their prices significantly, in line with soaring sugar prices. When sugar prices declined, the same manufacturers, rather than reducing retail prices, chose to blitz consumers with price-off coupons while waiting for the market to stabilize.

All in all, coupon promotions are endorsed by all levels in the marketing process, benefiting consumers, the trade, and manufacturers. An enthusiastic executive was quoted in Roger Strang's monograph, *The Economic Impact of Cents-Off Coupons*:

> The person who invented the cents-off coupon must have loved manufacturers, retailers and consumers alike. There is scarcely a more useful promotional tool in all of marketing.

Strang's conclusions about coupons are generally positive:

> Analysis has demonstrated that consumer coupons have an essentially positive impact on the economic system. The estimated total cost of couponing is small relative to other promotional techniques and resulted in a direct saving of over $500 million to the consumer in 1978. This saving can be realized at a time when the product is needed and usually in the shopper's preferred retail outlet. Coupons also provide an opportunity to experiment with new items. As a marketing technique, they encourage competition with a beneficial effect on price levels.

> The dramatic growth in coupon distribution indicates that manufacturers view it as a powerful and efficient technique for introducing

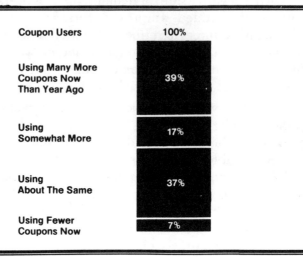

Source: A.C. Nielsen Co.

Increasing use of coupons among coupon-users. (Reprinted with permission.)

new products and building sales in their current lines. Retailers also gain from additional customers as well as the revenue from the handling allowance.

Consumers are turning to coupons to offset the inflationary pressures impacting their grocery shopping and this is reflected in their ever-increasing use of coupons.[2]

DO COUPONS INCREASE THE COST OF GOODS?

Various advocates of consumer interests have claimed that couponing as a promotional tool is wasteful and actually causes prices to rise. But coupon distribution and redemption continue to increase, and couponing has spread beyond the traditional consumer packaged goods categories that provided the initial impetus for coupon acceptance. Total 1980 expenditures for manufacturers' coupons accounted for only 0.3% of total consumer expenditures in grocery outlets, according to a U.S. Department of Agriculture study[3] reported by Anthony Gallo. Gallo, co-author of a forthcoming

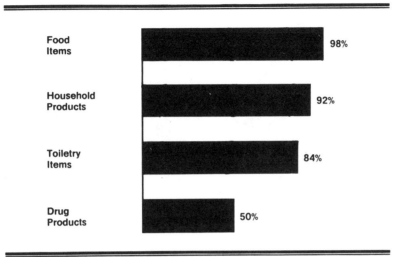

Coupon use by product class. (Reprinted with permission.)

publication tracing the growth of couponing in food marketing, believes that couponing pros and cons are complex:

> The net impact of manufacturers' coupons on consumers is difficult to judge. Such a judgment requires putting monetary values on such things as consumers' time, the value to society of new and innovative food products which might not get consumer distribution without extensive use of coupons, and the biasing of consumer choice toward couponed products. The availability of retailer private label products, which do not carry coupon administrative costs, gives consumers some choice about whether they want to pay for the coupon system. There is no hard evidence that food prices would drop in the absence of coupons, because manufacturers could shift to other types of advertising.[4]

PLANNING THE COUPONING PROGRAM

Planning a couponing effort rests on two basic areas for consideration: (1) the setting of specific objectives and (2) a precise and

Product	Percentage of total coupons redeemed	Percentage of total value of all coupons	Average face value per coupons
	Percent	Percent	cents
Beverages			
Soft drinks	1.7	1.8	24.2
Coffee, tea, cocoa	6.7	13.1	45.6
Milk products (except ice cream)			
Milk, butter, cheese	2.9	2.0	16.3
Meat, fish, poultry, eggs			
unprocessed (fresh)	0.2	0.5	65.8
Canned & processed	4.5	4.9	24.8
Fruits & vegetables			
unprocessed (fresh)	0.2	0.3	28.5
Canned & frozen-(includes orange juice etc.)	3.9	2.9	17.8
Cereal & bakery products			
Bread & rolls	3.5	2.6	17.2
Cookies, crackers, chips & snacks	2.5	1.8	16.7
Breakfast cereal	9.9	6.9	15.9
Flour & Flour mixes	3.3	5.0	36.2
Rice, pasta	1.4	0.9	14.8
Sugar & sweets			
Sugar, syrup, jellies	1.2	0.7	14.7
Ice cream, dessert, candy	3.4	3.0	21.2
Soups, baby foods, prepared meals (NEC)	9.6	10.6	26.2
Seasonings & dressings			
Seasonings & spices	1.9	1.2	26.2
Oils & salad dressing	4.0	2.7	16.0
Food total	60.9	61.1	23.5
Tobacco	0.8	2.3	62.1
Pet food	7.8	9.3	28.1
Household supplies[1]	12.8	11.6	21.4
General merchandise[2]	17.3	15.7	21.4
Nonfood total	39.1	38.9	23.7
Total	100.0	100.0	23.5

[1] Include bags, wrap, cleaning supplies.
[2] Chairs, dishes, motor oils, toiletries, toothpaste, etc.

Consumer redemption of manufacturers' coupons by product, November 1980.

Item	Percent of total value of all coupons redeemed for food Items	Estimated allocations of family food at home dollar	Manufacturer couponing intensity ratio
	Percent		
Beverages:			
Soft drinks	2.9	7.7	0.38
Coffee, tea, cocoa	21.4	3.7	5.78
Milk, butter, cheese	3.3	11.6	.28
Meat, fish, poultry, eggs:			
Not processed (fresh)	0.8	26.0	.03
Canned and processed	8.0	8.8	.90
Fruits and vegetables:			
Not processed (fresh)	0.5	6.7	.08
Canned and frozen (includes orange juices etc.)	4.7	7.4	.064
Cereal and bakery product:			
Bread and rolls	4.3	4.9	.88
cookies, crackers, chips & snacks	2.9	3.3	.88
Breakfast cereal	11.3	1.4	8.07
Flour and flour mixes	8.2	0.9	9.11
Rice, pasta	1.5	1.0	1.50
Sugar and sweets:			
Sugar, syrup, jellies	1.1	0.9	1.20
Ice cream, dessert, candy	4.9	5.8	1.20
Soups baby foods, prepared meals (NEC)	9.6	10.6	.88
Seasonings and dressings:			
Seasonings and spices	2.0	2.2	3.68
Oils and salad dressing	4.4	2.9	0.90
Total	100.0	100.0	1.52

Source: ERS survey.

Couponing's Growth in Food Marketing by Anthony E. Gallo, Larry G. Hamm, and James A. Zellner is available for $3.25 by writing to the Superintendent of Documents, U.S. Government Printing Office, Washington, D.C. 20402. Ask for AER-486.

Manufacturer's couponing intensity ratios for food products.

well-understood description of where the company stands prior to the program. Planning of the event must include where the company wants to be at the conclusion of the event; in order to determine how to get there, planning must also take into account the starting point.

In a presentation to the Association of National Advertisers (ANA) Couponing Workshop in 1977, Malcolm Douglas, director of sales promotion for Pillsbury, discussed the determination of objectives:

> In setting objectives for a couponing event in today's environment, it is important to remember that the rules have changed rapidly over the past four to six years. No longer can the couponing activity be viewed solely as a consumer event which will easily generate trade support in terms of retail displays and features. Nor does the announcement of a couponing program guarantee a solid, preemptive sales story for the retailer or for that matter, the consumer. Retail distribution patterns can preclude the need for retail display inventories as many retail outlets receive two to three deliveries per week. Selling a couponing event in its naked form is no longer news to the buyer unless it is dramatic. Finally, consumers have been so inundated by coupons in so many categories, so frequently, that a purchase response is more difficult to achieve. Therefore, objectives and strategies for a couponing event cannot necessarily be developed with a singular objective in mind, but through identification of a number of objectives which must be set and satisfied.
>
> The key now is to match objectives and strategies, along with financial considerations or constraints to develop the most effective couponing program.[5]

Clearly planning and executing strategy in a couponing program must combine overall performance objectives, in terms of incremental volume or tonnage, with specific objectives directed to trade and to consumers, both sides of the push/pull equation. At the very beginning of planning, certain benchmark readings must be established.

1. The size of the brand's consumer franchise in terms of dollars and units.

....

NEW YORK,_____1898.

RECEIVED OF_____

One FREE cake of The Procter & Gamble Co.'s
"AMBER" SOAP with my purchase of six cakes
of the same for 25 cents.

Full Name :_____

Address :_____

A turn-of-the-century free soap coupon used by Procter & Gamble Co. for its
"AMBER" Soap. (Reprinted with permission.)

2. The market share held by the brand within its category.

3. The average purchase cycle for products in the category.

4. Competitive couponing and other money incentive activities.

Concurrently, specific objectives must be set, usually keyed to one or more of the following goal areas:

1. *Generating Trial.* Trying a product or service through purchase includes an element of risk for the new user. If the performance of the product or service fails to meet anticipated satisfactions, the customer has lost its purchase price. A cents-off coupon that reduces the going-in price for a trial purchase can accelerate such a purchase and thus accelerate the total adoption process. Trial activities are not limited to new-product introductions. They are equally important in categories with high usage propensity in which the brand to be promoted enjoys only a low incidence of users. In this sense, "new potential buyers" are those who are nonusers of the brand, but are users of the category.

An interesting variant of couponing programs aimed at product trial are efforts centered around old products that have been reformulated, drastically or in part, and whose purchase among former users represents "new buying." Such products probably bear the added handicap of having to overcome earlier negatives. Coupons can be equally supportive of trial in this instance, since

Do Consumers Like and Use Coupons?

Definitely yes on both counts. Industry research ("What Consumers Think of Coupons 1980"—Nielsen Clearing House) indicates that 72% like them "very much", 57% "actively look for them". The same study shows that 76% of households used coupons in 1980—up 31% since 1971. Another company's research shows the following pattern of usage in "the past seven days":

	1977	1978	1979	1980	1981
% Using	55.1	61.1	63.7	63.6	64.3
Frequency	5.8	6.3	7.0	7.7	6.6
(Used per week)					

Who Uses Coupons?

Everyone. The Nielsen research indicates that the majority of consumers from all demographic, geographic and socio-economic groups use coupons. There has been particular growth in recent years in the use of coupons by households with an annual income of under $10,000 (up from 51% in 1975 to 69% in 1980). In 1980, coupons were used by 57% of non-white households and 69% of Hispanic households, with usage among both groups growing at a faster rate than the population as a whole.

Why Do Consumers Like and Use Coupons?

We believe it is because they benefit from a direct price reduction on a product of their choosing at the retail store of their choosing and at the time of their choosing. Most coupons are available broadly and can be used whenever the consumer is ready to buy an item. This contrasts with some other savings opportunities (such as special feature prices) which are available to the consumer only in certain stores and for a limited period of time.

Do Coupons Really Save Consumers Money?

The best judge of this may be the consumer. In the Nielsen research, 75% of consumers said that coupons were helpful in combating rising prices.

Another answer may be found in the industry statistics which indicate that consumers save nearly $1,000,000,000 through coupon redemption in 1981.

What About the Cost of Couponing?

The total cost of couponing is very minor and amounts to only 6/10 of 1% of sales in couponed categories (according to Dr. Roger A. Strang's book on "The Economic Impact of Cents-Off Couponing"), and two thirds of that goes to a direct price reduction to the consumer!

If coupons were eliminated, the consumers would lose the very substantial savings they now obtain from coupons.

What About Coupon Mishandling?

One way to improve couponing is to better control the dishonest few. Mishandling is a serious problem to be sure. The most often used industry estimate is that about 20% of all coupons redeemed are mishandled. However, this percentage varies considerably by the type and value of coupon and by the method of distribution.

There are a number of parties involved in active efforts to combat mishandling:

• Government agencies including the U.S. Postal Inspection Service, the FBI and IRS plus various federal and state law enforcement authorities.

• Industry groups such as the Audit Bureau of Circulations and the American Society for Industrial Security have undertaken special projects dealing with aspects of the mishandling problem.

• Many marketers, and/or the clearing houses they employ, continue to upgrade their coupon redemption facilities, adding sophisticated computer equipment to better detect and reduce misredemption.

All involved parties—including consumers—should support these efforts which benefit all.

Coupons are simply one marketing tool. They are an efficient way to:

• Encourage trial of new and improved products

• Reward loyal users

• Offer an immediate reason to buy the product

Coupons are a flexible marketing tool: they may be used in a variety of local or national ways. They can be tailored to reach prime prospects. They can be initiated quickly and simply. Coupons help to foster competition because small or new marketers, as well as large, established marketers, can offer them.

Questions & Answers About Couponing

Prepared by Promotion Marketing Association of America

pmaa

PMAA OBJECTIVES

PMAA is a national trade association dedicated to the following objectives:

1. To foster an understanding of the benefits of promotion marketing, including the use of premium incentives, to the consumer, trade, supplier and marketer.

2. To promote the highest levels of professional and ethical conduct by the supplier and marketer in the advertising and execution of promotion marketing to the trade and consumer.

3. To promote and protect the interests of those who use promotion marketing techniques in the sale of their products or services.

4. To monitor, promote and encourage an understanding of the laws and regulations which apply to the use of promotional techniques.

5. To encourage the interchange of ideas on sound promotional methodology and business practices.

6. To cooperate with federal, state and local government authorities for the good of the consumer, the community and the promotion marketing industry.

pmaa

420 Lexington Avenue
Suite 2031
New York, N.Y. 10170
(212) 867-3990

PR2882-rev.

How About Retailers?

Coupons provide a price reduction financed by the manufacturer. The growing use of couponing has been paralleled by a 71% reduction in retailers' percent of sales allocated to promotion activities from 1973 to 1979. As a result, industry statistics indicate that the marketing costs reflected in retail prices probably have not increased with the growth of couponing.

Retailers can use coupon events to draw customers to their stores. Couponing fosters competition at this level, too, in that any retailer large or small can be involved.

Couponing provides added short-term news, on top of normal practices such as everyday low prices, games, etc. Coupons frequently have a merchandising tie-in opportunity that can increase a retailer's coupon redemptions and total sales volume.

What Is the Real Role of Couponing?

As stated above, couponing is simply one marketing tool. Marketing contributes to our society by:

- its role in free enterprise; satisfying consumer need and desires; improving the standard of living.

- lowering unit costs by contributing to the development of mass markets, utilizing mass production and distribution techniques.

Successful manufacturers and retailers continue to employ coupons as a part of their promotion programs. These organizations constantly evaluate their existing and new marketing techniques to determine effectiveness and efficiency. If coupons were not effective or were somehow restricted, manufacturers would turn to other marketing tools to meet the same purposes as coupons. These could prove to be less efficient as well as less appealing to consumers.

PMAA's "Questions & Answers About Couponing." (Reprinted with permission.)

153

Coupon flyer used to generate consumer takeout of one or both types of Natural Sun orange juice.

former users who were turned off by the original versions of the brand, for whatever performance reasons, may consider the risk of repurchase even higher than for a totally new product.

2. *Maintaining and/or Strengthening a Brand's Franchise.* A brand's continued good health in the marketplace depends not only on the new buyers it may attract, but perhaps more importantly, on the number of users who keep buying it, the frequency of their purchases, and their product use-up rate. Couponing programs can benefit a brand by:

    a. Promoting the continuity of purchases among current users.

    b. Promoting more frequent purchases among occasional users, thus accelerating their product use-up rate.

    c. Expanding usage of the brand to additional household members.

d. Leading purchases to trade up to larger sizes or multiple packages of the product. As in the case of more frequent purchases, stocking up large quantities of the brand can satisfy both offensive and defensive strategies. The product has defensive strength if it is well stocked in the purchaser's home: The more product on hand, the less likely one is to purchase a competitive product.

3. *Enhancing the Brand's Position at Retail.* It is axiomatic, with the exception of mail-order sales, that consumer packaged goods will fail unless they obtain sufficient and proper retail distribution. Couponing programs can play an important role in obtaining retail distribution by:

a. Supporting new-product placements at retail by "promising" quick and substantial consumer takeout. By delivering on this promise, the manufacturer ensures a permanent home for the new brand on the retail shelf.

b. Supporting a better assortment for the brand, both in the number of units stocked and variety of sizes, forms, colors, and so forth.

c. Providing for tie-in activities such as retail floor displays and featuring in retailer advertising.

COUPONING METHODS

The number of couponing vehicles is large and keeps growing, as new channels for coupon distribution are created by new services. Overall, however, couponing methods divide into four broad groups:

Print Media Couponing.   By far the most coupons—close to 90% of all coupons issued—are distributed in the print media, which can be broken down into three categories: daily newspapers, including the "best food day" food section (usually on Wednesdays); Sunday newspapers; and magazines. Each print category shows a different breakdown by type of couponing carried:

1. Daily newspapers
    Single ROP (run-of-press) coupons

- Regular coupon redeemers have larger households and higher incomes than other shoppers do.

- Regular coupon redeemers spend significantly more money per shopping trip, irrespective of age, education, household size or income.

- 36% of all redeemers account for 70% of all coupon redemptions. These heavy redeemers (3+ coupons) redeem 5.3 coupons per shopping trip.

- 31% of all heavy redeemers save at least $2.00 per shopping trip by using coupons.

- Heavy coupon users make more unplanned purchases than other shoppers do.

- 22% of heavy coupon redeemers say they make unplanned purchases with money saved by redeeming coupons...often on the same shopping trip.

- The unplanned purchases of coupon redeemers are mainly of special "treat" type products that are relatively high-margin items for the retailer.

- 80% of heavy coupon redeemers regularly or occasionally use coupons to stock up on brands they use.

- 76% of heavy coupon redeemers say coupons and coupon advertisements regularly or occasionally make them aware of brands they have not tried.

- 73% of heavy coupon redeemers say coupons regularly or occasionally cause them to try new products.

Highlights of cents-off couponing and consumer purchasing behavior. (Source: Blair-Donnelly Report)

Coop (cooperative) ROP pages

Retailer (in-ad) coupons

2. Sunday newspapers

Single ROP coupons

Free-standing inserts

Solo coupon inserts

Coop coupon inserts

Sunday supplements

> On page coupons
> Tip-on coupons
>> Sunday comics
>>> Single ROP coupons
>>> Coop ROP coupons
3. Magazines
>> On-page coupons
>> Tip-on coupons
>> Gatefold coupons

Direct-Mail Couponing.   Approximately 3 to 4% of all coupons distributed reach consumers via direct-mail vehicles, a percentage that has changed very little over the past decade. Delivery of direct-mail coupons can be broken down as follows:

1. Solo mailings
   Broad-scale
   Selectively targeted
2. Coop mailings
   Broad-scale
   Selectively targeted
3. Envelope stuffers

Coupon Distribution in or near Stores.   A relatively new development in coupon delivery, in- or near-store couponing programs have been gathering momentum in recent years. Manufacturers are realizing that reaching people with coupons while they are shopping not only accelerates the usage of the coupons, but can further mobilize retailer attention and support. Various methods are used:

1. In-store
   In-hand distribution of single or multiple coupons (with and without samlping)
   Bonus couponing

Cash-register tapes

Swap tables

2.   Near-store

In-hand distribution—solo or coop programs (with and without samples)

Couponing Using the Package as a Carrier.   Representing about 6% of all coupons distributed in 1981, coupons distributed via product packages seem to be on the decline. Nevertheless, the package-as-carrier remains a powerful couponing medium, which can take several forms:

1.   On package
2.   In package
3.   Cross-ruff couponing
4.   Instantly redeemable coupons

MEDIA COUPONING

The use of media coupons goes back to the early 1920s and today they account for the bulk of all couponing activities.

Daily Newspapers

Black and white daily newspapers receive the lion's share of all media couponing. Appearing for the most part on the best-food days—usually Wednesdays—coupons in daily newspapers can take one of several forms.

Single ROP (Run-of-Press) Coupons.   Mostly used by manufacturers as part of a manufacturer's ad; sometimes inserted single standing.

Coop (Cooperative) ROP Pages.   Variation of single-coupon insertion. Coop programs came into being in response to increasing media costs. By syndicating a newspaper page—sometimes even a double-spread—to a number of participants, the cost per coupon can be reduced, often significantly. However, unlike single coupons, which are placed in a specific newspaper or newspapers by the manufacturer directly or through an advertising agency, coop ads are placed by the syndicator who then sells participations to as many manufacturers as feasible within the ad's space limitation.

Retailer In-Ad Coupons.   Placed by a retailer within the retailer's own ad, which in addition to the coupon(s), carries a range of features offered in the store during the promotional period covered by the ad. Such coupons are most likely to appear in "best-food" day ads. The important characteristic of these coupons is that they may be used only in the store, or account, offering them. Redemption for in-ad coupons may be paid by either the manufacturer or the retailer. If the manufacturer assumes liability, the arrangement should be formalized in a contract that sets up the conditions for redemption and establishes a ceiling for the number of coupons to be accepted. The ceiling normally is related to the amount of merchandise purchased by the account in conjunction with the promotion. On the other hand, the absorption of in-ad coupon costs by the retailer indicates willingness to allocate some of the retailer's promotional allowance to this effort.

Advantages of Daily Newspaper Couponing

1.   Daily newspaper couponing is relatively less expensive than other modes of delivery. A 1,000-line ad, a popular format, costs $8 to $9 per thousand circulation, while a participation in a coop ads—coupon only—ranges from $1 to $2 per thousand.

2.   Couponing in daily newspapers permits a large measure of planning and execution flexibility:

> *In terms of space:* For single-coupon insertions, manufacturers have a choice of various sizes, depending on overall advertising considerations. An early commitment and transmittal of copy may also gain the manufacturer preferential positioning within the ROP context. Coop ads are more limited in this respect. Insertion requirements in terms of mechanicals as well as rates are standard for coop participa-

			Number		
Coupons	1,528	1,722	1,833	1,670	1,688
			Percent		
Breakfast cereals	4.0	3.1	2.6	3.4	4.1
Flour mix products	6.2	1.8	3.8	5.0	4.4
Ice cream, candy, desserts	3.6	4.5	4.2	5.0	6.0
Oils and salad dressings	3.9	5.6	7.2	5.2	7.1
Soups, baby, and prepared foods	7.1	6.2	7.3	7.6	6.9
Soft drinks and noncarbonated beverages	2.8	8.8	10.2	4.9	2.1
Seasonings and spices	2.2	2.2	2.2	1.8	3.6
Cookies, crackers, chips, and snacks	3.5	3.0	4.3	3.3	6.4
Coffee, tea, cocoa	6.6	5.1	7.1	6.9	2.0
Sugar, sirup, jellies	2.0	1.9	1.7	2.4	2.5
Bread and rolls	2.2	3.3	2.3	2.2	0.7
Rice and pasta	0.9	0.6	0.3	1.0	7.0
Canned and processed meat, poultry fish	7.1	7.8	6.4	6.5	2.4
Milk, butter, cheese	3.1	1.6	2.7	2.0	5.7
Processed fruits and vegetables	6.5	7.3	4.2	4.7	2.1
Fresh fruit and vegetables	2.5	2.4	1.9	1.7	1.7
Unprocessed meat, poultry, fish	1.8	3.3	0.8	1.4	1.7
Total food	68.1	68.8	71.1	64.3	68.2
Pet food	1.1	3.3	1.9	2.8	2.3
Tobacco	.1	—	—	—	—
Household supplies	14.9	11.9	13.3	12.6	13.1
General supplies	15.8	16.0	13.7	20.3	16.4
Total Nonfood	31.9	31.2	28.9	35.7	31.8
Total	100.0	100.0	100.0	100.0	100.0

[1]ERS Survey of in-ad coupons in newspapers.

Retailer in-ad coupon percentage redemption in 50 major markets during four selected weeks in 1980.

SAVE 20¢

ON WISE
Puffed or Crunchy
cheez doodles® BRAND

—— PLUS ——

$2.00 VALUE OFFER!

$1.00 Cash Refund! + $1.00 in Coupons!

GOOD ON A VARIETY
OF GREAT-TASTING WISE SNACKS!

Yours when you mail in 5 proofs of purchase from Wise Puffed and/or Crunchy Cheez Doodles.

Print information in the space provided & mail to:

Cheez Doodles $2.00 Value Refund
P.O. Box 7164, Stratmar Station
Bridgeport, CT 06650

(Allow 4-6 weeks for delivery)

Please send me $1.00 cash plus four 25¢ coupons good on Wise snacks. I've enclosed 5 proofs of purchase (UPC codes) from Wise Puffed and/or Crunchy Cheez Doodles bags.

Name			
Street			
City	State	Zip	22

SAVE 20¢

on Wise Puffed or Crunchy
CHEEZ DOODLES
—8 OZ. OR LARGER PACKAGE—

Retailer: As our agent, please redeem for face value as specified. ANY OTHER USE CONSTITUTES FRAUD. You will be paid face value, or if the coupon calls for free goods, the regular retail price, plus 7¢ handling, provided you and your customers have complied with the terms of this offer and invoices proving purchase within the last 90 days of sufficient stock to cover coupons are shown on request. Send coupons to Borden, Inc., P.O. Box 1720, Clinton, Iowa 52734. NON-ASSIGNABLE. Customer must pay any sales tax. Void where taxed, restricted or prohibited. Cash value 1/20 of one cent. Limit one coupon per purchase. **Offer expires December 31, 1983.**

STORE COUPON

53000 121441

A combination coupon rebate flyer on Wise Puffed or Crunchy Cheez Doodles.

161

tions, regardless of the paper in which they appear. Single-coupon insertions, on the other hand, may call for different formats and sizes, depending on the layout of the newspaper as well as the rate structure.

In terms of timing: Newspapers come out daily, which allow coupon insertions to be timed precisely.

In terms of lead time: Closing dates for newspapers are much closer to issue dates than in other nonnewspaper print media. The shorter lead time enhances the appeal of newspaper couponing as a tactical vehicle for a manufacturer to respond quickly to market conditions, with rapid promotional action—offensive or defensive.

3.   Single couponing in daily newspapers allows manufacturers considerable latitude in targeting specific areas of need or opportunity. Depending on the syndicating service, a manufacturer's discretion is more limited in coop couponing. A manufacturer may decide to provide coverage in markets where a product is lagging—scoring low on the Brand Development Index (BDI) scale—or may choose to accelerate consumer takeout in markets where the product is doing well. With more than 1,600 daily newspapers available, a manufacturer's choice is wide enough to allow for specific pinpointing of effort. Further, where more than one daily newspaper serves a given market, the manufacturer can select the one that best reaches the targeted consumer.

4.   Both single and coop couponing provide opportunities for retailer tie-ins in terms of trade support, which result in increased pipelining to the retail floor, display activity, and price featuring—all coincident with the couponing event. One caveat, however, must be kept in mind: Retailers, particularly the larger accounts, require considerable lead time—as much as six to seven weeks—to prepare well for such a program. If such a tie-in is essential, the manufacturer's tactical, quick-response use of this vehicle is hampered.

Disadvantages of Daily Newspaper Couponing

1.   Redemption levels for daily-newspaper manufacturer coupons are low relative to other couponing media—approximately 3% of circulation, for both single and coop coupons, with the latter

holding a slight edge. Data on retailer in-ad coupon redemption are scarce since in-ad coupons do not generally flow through the normal redemption channels.

2. Misredemption of coupons circulated in daily newspapers is high enough to cause considerable concern. Industry sources now claim that misredemption exceeds 20% of all such coupons redeemed, some placing the figure at greater than 30%. Misredemption obviously increases the net cost per coupon redeemed above the budget intents of the manufacturer for a specific promotion of an item or line.

3. Circulation figures are meaningful when they represent net unduplicated reach. Reaching the same consumer several times with the same promotional incentive is wasteful, hence costly. A Westchester County commuter working in New York City reads *The New York Times* or *The Daily News* in the morning, *The New York Post* on the way home in the afternoon, and most likely has home delivery of the Gannet papers before evening. Potentially, this commuter has the opportunity to clip the same coupon three times. While media plans for single couponing in daily newspapers can be worked out to avoid most duplication, the potential for duplication is harder to avoid with coop couponing.

4. Although full-color printing has made some inroads in daily newspapers, the medium remains essentially a black and white one, which limits the creative options for advertising. Where color is used, substantial upcharges may apply.

Sunday Newspapers

As a medium, Sunday newspapers vary, often significantly, from daily newspapers in terms of content and reach dimensions. The Sunday newspaper is heavily weighted toward features, weekly summaries, and want ads over current news, which is the mainstay of the daily paper. The amount of advertising in Sunday newspapers greatly exceeds daily newspaper advertising; some special sections are printed in color, thus extending the advertising options. Readers spend more time with their Sunday paper, and some sections are still around and read in midweek.

1. *Single ROP Coupons.* Occasionally, single ROP coupons

appear in Sunday newspapers, but most of these coupons apply to purchases of goods or services other than consumer packaged goods. Restaurants and movie theaters, for example, may sometimes use this medium to present two-for-one offers good for a certain period of time with or without qualifications.

2. *Free-Standing Promotional Inserts.* Precisely because of the feature–news mix in the Sunday paper, much of the paper is printed and assembled in advance. Generally, only the news section is printed late in the day Saturday and added to the paper before newsstand and home delivery early Sunday morning. Coupon-bearing free-standing promotional inserts are a natural component in this enviroment. Whether designed as a single coupon, a multiple coupon, inserts from the same manufacturer, or a coop coupon program, inserts are in danger of acquiring a reputation for cluttering. Inserts carrying single or multiple coupons from the same advertiser are placed by the sponsor directly or through an agency, while coop inserts, carrying noncompeting coupons from several participants, are printed and placed in over a hundred major newspapers throughout the country by the coop syndicator.

3. *Sunday Supplements.* Unlike the coupon inserts, Sunday supplements carry some editorial content as well as advertising. In a sense, many supplements could qualify as magazines, generally published by groups other than the carrying newspaper, and made available for distribution with the Sunday paper on a market-exclusive basis. Coupon insertions in Sunday supplements come in two forms:

    a.   On-page coupons, using any of the standard-size ad configurations.

    b.   Tip-on cards, which are separately printed on heavier stock and then affixed to the supplement, usually on the back cover. A variant of tip-on coupons are bound-in, or pop-up coupons. They also are printed separately on heavier card stock and then bound into the carrier Sunday magazine.

4. *Sunday Comics.* In recent years, efforts have been directed at establishing the Sunday comics as a broad-spectrum couponing

medium. These efforts were accelerated with the introduction of coop couponing programs that expanded the range of products couponed in Sunday comics while greatly increasing the total number of coupons circulated in this medium. Today, coop programs account for the bulk of the couponing activity in Sunday comics, with single-coupon insertions in marginal use only.

Advantages of Sunday Newspaper Couponing

1. Overall, Sunday newspapers have a somewhat longer life than daily newspapers, which extends the opportunity for coupon exposure to potential users.

2. The good color reproduction possible in the magazine supplements and free-standing promotional inserts supports greater creative flexibility and impact.

3. Selectivity is generally good and provides well for pin-pointing of target audiences, in terms of three broad selectivity measures:

    In terms of readership: Since each supplement segment contains feature material appealing to specific interests, it also serves as a proper medium for advertising and coupons directed to people sharing those interests.

    In terms of space: The wide array of possible advertising units allows a wide range of choice.

    In terms of geography: Almost any combination of markets can be bought into—local, regional, or national runs—for whatever strategic demands are made by the marketing plan.

4. The free-standing promotional inserts offer participant exclusivity, avoiding competitive incentives within the same unit.

5. Costs for insertions are generally relatively low, depending on the supplement. Insertions of on-page coupons are less expensive than tip-ons or bound-in coupons. Free-standing promotional inserts generally show the most modest costs, particularly for small units of space.

Disadvantages of Sunday Newspaper Couponing

1. Redemption levels in Sunday supplements are generally low—below those obtained in daily newspapers for on-page coupons, although higher than that for insertions in free-standing promotional inserts and for tip-ons and bound-ins. As mentioned earlier, Sunday supplements are only lightly used for single-coupon insertions.

2. Lead times for insertions in Sunday papers are generally longer, which limits the tactical use of this medium and, to some extent, also restricts potential tie-ins with retailers.

3. Misredemption levels are still significant, but below those experienced in daily-newspaper couponing.

Magazines

The lion's share of magazine coupons is carried by the *Reader's Digest* and various women's magazines, particularly those directed to homemakers and sold mostly at check-out counters in retail stores. Similar to couponing in Sunday supplements, couponing in magazines can be inserted either on-page or as bound-ins. In addition, magazines can use gatefolds for single or coop insertions.

1. *On-page* coupons in a variety of ad units, with size and configuration dependent on the magazine's layout.

2. *Bound-in or pop-up* coupons—cards printed separately on heavier card stock and bound into the magazines.

3. *Gatefolds*—from the extra page or pages extended from a regular page or from the front or back covers and folded in to maintain the overall size appearance of the magazine. Gatefolds often carry multiple coupons, either for a single manufacturer or for several separate participants in coop configurations.

Advantages of Magazine Couponing

1. Media buys involving coupon insertions in one or more magazines can be fine-tuned:

To provide across-the-board mass reach.

To allow targeting of consumers having the profiles mandated in the marketing plan. Since magazines generally profile their own readers, media planners can select and combine the magazines that best fulfill their promotion specifications with least duplication. Further, most magazines offer regional and even single-market splits, which permits geographical segmentation.

To obtain appropriate placement, preferably adjacent to relevant editorial content. For example, it is more advantageous to place coupons for food items in a section carrying recipes than on the letters to the editor page.

2. Magazine life may extend for many weeks—depending on publication frequency—and during this time, each issue may be read by several persons. This pass-along feature of magazines increases the exposure of the coupons they carry to more people than indicated by their net circulation. Consequently, magazine coupons enjoy higher redemption levels.

Disadvantages of Magazine Couponing

1. The closing times for most magazines require longer lead times, which in turn call for longer planning and execution cycles, with the result that fewer opportunities exist for retail tie-ins.

2. Differences in page size, format, and configurations may require different ad sizes in one media plan if a combination of magazines is used.

3. Duplication of readership—hence duplication of exposure and waste—can result from using a combination of magazines. While both reach and frequently are critical in developing an advertising plan, frequency in terms of multiple exposures to a given coupon is not desirable.

4. Misredemptions must be closely monitored to prevent costly liabilities.

Summary—Media Couponing

Media couponing, with the exception of free-standing promotional inserts, tip-ons, and bound-ins, is often used as an adjunct advertising effort, couponing representing a subsidiary rather than primary objective. Problems may arise if advertising and couponing objectives are not in phase. For the most part, media couponing is highly flexible in terms of selectivity criteria and lends itself well to market-segmented strategies. On the negative side for magazines is the fact that the longer lead time to the closing of a print medium, the worse the opportunity for using media couponing as a tactical vehicle and the less likely it is to obtain meaningful retail tie-ins.

Print medium circulation costs vary, and they are not always related to potential redemption levels. With the exception of free-standing promotional inserts, tip-ins, and bound-ins, media coupon redemptions are generally low compared to other methods of coupon distribution. The free-standing promotional inserts redeem well, and their costs are average for print media. Tip-ons and bound-ins also have high redemption levels, but their cost is substantially higher.

Coop couponing in media has been gaining ground over single-coupon insertions. Primarily benefiting from cost versus redemption levels, coop couponing has also gained in recent years from vigorous marketing of free-standing promotional inserts and Sunday comics coop programs. Misredemptions remain the bane of media couponing, and only concerted efforts by authorities, coupon issuers, and the trade can reduce the damage they can cause to this otherwise popular incentive tool.

DIRECT-MAIL COUPONING

Through the distribution network of the U.S. postal service, promotional materials, with or without coupons, could be mailed to every single household in the United States. Mailing lists covering close to 80 million households can differentiate by state, city, and zip code all the way down to individual carrier routes. In reality, few mailings are truly massive. On occasion, some mailings to as many as

40 million are concentrating primarily on reaching average- and above-average-income families in A and B that is, highly populated counties. The more popular coop mailings, however, are mailed to fewer than 30 million households. Approximately 3% of all coupons circulated in 1981 were sent by mail, and this share level has held steady. Although this percentage appears small, in 1982 it represented some 4 billion coupons, which certainly qualifies direct-mail couponing as a major incentive tool.

Direct-mail couponing takes several forms:

1. *Solo Mailings.* Solo mailings are single efforts made by individual companies in mailing out one or more coupons for one or more of their products or services. A solo mailing may consist of a printed piece of heavier paper, folded over and sent out without envelope, or one or more pieces inserted in a regular or window envelope. Generally, coupons in solo mailings are attached to or printed on larger flyers containing additional advertising copy designed both to enlighten and to persuade the recipient to purchase. The coupon itself represents the actual incentive for quick action.

2. *Coop Mailings.* Coop mailings are generally put together by syndicators that purchase or maintain mailing lists and execute joint mailings to these lists for a number of noncompeting participants. Since postage charges are a substantial cost in all mailings, the ability of the syndicator to spread this cost among several participants makes coop mailings more attractive than solo mailings for many companies. Coop mailings are usually sent in oversized envelopes, with separate inserts for each participant. Some syndicators have tried, at one time or another, mailing out coupon booklets, and at least one syndicator of free-standing promotional inserts in Sunday papers has recently started mailing the same coop insert to 18 milion households.

Both solo mailings and coop mailings can be made *broad-scale*, mailed to all households in a given geographical area, or sent to a *selected target*, a specific group or groups identified in the marketing plans. By and large, however, even mass, broad-scale mailings incorporate some selectivity; mailers have learned that reaching some areas or groups is counterproductive, hence wasteful, just as reaching others is highly desirable.

3. *Envelope Stuffers.*   Stuffing coupons, piggyback fashion, in envelopes containing statements, direct-mail orders, or announcements of some kind follows the pattern set long ago by retailers, mostly department stores, in sending advertising materials together with monthly bills. Even though envelope stuffers account for only a small number of the coupons distributed by mail, repeated attempts are made to expand their use. The obvious appeal is to take advantage of the postage already paid for the mailing of the primary materials and, in effect, to enjoy free delivery. Attempts to use bank credit statements on a broad scale failed, apparently because the stuffing involved extensive, fragmented coordination with a large number of local banks. However, another effort calling for the insertion of an envelope with coupons into a mass mailing by a company soliciting magazine subscriptions has been repeated several times. Envelope stuffers naturally reach only the people or households relevant to the primary carrier. This selection may affect to varying degrees the performance of the promotional program represented by the coupons. Good response may depend on how close the target audience of the coupons matches the audience provided by the carrier.

Mailing-Lists Management

It has been said that virtually all types of mailing list configurations can be found. Given the traffic in names generated by direct-response programs, subscription solicitations, and charitable contributions together with zip-coded socioeconomic profiles available from census sources, the direct-mail list-maintenance business has grown rapidly in the last 20 years.

Some companies maintain huge *general lists* covering all or most households in given areas. These lists, based on individual addresses, are compiled from a variety of secondary sources—for instance, census data, car registrations, telephone registries. These lists are usually further refined and updated by continuous inputs obtained at the local level, including periodic checks by individual postal carriers.

Targeted lists also require a great deal of secondary compilations as well as primary search for data. A new-babies list, for example, may rely on names generated from local birth announcements, route lists of diaper-service companies, birth registrations, maternity-ward records, and, at times, from direct contact with individual obstetricians. All this information from all sources is received by the mailing-list manager, usually on a continuous flow basis, and is purged and merged with previously obtained data, so as to each time produce a list of valid, nonduplicated names.

Proven-response lists, as a rule, compile the names of people who have already responded at least once to a direct-response message or offer. The rationale here is that such people are predisposed to read and react to direct-response propositions, and thus their names and addresses are valuable to others seeking to market similar product or services.

Questions about Mailing Lists

Precisely because mailing lists are so critical to the success of direct-mail efforts, the validity of any list used must be carefully qualified against a promotion's objectives.

1. List Coverage
    a. What are the list's coverage parameters?

        In regard to overall reach?

        As a percentage of all people or households in the specific target area or group desired?
    b. Is the list exclusionary of certain areas or groups?

        Does it exclude specific income groups—for example, low-income households?

        Does it exclude specific areas—for instance, C or D (sparsely populated) counties?

        Does it exclude high-risers?

        Does it exclude central-city homes?

        Does it exclude households headed by females?

        Does it exclude singles households?

        Does it allow for duplicate mailings to homes where two singles live together?

2.   List Validity
   a.   How reliable is the provenance of the names on the list?
   b.   How often is the list updated? A new-babies list, for example, is generally obsolete within a year and thus of little value to a marketer of disposable diapers. General lists are subject to a 15 to 20% turnover each year due to household mobility. As a consequence, most general mailings are addressed to "occupant" or "resident," in order to ensure delivery of a mailing, which if addressed by name to a person who has moved would be dumped under third-class postal regulations.

Advantages of Direct-Mail Couponing

1.   Although they are more costly to circulate, direct-mail coupons are redeemed at a higher level than those inserted in any of the print media.
2.   Direct-mail couponing allows for considerable selectivity:

   In terms of geographic coverage.

   In terms of various socioeconomic criteria. While zip-coded census data do not include profiles of individual households, it is possible through statistical manipulation to determine which tracts represent above-average potential and to skew programs to those tracts.

   In terms of pinpointed reach, using targeted tests or proven-response lists.
3.   Direct-mail couponing offers less opportunity for mis-redemptions since deliveries are made to individual addresses. Direct-mail avoids the potential for collusion in misredemption schemes that is possible for coupons included in newsstand media. Also, the security of coupons in transit through the U.S. postal system is very good.

Disadvantages of Direct-Mail Couponing

1.   Solo mailings can be scheduled as needed, but coop mailings are less frequent and may not be available just when such an effort is

indicated in the marketing plan. Furthermore, since participants in coop mailings usually enjoy exclusivity of product or service class, would-be participants in a coop mailing might frequently be preempted by competitors.

2.   Clutter, long the bane of advertising media, has now become a problem in coop mailings as well. A recent mailing, for example, contained six coupons, which were thoroughly overwhelmed by the accompanying 14 direct-response offers. It remains debatable whether coop mailings can continue as they are and provide a proper and effective environment for couponing programs.

3.   Depending on the list used, waste can become a critical cost. Each delivery is prepaid, so any mailing that does not reach its destination is wasted. "Nixies"—mailings returned to the post office as undeliverable—run as high as 50 to 60% for some of the targeted lists, particularly if the pieces are specifically addressed to individuals. The broader lists used in large mailings for mass penetration are generally updated more frequently; their nixie level averages around 10% and sometimes less, since "occupant" and "resident" designations are used. Monitoring of nixies is costly; the post office only returns undelivered mail if it carries first-class postage. Undelivered third-class mail is destroyed.

Summary—Direct-Mail Coupons

Direct-mail coupons, whether delivered solo or coop, have long been a mainstay of promotional plans in many consumer packaged goods companies even though direct mail accounts for only 3% of all coupons distributed. Direct-mail programs can be highly selective, able to key on specific groups targeted in marketing-plan objectives. The costs for direct-mail programs can be controlled through careful and judicious selection of the proper mailing lists. Selection efforts can lower the rate of undeliverables while at the same time furthering the delivery of coupons to the most desirable prospects.

COUPON DISTRIBUTION IN OR NEAR STORES

Large-scale couponing programs in or near the point-of-purchase were first tried in the mid-1960s. Even though their share of coupon circulation is very small, in- and near-store programs have had significant growth in the last five years. With the continued fragmentation of advertising media and spiraling advertising costs, efforts to shift some of the burden for moving merchandise to promotional efforts at the point-of-purchase are increasingly important. The concept underlying such coupon distribution is simple: Reaching people in shopping traffic with a monetary incentive that can be used immediately while they are in a shopping frame of mind, increases the likelihood that more persons will make the purchase for which the coupon is intended. This coupon-inspired purchase, however, is only half the equation. It is the other half that lifts in- and near-store programs out of the context of routine, general couponing efforts into total marketing events. Given the promise of increased and accelerated consumer takeout in their stores, retailers pipeline incremental merchandise to the retail floor and tend further to support the couponing programs with price featuring and display activities. All in all, store-related programs represent an integrated application of push and pull principles.

Coupon distribution to shoppers in or near stores can be conducted by in-hand distribution, cash-register tapes, swap tables, dispenser units, and bonus couponing.

In-Hand Distribution

As a result of the person-to-person contact by trained couponers either in or near the store, the couponer can actually deliver a short verbal advertising message, answer questions, respond to possible objections, and urge immediate purchase. Further, these couponing programs can be highly selective:

By site: Programs can be conducted nationally, regionally, or locally, in urban or suburban areas, in low BDI or high BDI markets, and so on.

By sight: Potential recipients can be screened visually for the desired group—for instance, people with grey hair, teenagers, or older women.

By verbal screen: In- or near-store coupon distribution is the only vehicle that allows verbal screening of recipients. Through questions, the couponer can screen out people who don't own a dishwasher, don't have a dog, or don't have babies, while concentrating on people who use competitive brands, on heavy users of the category, and so forth. Care, however, should be exercised in the use of verbal screens. The more extensive the screen, the lower the overall distribution productivity and the higher the cost per coupon handed out.

In-store couponing programs—whether combined with product demonstrations or not—are most effective if they occur near a display of the product. In that position, the product/coupon presentation can be followed up by the actual placing of a unit in the shopper's cart. If the couponing station for refrigerated or frozen items cannot be near the refrigerator or freezer case, spot refrigerators or freezers should be used. The couponer station should always be placed in locations of high store traffic. Low-traffic aisles or areas lower the program's productivity.

Near store couponing programs generally reach more shoppers than in-store efforts since the couponers can take advantage of higher traffic flows. The couponer station can be set up at the busiest store entrance, usually an entrance from the parking lot. Nevertheless, immediate redemptions will be somewhat lower, since the coupon distribution is a few steps removed from the retail floor and not in close proximity to product displays. Sampling through demonstrations tends to accelerate immediate takeout; but samples that must be taken away and used in one's home may actually delay purchase, at least until the next shopping trip.

Strategically then, for new products in partially or totally commoditized categories and high price elasticity, it is better to coupon only—using a higher face value coupon—than to give away a sample. The *trial-through-purchase* approach results in an actual purchase. The shopper, having "risked" money on the purchase—despite a high-value coupon—is more attuned to giving the product a fair trial, and the retailer, having rung up a sale, is more convinced that the product is viable and deserving of a permanent home on the shelf.

While most coupon programs—including those conducted in or near stores—are designed with an offensive strategy in mind, in- or near-store programs are also highly effective when following a defensive approach. For example, an in-store program conducted during a competitive introduction, and receiving full trade support in terms of increased pipelining, featuring, and display activities, can effectively blunt the impact of the new entry, despite that entry's being backed up by heavier introductory expenditures.

Legal Considerations

In-store programs, as well as near-store programs conducted within the perimeters of specific stores, technically bring into play the provisions of the Robinson Patman Act, which requires equal and proportionate treatment for all retail customers. This legal requirement may not be a major problem, since the smaller stores—mostly independents—whose competitive position the act was designed to protect, do not, by and large, welcome coupon promotions and carry more limited stock assortments. Nevertheless, certain steps may counter potential legal problems and should be reviewed carefully by companies considering such promotions.

1. Media announcements of the planned in-store program can be placed in trade publications within the trading area, inviting all retailers interested in participating, and offering certain options of alternative promotional support—for instance, pads of "take-one" offers.

2. The availability of the program to trade factors can be made contingent on their purchase of a set number of cases for each day of in-store couponing. Thus, chain accounts could buy and schedule for their stores while wholesalers could act on behalf of their client retailers.

3. A down-the-street couponing program can overlay the larger in-store program. Special couponers arrange to visit the smaller stores and coupon their customers for a relatively short period of time, provided that the store carries the couponed product and that permission for the couponing is given by the store manager. Coverage is routed on a down-the-street basis and is limited to stores not receiving the regular program. Accurate and complete logs should be kept of all couponing calls and their duration, whether and how well the store stocked the product, and the number of coupons distributed. Where possible, the log should include the store manager's signature.

Advantages of In- or Near-Store Couponing Programs

1.   Distributing coupons to potential customers while they are shopping can dramatically increase both immediate and total redemptions.

2.   The opportunity for dialog between the couponer and the customer can help in persuading nonusers to try the product.

3.   In-hand programs allow considerable sales leverage at a time when such leverage may actually be declining—retailers having abandoned their commitment to full assortments and increasing costs of sales coverage forcing reductions in many sales organizations.

4.   In- or near-store programs experience minimal misredemptions. Since the coupons are under control until they are personally handed to ultimate users—usually one coupon per household—the chances for collusion and misuse are marginal.

5.   In- or near-store programs are highly flexible, allowing for many measures of selectivity. In effect, coverage could be tailored to the individual stores, while at the same time, the "mass" characteristics of the couponing program could be maintained.

6.   Critical trade support is readily obtained by these programs because they are conducted in or near specific retailing outlets. Once the program is accepted by a retailer, the retailer must support it, at least by pipelining incremental merchandise, or customers may be antagonized.

7.   Couponing events on the retail floor may gain the retailer an enhanced image among the customers.

8.   Strategically, such programs can help establish new distribution, expand existing distribution to new items, accelerate consumer takeout several times normal, and strengthen the product's permanent home on the shelf.

Disadvantages of In- or Near-Store Programs

1.   Precisely because in- or near-store store programs can deliver superior results, their success requires considerable work. It makes little sense to have couponers distribute coupons and urge immediate

purchase if stocks on the retail floor are low or if the store runs out of the product altogether. Apart from the logistics involved in the execution of the program itself, incremental merchandise must be sold and its flow from warehouse to retail floor must be assured. Unfortunately, not all sales organizations are equally motivated or capable of investing the needed effort.

2. Going-in costs are higher than with other couponing vehicles, which may deter some marketing people from using in- or near-store programs regardless of how well the results compare with the results of other programs. Indeed, if in- or near-store programs are viewed strictly as coupon circulation vehicles, their cost may seem prohibitive. But if all other contributory elements are taken into consideration—critical factors in the marketing process—in- and near-store programs will generally stack up at least as dollar efficient, as well as highly effective compared to other couponing efforts.

3. Coop programs are occasionally offered, but their success depends on the amount of coordination possible among the various salesforces, the trade, and the company executing the program. Much of the concentrated focus needed to generate the proper sales leverage in solo programs is very hard to marshal in a cooperative promotion.

4. Scheduled in- or near-store couponing programs are vulnerable to announced bonus-couponing offers, since some retailers are not willing to allow such programs at a time when they are committed to double, or even triple, the cents-off value of the coupons distributed. One option for the manufacturer is to offer coupons whose value exceeds the retailer's upper limit for bonus offers and hence place no monetary obligation on the retailer.

Cash-Register Tapes

From time to time, some trade factors distribute coupons printed on the backs of cash-register tapes. The coupons are usually printed in one color and without separation. Fast-food establishments have occasionally used this medium to boost patronage. Depending on the length of the tape, a customer could receive several coupons for the same product or service. Again, depending on the length of the tape and volume of shopping represented, a customer may end up with only half or two-thirds of a coupon. A variant of cash-register tapes are coupons printed on shopping bags. This distribution vehicle received some experimentation, but failed to generate much interest.

Swap Tables

Some supermarket chains have set up swap tables, where customers dump coupons for products they don't want or need and rummage around for coupons left by others. Concerns about potential misredemptions resulting from unmonitored dumping and retrieval of coupons has limited the use of swap tables and may eventually do away with them altogether.

Dispenser Units

At one time, attempts were made to install dispenser units in supermarkets, whereby a shopper could obtain a coupon booklet by inserting a quarter in the machine. To induce the trade to allow these dispensers on the retailing floor, appropriate private-label coupons were included side-by-side with manufacturer coupons. This couponing method did not expand beyond earlier experiments in stores in Southern California. It is likely that original equipment costs, problems of maintaining and supplying the dispensers, and potential misredemptions combined to make the program less than cost efficient. No doubt, we will see additional experimentation in this area in the years to come.

Bonus Couponing

While bonus couponing is not strictly a form of couponing, it is an incentive overlaid by retailers on regular manufacturer coupons and thus fits appropriately in this group of promotional tools. Bonus couponing is the intermittent practice by retailers of doubling, even tripling, the discount they give their customers based on the face value of manufacturers' coupons. A 10¢ coupon is redeemed for 20¢ or 30¢ against purchases of the couponed product. Primarily a retailer's "price war" phenomenon, the bonus-couponing practice has recently gathered momentum and is being used today as much defensively as it was earlier used offensively. Besides being a rather costly endeavor—especially in view of the narrow profit margins in the supermarket industry—bonus couponing has also ceased, by and large, to produce a meaningful competitive edge. Most, if not all, major retailers immediately respond in kind when one of their number offers such a program to shoppers. Recently, many retailers have reduced their bonus couponing liabilities by setting limits on the amounts of "matching" monies they will provide on manufacturers' coupons. Some retailers exclude certain product categories, such as coffee and cigarettes. A few retailers have applied the incremental incentive of bonus couponing to those days of the week when store traffic is traditionally light. However, the effectiveness of this approach still depends on the competitive reaction displayed by other retailers in the same market.

Summary—In- and Near-Store Couponing

With few exceptions, the bulk of couponing programs adjacent to or on the retailing floor is accounted for by in-hand distribution of

In-store couponing of Colgate's Fresh Start in Dallas.

In-store couponing of Pepsi-Light in the Northeast.

coupons in or near stores. These programs are relatively new, but they are increasingly popular because they help manufacturers bring to fruition their marketing efforts. It has been said that nothing happens until a sale is made. It must be added that no sale can be made until the product is on the retail floor, in the proper assortment and quantities. In- and near-store couponing programs are highly effective in this regard.

COUPONING USING THE PACKAGE AS CARRIER

In- and on-pack coupons account for only 6% of all coupons distributed, but they remain popular, perhaps because they entail minimal circulation costs since the package itself acts as carrier. Using a package to carry a coupon allows a manufacturer to circulate coupons for the carrier product itself, for other products, or both. Sometimes, coupons for products sold by other manufacturers are also included, usually in some kind of reciprocal arrangement. The insertion of such coupons in or on the package is usually prominently flagged on the package itself in order to attract shoppers' attention and thus provide incentive impact for both the carrier brand and the couponed brand.

A number of considerations should govern the use of this promotional vehicle:

1. The consumer profile of the couponed product should match the consumer profile of the carrier brand. If this match is missing, most of the coupons will be wasted.

2. Longer expiration periods should be used for in- and on-package coupons so that the particular product-run carrying the coupons will sell out to consumers while the coupons are still valid. Often, no expiration dates are given for these kinds of coupons. The Federal Trade Commission has directed manufacturers that coupons enclosed in consumer products must either contain no expiration date or a date that allows potential users a minimum of six months to use the coupons so that most of the stock containing the coupons can be sold before the expiration date.

3. In-pack coupons that may come in contact with food must be printed on FDA-approved paper with "edible" inks also approved by the FDA. Sometimes, particularly if more than one coupon is involved, the manufacturer may use a small approved cellophane or plastic envelope for the coupon(s), which is dropped into the package while it moves along the production line.

4. Problems may be encountered if a particular account refuses to take in the promotion because it does not carry the couponed products although it stocks the carrier brand. On the other hand, obtaining distribution for a new entry may be helped if coupons for the new product are distributed by means of a carrier representing a well-known and frequently purchased product. This strategy has been used primarily by companies to introduce line extensions to existing popular brands.

5.   The reach of in- or on-pack coupons is limited to those people buying the carrier product. Further, such coupons can be used only after the carrier brand is purchased, and as a result, their impact may be staggered over a considerable period of time.

Couponing programs using product packages as carriers may be executed in several ways.

In-Pack Coupons.   Single or in several configurations, these coupons may be used by the couponing manufacturer for the manufacturer's own product or products, for noncompetitive products sold by others, or for any combination of such products. Using an in-pack coupon for the carrying brand itself is primarily designed to generate repeated purchases of the product. If the product-in-use lives up to its level of anticipated satisfactions, the coupon continues to lower the risk of making a follow-up purchase of the same product. Often, a number of purchases are necessary for the consumer to gain the type of experience needed to generate a switch to a product not regularly purchased or used before. The situation is even more critical for a product that is new on the market.

Cross-Ruff Coupons.   Cross-ruff coupons delivered in-pack for products sold by the same manufacturer—assuming matching consumer profiles—will derive strength and, in effect, enjoy a halo effect, from the carrier brand. Such carry-over effects can be quite helpful to a new entry, which can gain consumer credibility from its implied "sponsorship" by a well-known and accepted brand.

While the same sponsorship values do not exist with cross-ruff coupons offered by other companies, such coupons help the carrying brand by providing, through their money-saving feature, a meaningful incentive to the purchase of the carrier product. For such an incentive to be effective, however, it must be highlighted on the package itself, preferably on the front panel. The effects of cross-ruff coupons are greatly enhanced when the purchase of the couponed products provides a tie-in usage with the carrier brand. Obviously, such a tie-in provides a measure of relevance, as in the examples of a cheese-spread coupon with the purchase of a box of crackers and a toothbrush coupon inserted in a toothpaste package.

On-Pack Coupons.   These follow the same patterns as in-pack coupons with one exception: The coupon or coupons carried on-pack are printed on the back or side panels of the package itself. Two particular problems are connected with this promotion type:

Special packages carrying the printed coupon or coupons must be specially designed and run.

Care must be taken in designing the package and the coupon(s) to reduce the potential mutilation of the package on the shelf, however, marginal, by people wishing to get the coupons and not willing to buy the product. The higher the value of the coupon(s), particularly if cross-ruff coupons are used, the more serious this problem can be.

A variant of on-pack coupons are coupons printed on outer wrappers—for instance, the multiple-pack sleeves designed to carry six bottles of soft drinks or four cans of tomato sauce. In this instance, the wrapper, or sleeve is printed with the coupons and properly flagged, while the product itself comes from the regular production runs. A second variant is the reversible label, where the coupon or coupons are printed on the reverse of the product label, which is then affixed to the product package with spot gluing. Generally used with canned products, the coupon offer is highlighted on the front side of the label.

Instantly Redeemable Coupons.   Instantly redeemable coupons are designed to generate immediate purchases of the product, rather than a later purchase in a subsequent shopping trip. Obviously, customers must be able to remove these coupons in the store without damaging the package, which should be able to be restocked if a customer decides against purchase at the check-out register. Coupon-carrying *neck tags* are often used for this purpose since they can easily be removed. Experiments have also been made with pressure-sensitive coupons that are affixed on the outside of the package and easily peel off. But problems due to the residual glue, however little, have prevented wide adoption of this method. It should be stressed, however, that instantly redeemable coupons are used, in most cases, as a desperation tactic to infuse vitality into a product that has been languishing on the shelf and whose permanent retail home is consequently threatened. These coupons should not

On-pack coupons for Waldbaum's private-label cereals.

only be easy to remove and use on the spot, it is often important that they be easy to affix, even after the product is in the store, by company salespersons or agents hired for the purpose.

Summary—In- and On-Pack Coupons

The use of in- and on-pack coupons is popular primarily because the incremental distribution costs are slight. To be effective, in- or on-pack coupons should discount products that closely share consumer targeting with the carrier brand. Their effectiveness is further enhanced if the couponed product has tie-in usage opportunities with the carrier product. In- or on-pack coupons benefit the products couponed and the carrier brand, whose purchase is also encouraged by the fact that it bears a coupon for another product. These coupons, highlighted on the front panel, are definitely becoming part of the sales proposition and must conform to FTC policy whereby the package label must inform the consumer of all conditions governing use of the coupons, including expiration date and the specific product—size and type—for which it can be redeemed. The effectiveness of in- or on-pack coupons is automatically limited as distribution is limited to the specific run of the carrier package. Also, coupon impact is staggered because usage of these coupons can be exercised only after the carrier product is purchased. For this reason, the use of in- and on-pack coupons is generally supplementary to other couponing and promotional programs.

COUPON REDEMPTION

The number of coupons likely to be redeemed as a result of a given couponing event has important implications for the strategic objectives of such a coupon campaign and represents essential information for establishing the liability parameters of the couponing event. Much of the liability extends to subsequent years as the flow of redeemed coupons continues to reach ultimate redemption centers long after the coupons are first circulated. According to industry sources, although coupons are used by consumers early, within the first year of distribution, it will take three years, on the average, before all coupons generated by a specific promotion are ultimately redeemed. Such a time lag requires sufficient accruals, year to year, and hence companies must make adequate provisions for such funds.

As the number of coupons circulated and redeemed has rapidly increased in the last decade, so have financial commitments to this area of promotional activity. The procedures required to receive,

THE COUPON PROCESS

Issued 102 Billion   **Redeemed 4 + Billion**

WHO REDEEMS COUPONS — RETAILERS

	FOOD STORES 92.5%	DRUG STORES 5.0%	ALL OTHER 2.5%
RETAILERS			
COUPONS	3.7 BILLION	.2 BILLION	.1 BILLION

WHO CLEARS COUPONS

	COMMERCIAL CLEARINGHOUSE 85.0%	ASSOCIATIONS 10%	WHOLESALERS 2.5%	RETAILERS 2.5%
CLEARERS				
COUPONS	3.4 BILLION	.4 BILLION	.1 BILLION	.1 BILLION

WHERE COUPONS CLEARED FOR RETAILERS

	MEXICO 75%	HAITI 12.5%	USA 12.5%
LOCATION			
COUPONS	3.0 BILLION	.5 BILLION	.5 BILLION

WHO REDEEMS COUPONS — MANUFACTURERS

	2,000-100%	20 LARGEST 1%	750 MEDIUM 37.5%	1,230 SMALLEST 61.5%
MANUFACTURERS				
COUPONS	4 BILLION-100%	2.5 BILLION 62.5%	1.2 BILLION 30.0%	.3 BILLION 7.5%

WHERE COUPONS REDEEMED BY MANUFACTURERS

	USA 55%	MEXICO 45%
LOCATION		
COUPONS	2.2 BILLION	1.8 BILLION

The coupon process—estimate of total coupons issued and redeemed in 1931. (Source: Coupon Handling Practices, September 1982.)

187

process, investigate provenance, and pay for the coupons presented to manufacturers for payment have been severely strained. Handling the redemptions resulting from the more than 100 billion coupons circulated in 1981 alone—the yearly number will exceed 150 billion mid-decade—and disbursements of more than $2 billion in 1982 has propelled coupon redemptions into a significant industry in and of itself.

Coupon redemption encompasses four areas of concern:

1. *Coupon Redemption Levels.* As indicated earlier, redemption levels differ according to the distribution medium. Redemptions also vary by product class and are affected by the relationship of face value to retail price.

2. *The Couponing Redemption Process: Planning and Monitoring Functions.* The process for the redemption of coupons circulated by a company must include thorough planning, from initial estimates of anticipated redemptions to timely reporting on the number of coupons redeemed.

3. *The Couponing Redemption Function.* Coupon clearinghouses act as agents for the principals—either retailers or manufacturers—in handling most of the coupons redeemed. In-house centers handle the rest.

4. *Misredemptions.* If anything can impede couponing, it is increased misredemption across the whole spectrum of products couponed. Some of the companies using coupons may have to abandon this otherwise powerful promotional tool.

Coupon Redemption Levels

That customers have become increasingly responsive to coupon promotions is shown by the growing number of coupons circulated and by the growing number of coupon carriers—mostly coop in nature—reaching the public. The supermarket may represent the last cash business in the United States, and it is easy to discern why consumers, concerned with inflation and consumer packaged goods prices, find coupons of at least some instant relief.

Many factors affect the number of redemptions obtained, some rooted in the product itself, others in the dimensions of the offer made and the carrier bringing it to consumers. Still other influences on redemption derive from retail realities and competitive activities.

1. *Product-Related Factors.* Clearly, the brand/product category couponed and its standing among consumers affects the redemption rates of its coupons.

    a. *Brand Awareness.* Consumers tend to be suspicious of brands unfamiliar to them; hence, brand awareness is conducive to higher redemption levels. Further, lack of familiarity keeps consumers from developing a clear value image for a brand, which affects their decision as to whether a coupon is "worth it." A frequent question is whether a new product launch should be accompanied by a coupon offer concurrent with the start of advertising. Usually, the more prudent course of action is to delay couponing for several weeks, until a reasonable level of brand awareness has been established.

    b. *Brand Loyalty.* Consumers using a particular brand as part of the brand's core group obviously welcome coupons lowering the purchase cost of a product they buy regularly. A general rule is that the larger the share held by the brand, the higher the redemption levels achieved. Still, while significant brand loyalty may help obtain trade support for a coupon promotion—which may actually have been offered in order to generate "push" results in the first place—most manufacturers see few benefits to be gained from giving discounts to regular customers.

    Nevertheless, in at least one instance, a coupon event for a leading brand can be highly salutary. Such an event, planned as a defense against the entry of a potentially strong competitor, can be successful precisely because the brand already enjoys a large market share. By accelerating purchases of the established brand—with the coupon—customer switchovers to the new competitive product are staved off.

c. *Frequency of Brand Purchases.*   The shorter the purchase cycle is for a brand, the greater the likelihood of its coupons being used. Conversely, the longer the coupon is held—given a brand with a longer use cycle—the more likely it is that the coupon will be mislaid or that competitive coupons or other money offers will prevail against the original coupon.

d. *Product-Category Purchases.*   Similar to the effects of usage cycles within a category, differentials in purchasing cycles between different product categories also affect redemption levels. The more commoditized the product category, the higher the usage of coupons is for products in that category. The accompanying data compiled by A.C. Nielsen indicate the differentials—on average—between several product categories, with meat and dairy products and beverages showing best redemption levels.[6]

However, the inroads made by generics in many of the major supermarket chains may impact the more commoditized product categories, where switching away from branded products occurs more readily.

2. *Redemption Differentials Related to Media.*   Redemption rates depend on the medium carrying the coupon. According to A.C. Nielsen's 1981 *Coupon Distribution Trends,* redemption levels range from a high of 18.4% for regular in-pack coupons to a low of 2.1% for coupons circulated in Sunday magazines. Not included in the redemptions are coupon redemptions generated by in-store programs, which average more than 34%.

All figures represent averages for all products couponed in a given medium. Some products may redeem at a much higher rate than the average reported for the medium, while others may do worse.

The following A.C. Nielsen chart further qualifies the 1981 averages by medium of circulation in providing additional breakdowns by product category.

3. *Coupon Cents-Off Values.*   It is not axiomatic that the higher the cents-off value provided by a coupon, the higher the redemption rate. While such a direct relationship does hold for like products at like prices, the relationship is not true across the board

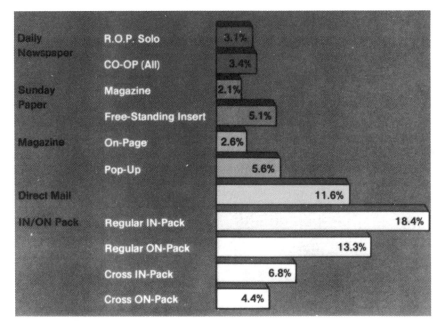

Average coupon redemption rates by media on grocery products. (Reprinted with permission of A.C. Nielsen.)

for products at different price levels. A 20¢-off coupon, for example, does not necessarily redeem better than a 10¢-off coupon if the first product retails at $2 and the second one sells for 49¢. This situation again turns on the price value relationships discussed earlier. A discount of 20¢ on a $2 item represents a 10% discount; a coupon for 10¢ off a 49¢ item is twice as valuable, a 20% discount off retail.

As retail prices responded to inflationary pressures and went up, year to year, so did the average cents-off face values of coupons. As shown in the A.C. Nielsen chart for the years 1977 to 1981, the average face values of coupons for products sold in grocery outlets increased almost 33%, from 14.9¢ to 19.8¢.

This trend toward higher coupon face values is further illustrated by the declining percentage of lower value coupons and the growing percentage of higher value coupons in circulation.

The distribution of 10¢-off coupons declined 34% from 1979 to 1981, while the circulation of coupons with face values of 25¢ and higher increased by 51%.

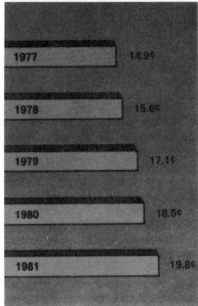
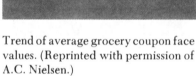

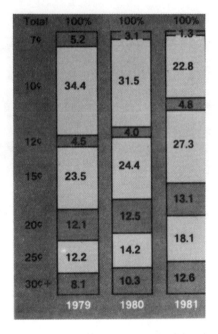

Trend of average grocery coupon face values. (Reprinted with permission of A.C. Nielsen.)

Percentage of grocery-coupon distribution by face value. (Reprinted with permission of A.C. Nielsen.)

Not included in cents-off face values of coupons are the handling costs to the retailer and the redemption center used by the manufacturer. The current per-coupon handling charge paid to retailers in return for their accepting and processing coupons is 7¢ and will soon be increased to the 8¢–10¢ range. Not too long ago the charge was 5¢. The fees charged by the redemption centers acting as agents for manufacturers vary widely and are generally set by contract. The average fee is 2¢ per coupon processed.

4. *Retail-Related Factors.* Product availability remains one of the most critical factors affecting coupon redemption rates at retail. Consumer decisions to use coupons are generally volatile, more so as switching between a number of like brands has become increasingly acceptable. At the same time, the lessening trade commitment to full assortments has caused significant out-of-stock conditions for many items, sometimes whole lines. While product availability accelerates

redemptions, out-of-stocks not only defer purchases but switches planned purchases to competitive brands. Coupons often go unused, their effectiveness having been lost altogether by the time subsequent purchases of the product come around. Many coupon promotions are designed specifically with the trade in mind, in an effort to increase pipelining to the retail floor. But running such a promotion without sufficient stocks at retail is obviously wasteful.

5. *Competitive Activities.* As in all marketing areas, competitive activities influence a coupon's redemption level.

The Coupon Redemption Process: Planning and Monitoring Functions

The systematic approach to redemptions developed by the Promotion Services Department at General Mills (GM) is illustrative of one of today's best coupon-redemption systems.[7] Each step in the GM process represents a separate function.

Estimating Redemptions. Since redemption rates determine both cost and effectiveness factors in a given promotion, working up redemption estimates for alternative couponing programs enables the department to select the best promotional alternative.

Data for such estimates may be generated from similar past couponing experiences with the brand.

If such experience is not specifically available—particularly in the case of new products—General Mills has developed its own estimating formula based on experiences with other brands, averages provided for the industry, and certain assumptions.

According to David Levi, manager of GM's promotion department, "the concept of developing a formula for calculating redemption estimates is based on the following assumption: that redemptions are a function of the *coupon value, distribution vehicle,* and *brand.* Therefore we need a formula that includes factors that measure the differences in value, couponing vehicle, and brand. We use ratios as a way of expressing these differences, and so our formula includes a *value ratio,* a *vehicle ratio,* and a *brand ratio.* A ratio, however,

Promotion vehicle	Nielsen averages (%)				Vehicle ratios
Direct mail	10.5	÷	10.5	=	1.00
Magazine pop—up	4.3	÷	10.5	=	0.46
Magazine on—page	2.5	÷	10.5	=	0.24
Free—standing insert	5.0	÷	10.5	=	0.48
Sunday supplement	2.1	÷	10.5	=	0.20
Newspaper ROP	2.9	÷	10.5	=	0.28
Newspaper Coop	3.3	÷	10.5	=	0.31

Coupon value ratios.

means nothing unless we know what it is a ratio to. For convenience *we calculate the value ratios against our most common value, our vehicle ratios against our highest redeeming vehicle, and the brand ratios against our highest redeeming brand."*[7]

As an illustration, Levi has applied the GM formula to a 15¢ coupon promotion for the hypothetical product "Wheat Flakes."

1. Since the most common value at GM was 10¢ at the time this example was presented, the *value ratio* was calculated against 10¢.

Assuming that in GM's experience a 15¢ coupon redeems 20% higher than 10¢ coupons, a 1.2 value ratio is obtained.

Assumptions:

    10¢ is our most common value

    Value tests show 15¢ coupon redeems 20% higher than a 10¢ coupon for a value ratio of 1.2

Value ratios:

    10¢ — 1.0
    15¢ — 1.2

Vehicle ratio calculations for different promotion vehicles.

2.   The next step is the calculation of *vehicle ratio* for the proposed "Wheat Flakes" promotion. Using A.C. Nielsen's average redemption figures rather than GM's own experience, Levi used direct mail, the highest redeeming medium, for his base. Thus, while the direct-mail vehicle ratio is 100%—the benchmark—free-standing inserts redeem at 48% of the direct-mail rate and ROP newspaper coupons at 28% of the direct-mail rate.

3.   The calculation of *brand ratio* comes next. While the assumption has been made that the GM highest redeeming brand generates a 15% redemption level with a 10¢ direct-mail coupon, no comparable 10¢ direct-mail experience is available for "Wheat Flakes." Hypothetically, however, some redemption data are available from other couponing vehicles and values. These data are translated to 10¢ direct-mail equivalents yielding a 12.0% average redemption level and a 0.8 *brand ratio*, which is the ratio of the 12.0% direct-mail equivalent for "Wheat Flakes" to the highest redeeming brand 10¢ direct-mail equivalent.

4.   Finally, an estimate of projected redemptions for an ROP newspaper "Wheat Flakes" 15¢ coupon can be constructed. Given a starting point of 15%—the highest redeeming brand 10¢ direct-mail equivalent experience—a *brand ratio* of 0.8, a *value ratio* of 1.2, and a *vehicle ratio* of 0.28, the redemption estimate is 4.0%.

Value	Description	Date	Promotion S & F	Project red. %	Value ratio	Percent Adj. to 10 value	Vehicle ratio	Percent Adj. to direct–mail equivalent.
10¢	Magazine pop–up	2/78	302	5.0			0.46	10.9
15¢	Magazine on–page	5/78	303	3.5	1.2	2.9	0.24	12.2
10¢	Supplement	6/78	304	2.6			0.20	13.0
15¢	Coop ROP news	8/78	305	4.4	1.2	3.7	0.31	11.9
							Average	12.0

$$\text{Brand ratio} = \frac{\text{Average 10¢ direct–mail equivalent}}{\text{Highest redeeming brand's 10¢ direct–mail equivalent}} = \frac{12.0\%}{15.0\%} = 0.8$$

A brand ratio calculation for "Wheat Flakes"—1978.

Highest redeeming brand – 10¢ direct mail	15.0%
Wheat Flakes brand ratio	0.8
Wheat Flakes 10¢ direct – mail estimate	12.0%
Value ratio for 15¢ coupon	1.2
Wheat Flakes 15¢ direct mail estimate	14.4%
ROP newspaper vehicle ratio	0.28
Wheat Flakes 15¢ ROP newspaper estimate	4.0

A redemption estimate for a "Wheat Flakes 15¢ ROP coupon.

5. An additional step helps in reviewing redemption estimates for other media. Using the 14.4% "Wheat Flakes" 15¢ direct-mail estimate, alternative redemption estimates can be obtained from other vehicle ratios.

After these calculations have been completed, the decision can be made about which vehicle to use for the promotion. If a couponing program is being considered for a totally new product, which obviously cannot provide prior couponing redemption experience, experience with similar products is initially helpful.

Coupon Code Assignment. Each coupon promotion receives a unique coupon code that identifies all redemptions generated by the promotion. The GM code contains a description of the promotion, including the distribution vehicle, outdate, and circulation. Additional information may be encoded as desired.

Other couponing vehicles	Vehicle ratios	Wheat Flakes 15¢ direct mail (%)		Wheat Flakes 15¢ coupon estimate (%)
Magazine pop – up	0.46	X	14.4	=	6.6
Magazine on – page	0.24	X	14.4	=	3.5
Free – standing insert	0.48	X	14.4	=	6.9
Sunday supplement	0.20	X	14.4	=	2.9
ROP newspaper coop	0.31	X	14.4	=	4.5

A 15¢ coupon redemption-estimate schedule for "Wheat Flakes."

Preparation of the Promotion Schedule and Estimate.   At GM the promotion schedule and estimate launches the official record of the proposed and approved couponing program. (The same form is used for promotions other than couponing.) The document serves several purposes:

Describes the promotion in detail.

Records all the information that will be entered in the computer coupon-redemption reporting system.

Shows the total promotion cost, calculated by area of expense, and which portion will be charged to the brand's promotional budget, thereby reducing the funds budgeted to it for future promotions during the fiscal year.

Records management approvals.

In addition, a promotion log is used to keep track of all documents related to each promotion, including the logging of supplier contracts, verification of the vendor's performance before approval of disbursements, and the preparation of the appropriate artwork.

Advising Sales of Incoming Promotions.   Summary reports of all coupon programs committed to for the following two months are issued monthly to the sales department. Circulation figures are further reported by sales region. Detailed sales letters are also prepared for each promotion. Since sales departments often need significant lead times to incorporate incoming promotions in their sales presentation calendar, most companies operate on considerably more than two months' advance notice for promotions.

Redemption Reports.   Monthly computer reports track current-month as well as cumulative redemptions by brand and by specific coupon code, which enables the promotion department to analyze actual versus projected figures and to update liability projections. The data generated by each promotion become part of the GM data bank, which, in turn, is available to help in the calculation of future brand and vehicle ratios.

Designing the Coupon

The physical appearance of the coupon is the subject of careful planning. The size and the overall impression it makes on the consumer determine the response of shoppers and the trade. The product presentation itself, including package spotlighting, may heighten redemptions. Finally, the coupon's legal copy must adequately caution coupon users and delineate the proper handling that safeguards against misredemption. If all other factors are equal, the success of a particular couponing program can rest with coupon design. A.C. Nielsen suggests the following steps in designing a coupon.[8]

1. Keep to generally accepted industry standard sizes, primarily the dollar-bill-size coupons and the one-third IBM-card size. Odd shapes make handling difficult throughout the redemption process. Still, there are times when space availabilities may necessitate special coupon sizes. A coupon inserted in a small cigarette sample box, for example, cannot conform to standard size.

2. The face value of the coupon must be prominently displayed, in large type on at least two corners of the coupon. "Free" coupons, whose face value depends on the particular retail price charged for the product—often presents problems. As stressed by Robert Popaditch of Jewel Food Stores at a 1977 ANA workshop:

> Free coupons are another problem to us. What's the value on it? My price is 49¢, and my competitor's is 59¢. Am I being cheated? Are you being cheated? And what's to prevent me from raising my price to 69¢ while your free coupon is running. The checker has to put a value on a free coupon. What's to prevent her from putting 89¢ on it, giving the customer the 49¢ value, and pocketing the rest?[9]

The self-destruct type of coupon—designed to permit use of one of two versions, each carrying a different face value and different redemption conditions—presents another set of problems. According to Daniel Wilkenson Jr. of the Virginia Food Dealers Association:

> The either/or coupon is extremely popular but does represent some misredemption problems too. At the check-out, the sticky-fingered checker can [on a 12¢/25¢ coupon] redeem for 12¢, pull out 13¢, and he's made himself a few bucks over a period of time. Most of these

coupons come to the clearinghouse intact. How much was it redeemed for? We've got no way of knowing. We notice that the higher values have the higher redemption rates. Since there's no way in the world to know which value was redeemed, you have to give the benefit of the higher value. And this invites a certain amount of rip-off that's absolutely uncontrollable.[10]

3. The words "store coupon" should be prominently displayed on the coupon so there is no doubt in the minds of shoppers and trade alike as to its purpose.

4. The paper stock on which the coupon is printed should have the weight and texture for easy handling.

5. Simplicity and clarity are the hallmark of a good coupon. The design should be clean and uncluttered. Both offer terms and coupon face values must be easily understandable by shoppers and clear to check-out clerks. On this subject Wilkenson declares:

> The coupons that bother us most are what I call "cutesy" coupons. You get real cute on some of these things. Here is one that says to the customer: "Sara Lee will donate 10¢ to the Muscular Dystrophy Association for each coupon redeemed in accordance with 1976 tie-in condition." What's the value of this coupon? We presume it's 10¢. But in the copy to the grocery it says, "As your agent, redeem this coupon for a retail customer in accordance with the terms of this offer. We will reimburse you 10¢ plus 5¢ on the purchase of one package, or 25¢ plus 5¢ on the purchase of two." They're going to give some money to charity, but nobody knows what the coupon is worth to the consumer and it can be either of two things to the retailer.[11]

6. Accurate monitoring of redemptions requires that coupons be properly coded. Such codes may include market data identifying not only the specific distribution vehicle involved but also the market or markets in which the coupon is circulated. The codes should stand out and be highly legible. Since coupons are sometimes partially torn, codes should appear in two different places on the coupon. Redemption houses have recently been experimenting with optical scanning to accelerate processing, which requires coupon codes printed with magnetic ink.

7. Each coupon should carry the full text of the legal copy directed to the retailer who, as redemption agent acting on behalf of

the coupon issuer, is cautioned as to the conditions under which coupons submitted for payment will be honored. Such copy should include a statement that the manufacturer issuing the coupon retains the right to request proof that the retailer has purchased sufficient merchandise to cover the number of coupons redeemed.

8.   The address of the redemption house should be printed clearly.

9.   Expiration dates, if used, must be prominent in order to avoid confusion by both consumers and check-out clerks. Some trade factors are no longer observing expiration dates, and some manufacturers, to avoid confrontations with influential retailers, are doing likewise. In any case, short expiration dates can create irritations and antagonize customers, rather than gain friends for the coupon issuer. On the other hand, there are some indications that shorter expiration limits may accelerate redemptions. This in addition to their advantage in providing more precise time limits for the financial liability undertaken by the coupon issuer.

A study undertaken by Donnelley Marketing measured the redemption flow of ROP coupons with 4 and 9 months' expiration dates.[12] The study concludes that shortened time periods can compress coupon usage into a shorter time span without measurable loss in total response. Further studies in this area are needed to ascertain specific determinants.

10.   It is desirable to emphasize the one-to-one rule of redemption—namely, that only one coupon will be accepted for each package purchased.

11.   If space allows, printing the product picture on the coupon itself can be helpful.

The Coupon-Redemption Function

Coupons flow, from shoppers who redeem them in retail stores, ultimately to manufacturers' redemption centers. Redeemed coupons are turned into the cage on the retail floor by check-out clerks at the end of their shifts. There they are counted, bundled, and usually sent on to chain headquarters or to a clearinghouse. Some independents themselves sort out the coupons by manufacturer and ship them directly to different manufacturer redemption centers.

Chain or divisional headquarters accumulate coupons received from all outlets in the chain and usually send them to a retailer clearinghouse.

The retailer clearinghouse verifies coupon counts and pays the individual retailer or the chain the total face value of all the coupons submitted plus a retailer standard handling charge, now set at 7¢ per coupon. After sorting the coupons by manufacturer, the retailer clearinghouse sends them, with appropriate billing, to the applicable manufacturer redemption center.

Some independents and an increasing number of chains are bypassing retailer clearinghouses, choosing instead to send coupon submissions directly to manufacturer redemption centers with the aim of expediting payments. This practice may be due to those retailer clearinghouses that wait for payments from manufacturers before making their own disbursements to retailers.

Some large manufacturers, including Procter and Gamble, General Foods, R.J. Reynolds, and General Mills, operate their own in-house redemption centers. While perhaps advantageous to major manufacturers, the expenses of setting up, operating, and managing a redemption center are excessive for most manufacturers, who generally prefer to use outside suppliers.

Redemption-Center Reports. Redemption centers can supply a wealth of actionable information, both for financial control and sales development purposes. Such reports are issued frequently, usually at monthly intervals, and they usually include information in two areas—coupon-related data and retailer-centered data.

1. A basic management report provides detailed information for each coupon code:

   Name of brand, further detailed (when relevant) by type, size, color, and flavor

   Date of distribution (initial run in the case of in- or on-pack couponing programs)

   Vehicle used for distribution

   Face value

   Area of distribution—national, regional, and specific markets

   Estimated total redemptions—in number of coupons and as a percentage of circulation

Projected total redemptions based on redemptions to date—in number of coupons and as a percentage of circulation

Redemption for the immediate past period (usually the past month)—in number of coupons and as a percentage of circulation

Disbursements during the immediate past period

Cumulative disbursements

Redemption-center fees together with applicable postage costs

2. A report detailing disbursements to retailers is a companion document to the basic management report, and it identifies retailers redeeming above average numbers of coupons for a given brand or brands and relates that information to sales for increased pipelining follow-up. This information will help spotlight developing trends as well as potential misredemptions. The report may include:

Coupons redeemed by each retailer by coupon code for the immediate past period and on a cumulative basis—quantity and total face value.

The aggregate of coupons, by coupon codes, redeemed by all stores in a chain—quantity and total face value.

Record of payments by individual retailers—the invoice numbers, dates, and amounts paid.

Discrepancy checks, to compare the amounts billed by a retailer with the amounts verified and paid by the redemption center.

Additionally, specially tailored reports may be requested and programmed for, based on a manufacturer's particular informational needs.

MISREDEMPTIONS

The veracity of the oft-repeated statement that "coupons are money" motivated many to reach for the money without using the coupons for the purpose they were intended. Coupon misredemption has taken form as widespread and well-organized fraud, bringing into collusion consumers, retailers, and clearinghouses. As defined by the U.S. Postal Service, the elements of coupon fraud are twofold: a scheme to defraud and the use of the United States mail. The involvement of the mails is not limited to coupons submitted for redemption by mail; mail involvement may extend to the check drawn in payment of the coupons and mailed out to the person or persons attempting to perpetrate the fraud.

In the late 1970s hundreds of thousands of 25¢-off "Breen" detergent coupons were submitted by over 300 retailers to the "CFCP Clearing House" for redemption. The coupons were carried by a free-standing insert in three New York–area newspapers and generally resembled all the other coupons circulated in the insert— except for one important detail: The product did not exist. Both "Breen" and "CFCP Clearing House" were fictions, created by the U.S. Postal Service expressly to help uncover some flagrant coupon misredeemers. Some 100,000 "Breen" coupons—some claim a much greater number—were submitted for redemption by more than 1,600 individual accounts. Further, even though this coupon circulation was limited to New York, submissions were received from 40 states. In some instances, redeemers were identified as individuals working out of their homes, newsstand operators, hardware-store operators, and other nontraditional retail establishments.

The seriousness of the misredemption problem receives constant attention from all concerned given that couponing is a favored promotional vehicle. Nevertheless, with misredemption costs already exceeding $200 million a year, industry efforts to stem misredemptions have greatly accelerated. A National Coupon Fraud Coordinator appointed by the U.S. Postal Service has resulted in increased indictments and prosecutions. The industry itself, through the efforts of the Grocery Manufacturers of America and many major manufacturers, has tightened its procedures and controls.

Some favorite coupon misredemption ploys were outlined by H.R. Wientzen of Procter & Gamble in a talk at the ANA Advertising Financial Management Workshop in 1979 and are summarized below.[13]

1. *The Fraudulent Clearinghouse.*   The ease of entry in this field has sometimes attracted marginal operators, who have been able to generate substantial amounts of money by adding fraudulent coupons to legitimate submissions received from retailers. Others have created fictitious retailer accounts and have submitted coupons in their names. Fraudulent operators are aided in their efforts by easy access to a large number of coupons—primarily from coupon-bearing "best-food"-day newspapers and magazines—and their use of "coupon-clipper" networks to obtain coupons.

2. *Redemption of Coupons Submitted by Individuals Rather Than by Legitimate Retail Outlets.*   Individuals defraud by creating one or more bogus accounts and submitting coupons obtained fraudulently, using the addresses of themselves, family members, and friends to receive payments.

3. *Charitable Group Redemption.*   Unwittingly, members of organized charities will sometimes collect coupons for sale at a fraction of their face value to unscrupulous retailers or other operators who will misredeem them. Individuals donating the coupons, and even the leaders of the group, may be unaware that they are parties to an illegal scheme.

4. *Counterfeiting.*   Reproducing black-and-white newspaper coupons is relatively easy. It is even easier if the counterfeiter can gain access to press plates, which are often readily available in press rooms.

5. *The Large-Scale, or Bulk, Operator.*   The large-scale, bulk operation recruits large numbers of "coupon clippers," who are usually paid by the pound for newspaper and magazine coupons. The operator submits these coupons for payment through far-flung networks of marginal clearinghouses, retailers, and bogus accounts.

6. *Trade Schemes.*   Individual retail stores are sometimes a source of misredemptions, which are carried out by their employees, or even their owners, who may be receptive to actions that serve to supplement their income. A check-out clerk can drop a few coupons brought from home in the cash-register drawer and remove cash equal to the face value of the coupons. These coupons mingle with coupons properly redeemed by shoppers and all of the coupons are submitted for payment through regular channels. This sort of misredemption is extremely hard to police.

Besides the measures initiated by the U.S. postal service, steps to reduce, if not eliminate, misredemptions altogether are being taken by major retailers and manufacturers and by manufacturer redemption centers. Above all, manufacturers must convey total intolerance of misredemptions, and they must be ready to take a hard line by rejecting the redemption of coupons of questionable provenance. Too often payments are authorized for fear of antagonizing a particular trade factor. Manufacturers must demand proof that specific procedures are followed regarding the retrieval and destruction of unsold copies of newspapers and magazines to prevent their falling into the hands of misredeemers. Lacking proof of strong controls over a particular vehicle, the manufacturer should refuse to use it for coupon circulation purposes. Tight security must also be maintained at the printing plant.

The security arrangements used by the Wessel Company, a couponing lithographing operation in Elk Gove, IL, are typical of current efforts to prevent the misuse of printing facilities and the theft of coupons from loading docks. Wessel's measures include bonding of all employees, television surveillance of loading docks, total destruction of printed waste, blind packaging with theft-resistant plastic outer coating, and bonding of all drivers. All coupons are consecutively numbered and printing is done with phosphorous ink, detectable under ultraviolet light, in order to deter counterfeiting.[14]

In his book on couponing, Russell Bowman suggests that manufacturers implement a ten-step program to control misredemptions.[15]

1. Periodically update the coupon's legal copy to assure the inclusion of a clear message that fraud will not be tolerated.

2. Communicate promptly and clearly to all concerned in any suspicious situations that the company is fully prepared to investigate and, if necessary, prosecute. The company posture on couponing can be an important deterrent.

3. Make available to salespeople and the retail trade point-of-sale guidance signs to indicate what is coupon "fair play."

4. Merchandise coupon drops well in advance to provide salespeople and retailers the opportunity to order backup stock. Out-of-stock often leads to misredemption resulting

from brand-switching rather than from criminal intent. The retailer is put at a disadvantage with customers at the check-out counters.

5. Promote the trade and consumer benefits of couponing in sales literature, at point of sale, and in consumer and trade advertising. Coupons are profitable to the trade and offer a genuine bargain to shoppers.

6. Use reasonable expiration dates on coupons, depending on the method of distribution. On-pack coupons obviously take longer between print production and presentation by a shopper at check-out than ROP newspaper coupons, most of which are presented a few days after they are printed.

7. Select a coupon-distribution method that affords the company specific safeguards against massive misredemption attempts. Sequential numbering is a strong deterrent, which can be used in free-standing inserts, direct mail, and tip-in coupons.

8. Company financial executives must comprehend the importance of prompt payment of legitimate retailer invoices. The retail trade should not have to float a reserve to cover the manufacturer's couponing program.

9. Involve legal counsel at the first sign of any serious challenge to the integrity of the program (whether the problem originates with a consumer, the trade, or a retail clearing-house).

10. Use the same common sense in handling coupons as in handling money.

Responsible trade factors must be equally diligent in fighting misredemptions. Theirs is primarily an educational task, one of teaching their employees how to prevent customer misredemptions and informing employees of the penalties for misredemptions on their part. Cash-register signs and store banners should spotlight the campaign against misredemption to customers and store personnel alike.

Most of the responsibility for controls falls to the manufacturer redemption centers. Controls are applied as coupons are received

* ☐	Is the coupon rectangular, square or triangular?
* ☐	Is the coupon located in the lower outside corner of the advertisement?
* ☐	Is the coupon outlined by dashes?
* ☐	Is the amount of copy (and any art) about what most people would expect to see on a coupon?
* ☐	Is the placement (layout) of copy and any art as most people would expect to see it?
1. ☐	**Is the coupon an artistic cliche, thus likely to be immediately recognized as a coupon?**

* ☐	If the advertisement is full color bleed, is the color dropped out from behind the coupon to leave it white?
	OR
* ☐	If the background of the advertisement is white, is there a tint of color behind the coupon?
* ☐	Is the coupon made to look like a separate, "to-be-removed" part of the advertisement?
* ☐	Is the advertisement free of any elements that tend to camouflage the coupon?
2. ☐	**Is the coupon as visually strong as possible?**

* ☐	Does the headline say what the coupon is for?
* ☐	Does the artwork show what the coupon is for?
3. ☐	**Do the artwork and headline together make immediately clear what the coupon is for?**

A. ☐	**WILL READERS INSTANTLY RECOGNIZE THAT SOMETHING IS BEING OFFERED (the job of the coupon) AND EXACTLY WHAT THE OFFER IS (the job of headline and art)?**

Reader's Digest checklist for effective coupon advertising.

* [ ] Will whatever is being offered (e.g., money off on purchase, an item free or for sale, prizes to win, etc.) have a strong appeal to the people at whom the advertisement is aimed?

* [ ] Do the headline, the art and the copy enhance the inherent appeal of the offer?

1. [ ] **Will enough of the right people want what is being offered?**

---

* [ ] If the coupon is for money-off at purchase, is the amount likely to be high enough—but no higher than necessary—to get an acceptable amount of the kind of response desired (i.e., new users, continued purchase by current users, purchase of the advertised brand instead of a store or generic brand)?

* [ ] If the coupon is to order what the advertisement offers, is the price (for comparable quality) lower than people can get easily at nearby stores?

* [ ] Is the offer made on a "we will bill you later" basis; or can readers purchase with credit card numbers?

2. [ ] **Will enough of the right people want what is offered at the price they must pay?**

B. [ ] **DOES THE OFFER HAVE THE STRONGEST POSSIBLE APPEAL TO THE LARGEST POSSIBLE NUMBER OF THE PEOPLE TO WHOM THE ADVERTISEMENT IS DIRECTED?**

---

* [ ] Is the coupon physically easy to remove and fill·in and send; or easy to use for money-off with purchase?

* [ ] If the coupon is for money-off purchase price, will the amount offered be subtracted at time of purchase?
OR

* [ ] If the coupon is for "refund after purchase," will readers likely find that easy to do?

* [ ] If the coupon requires providing information, will a first glance likely give readers an impression that it is easy to do?

* [ ] If they start, will they find that it actually *is* easy to do?

* [ ] Will readers likely find responding completely free of any embarrassment, awkwardness or feeling of "being used."

1. [ ] **Relative to how much (or how little) people want what is offered, is what you ask them to do likely to be considered by <u>them</u> a "bargain" in terms of what they must do or put up with to get it?**

C [ ] **IS IT EASY AND CONVENIENT TO RESPOND?**

Reader's Digest checklist for effective coupon advertising.

and processed, and the tracking of redemptions by individual retailer accounts, particularly those who may have roused suspicion, helps spotlight questionable submissions. At Nielsen's Clearing House, for example, processors are trained to look for specific conditions. If one of these conditions occurs, the spotter refers the coupons to the client for disposition. Among the conditions watched for are:

Unusual quantities of any one coupon

Unusual quantities of old coupons

Mass or gang-cut coupons

Coupons that do not show consumer handling

Coupons appearing purposely wrinkled

Coupons with a different appearance from others of the same distribution

Coupons received from a retailer in multiple packages.

NOTES

1. Russell D. Bowman, *Couponing and Rebates* (New York: Lebhar–Friedman Books, 1980).
2. Roger Strang, *The Economic Impact of Cents-Off Coupons* (Nielsen Clearing House, 1980), pp. 22–23.
3. Anthony E. Gallo, "Coupons: Part 1," *National Food Review*, Spring 1982, pp. 11–18.
4. Gallo, "Coupons," p. 15.
5. Malcolm Douglas, "Setting Objectives and Strategies for Coupon Promotions" (Paper presented at the ANA Couponing Workshop, May 24, 1977), pp. 1–2.
6. "Coupon Distribution and Redemption Patterns by Product Group," *NCH Reporter*, 2 (1981), pp. 2–7.
7. This material was presented by David Levi and Owen Erstad of General Mills at the PMAA seminar held in Chicago in the Spring of 1980.
8. "The Do's and Don't's of Couponing," *NCM Reporter*, Nov. 1, 1982, pp. 11–12.
9. "Trade Attitudes Toward Couponing," (Panel discussion presented at the ANA Couponing Workshop, New York, 1977), p. 7.
10. "Trade Attitudes," p. 13.
11. "Trade Attitudes," p. 14.

12. "Coupon Expiration Dates Influence Behavior," *Findings* No. 8, November 1982.
13. H.R. Wientzen, "Identifying and Controlling Coupon Misredemption," Paper presented at the ANA Advertising Financial Management Workshop, 1979.
14. "Coupon Rip-Off," *Media Decisions*, May 1979, p. 63.
15. Bowman, *Couponing*.

SIX

Money Promotions: Refunds and Rebates

Refunds are generally viewed as promotional incentives that offer purchasers a return of some or all of the money they paid for a purchase when proof of that purchase is sent to the manufacturer. Technically, there is little difference between refunds and rebates. Both refer to the same cash incentive manufacturers will allow a shopper on their products. In practice, refunds are primarily used by consumer packaged goods manufacturers, while rebates are offered by sellers of large-ticket items such as appliances and cars. The emphasis in the case of rebates is on specific price reductions paid to buyers directly by the manufacturer. In general, the average value of a rebate is significantly higher than that of a refund. For the purpose of this chapter, however, the term *refund* is used to cover the entire range of refunds and rebates.

Refunds may be made in cash, by check, or by bearer draft. At times, a manufacturer may use a "free" coupon which entitles the recipient to receive free, at retail, a like product to the one he or she purchased in the first place. In another variant, buyers earn cash awards in certificate form, which can be used for off-price discounts on a subsequent purchase. The money value of these certificates can be substantial—for example, a $100 certificate offered by an airline to people taking a specific flight, which can be applied as a sizable discount on the next booking. Obviously, this approach primarily suits relatively expensive merchandise and services.

Refund offers have also been used in conjunction with other consumer incentives. The refund submission, for example, may not only serve to claim the amount promised but may also be used as an entry to a sweepstakes program offering a wide range of prizes. Some manufacturers have used refund mailings as carriers for coupons and money incentives on other products in their mix.

Overall, refund promotions are designed to accelerate and expand consumer purchases of the promoted item. More specifically, refunds are designed to cause one or more purchases; repeat purchases are achieved by asking for multiple proofs-of-purchase of a product and making the refund value sufficiently high to generate repeat actions until the terms of the refund are met. Such repetitive purchases are particularly important in the case of new products, where adoption hinges on extended usage, and several purchases are needed before a regular usage pattern sets in. Similarly, a product's position at retail can be defended against a new entry through a multiple proof-of-purchase refund offer that keeps product users out of the market for a while longer, thus denying the new product a strong foothold and perhaps topping it altogether.

Alternatively, multiple purchases, with or without specific "mix" requirements, can be specified for several different products of the same manufacturer. Such programs are primarily designed as dealer-loader programs and are often executed in conjunction with other trade-supported feature and display activities. Refunds are often used to stave off competitive activities, particularly those that offer specific price incentives. Here too the emphasis is at point-of-purchase, with both push and pull concerns taken into account. Coupons are often circulated together with the refund offer. In effect, such a piggyback approach offers the consumer both immediate and later savings, which enhances the impact of both incentives.

CIRCULATING THE REFUND OFFER

Basic to most refund offers is the requirement that special forms, circulated by manufacturers offering the refunds, be used in submitting a request for a refund. This requirement limits the offering of refunds to media that can carry such forms, although other media may be used to advertise the refund and attract people to the retail outlet carrying the product and the refund forms.

1. *Print Media.*   Print includes the whole range of print carriers, from daily newspapers to magazines to free-standing inserts. Often, the refund offer is only part of the body copy in an advertisement that "sells" the product, with the offer designed to "close" the sale.

2. *Direct Mail.*   Similarly to print, direct mail can be used to circulate refund offers either solo or in coop vehicles. Such offers may be made in conjunction with other incentives—for instance, coupons—and the offer could carry sufficient body copy for a strong product sell.

3. *Point of Sale.*   Tear-off pads, usually containing 50 to 100 refund forms, are in common use. The pads may be placed on the shelf where the product is sold, attached to special product displays, or displayed on the store's consumer information bulletin boards.

A take-one refund offer for Maxithins.

In years past, after all refund forms had been taken, the pad back-up card—called by some the "sorry-copy" card—often directed interested shoppers to write in to request a form. But given the problems and abuses more recently encountered by manufacturers in this area, few are now willing to provide additional forms after the initial supply is gone.

4. *On/In Package.* Often, refund offers are printed on the package itself or inserted in it. These refund offers may be for the carrying product or for other products sold by the same manufacturer. Generally, the offer is flagged on the front of the package so that it may be easily seen by shoppers and hence provide immediate incentive action. Since a special packaging run is required, the promotion is planned to last as long as it takes for supplies of the

Examples of refund neck tag offer on Hunt's Prima Salsa.

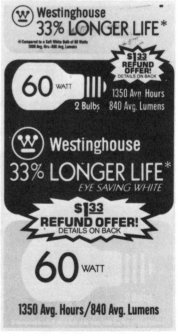

An on-pack refund offer by Westinghouse.

$1 33 REFUND OFFER!

Buy three packages of Westinghouse Eye Saving White bulbs and get an in-the-mail $1.00 cash refund *plus* a 33¢ store coupon, good on your next purchase of Westinghouse Eye Saving White bulbs — the light bulbs that have 33% longer life.

To get your $1.33 cash/coupon refund, buy 3 two bulb packages of Westinghouse Eye Saving White light bulbs and mail 3 proof-of-purchase symbols (one from each package) with the coupon below to:

Westinghouse $1.33 Refund
P.O. Box 7550
Stratmar Station
Bridgeport, Conn. 06650

Void where prohibited or restricted.
Two rebates per household, group or organization.
Offer expires March 31,1983. Please allow six weeks for refund.

- -

Please send me my $1.33 cash/coupon refund. I am enclosing one proof-of-purchase symbol from each of 3 two bulb packages of Westinghouse Eye Saving White light bulbs.

PLEASE PRINT

NAME _____

ADDRESS _____

CITY _____ STATE _____ ZIP _____

- -

Westinghouse Electric Corp.
Lamp Div., Bloomfield, N.J. 07003

Made in U.S.A.

90-T192-6

EYE SAVING
46677 10003
PROOF OF PURCHASE

2 Bulbs

60W/W

60 WATT

*Compared to a Soft White Bulb of 80 Watts-1000 Avg. Hrs.-860 Avg. Lumens

An on-pack refund offer by Westinghouse.

215

specially packaged product to move through channels. It is sometimes difficult to pinpoint the effectiveness of a refund program or to direct it to counter specific trade or competitive problems. Refunds, in this context, represent a promotional approach that appeals primarily to the product's customers and only marginally attracts new users.

INVOLVING THE RETAILER

As with all money promotions—indeed with all promotions—the proof of success is action at point-of-purchase. Retailer-personalized involvement with refund offers can be beneficial not only by providing a stronger "push" in terms of loading up at retail while feature-supporting the offer accountwide, but also by helping to increase potential consumer response to the offer.

Even though a refund offer is made and paid for by the manufacturer, the offer can be circulated under the various names of the participating retailers. Retailers thus involved will be motivated to stock up so their own customers will not be disappointed.

Westinghouse's Soft White alternative refund offer.

Westinghouse's Soft White alternative refund offer.

A take-one Bic mail-in refund pad.

While similar to in-ad coupons, refund offers differ in one major respect: Control remains with the manufacturer throughout. Further, by limiting the offer to retailers who are willing to participate, the manufacturer can avoid wasted circulation and perhaps save the cost of advertising altogether, if retailers consent to insert the offer at local rates paid from coop advertising funds.

A multiple-purchases refund offer on seven Hunt-Wesson products. (Reprinted with permission.)

STRUCTURING AND PROCESSING
THE REFUND OFFER

Clarity, simplicity, and completeness rule a well-structured refund offer. In a release prepared by the Promotion Marketing Association of America (PMAA) in April 1981, the following information was judged pertinent data—as applicable—to be used in refund offers and their advertising:

Brand name

Eligible size(s), flavors, varieties, and so forth

Proof-of-purchase requirements (specify tops, bottoms, seals, UPC, labels)

Offer name, box number, and complete address

Expiration date (if any)

Certificate requirement (if any)

Geographic limitations (if any)

Limitation on number of refunds per consumer (if any)

Additional recommendations to facilitate the processing of refund offers were suggested by A.C. Nielsen:[1]

1. Bulk proofs should be avoided. Letters are normally machine processed at the post office, but bulky letters are set aside for manual handling, which results in delayed delivery and potentially costly postage-due charges.

2. The terms of the offer should be kept simple and, if possible, should illustrate any required proof.

3. The terms of the refund offer should fully spell out all promotion limitations—that is, one per family, household, address, group, and so forth. The offer should further specify, prominently, if the refund form/certificate is an absolute requirement and whether it can or cannot be reproduced in any way. Advertised expiration dates must take into account the way in which the offer is circulated. On/in pack offers, for example, require a more extended expiration date.

4.   Specify the allowable delivery time for the refund on the actual form/certificate itself. Some 4–6 weeks should be allowed if refunds will be sent first class and 6–8 weeks if they are to be mailed third class. With mail deliveries continuing to slow down stated response, times may have to be further extended.

5.   The clearinghouse, whether an outside supplier or an in-house facility, should have enough time to gear up for the program and should be immediately advised if an offer is extended or redistributed.

REFUND VALUES

Refund values must be meaningful to the consumer in order to bring about the desired action. In exercising the refund, a consumer will incur some out-of-pocket expenses—postage, envelope—and these costs will enter a consumer's calculation as to whether to respond to a refund offer or not. Assuming though, that a worthwhile base value has been determined—usually $1 and up—how high is up? The answer depends on several criteria:

1.   The number of purchases that must be made to qualify for the refund. Obviously, the higher the number of proofs of purchase, the larger the reward required to bring the refund offer to fruition.

2.   The amount of incentive judged necessary to bring about a purchase. Purchases may also hinge on the life-cycle stage the product is in and the market share it enjoys at the time of the offer. Clearly, the higher the offer, the better the returns one can anticipate.

3.   The competitive pressures on the product. Refund offers are often made in response to competitive pressures. The amounts offered will therefore depend on what the competition is doing and on whether the effort is to be offensive or defensive. Ideally, a refund provides shoppers with a competitively favorable price/value ratio for the product.

Strategically, if the refund offer is designed to generate immediate sales—to shore up, for example, lagging product movement—its value should be high and the number of proofs of purchase should be minimal. Conversely, if the money available for the refund program is limited, the number of proofs of purchase required will be higher and the refund value will be kept to a modest level.

Response Levels

Average refund response levels differ by media. On/in pack offers usually generate the highest level of response, which is understandable since most submissions come from current users who are predisposed toward the product and who can more easily accumulate the proofs-of-purchase through regular purchases. The juxtaposition of product and refund offers at point-of-purchase makes the retail floor the second largest percentage generator of refund submissions. The smallest response is given to offers circulated in various print media.

A 1977 survey by Nielsen sets the average returns from on/in pack insertions at 3.8%, from point-of-purchase at 2.5%, and from print media at 0.5%. These figures, however, do not indicate the wide ranges involved—for instance, submissions generated by refund offers at point-of-sale range from 1.5% to 4.5%—and do not totally reflect current return levels. With the current great attention given refunding by individuals and by organized groups, response levels may already have reached levels twice those of 1977.

Slippage

In projecting liabilities from refund programs side by side with resulting increases in sales, manufacturers must consider the number of people who will buy a product or products with the intention of submitting the appropriate "qualifiers" for a promised refund and then fail to do so. In effect, a slippage occurs when some products are purchased as a result of the refund offer although ultimately no liabilities will be accrued against these purchases because no requests for refunds will be made against them. Payout calculations must include the slippage factor from the outset of planning the refund program. While little normative information for various product categories is publicly available, there are indications that more than half of those who intend to exercise a refunding option and make at least one purchase fail to do so. This percentage gets smaller as the refund value increases, thus making the effort on the part of the consumer more worthwhile. For every refund request submitted, it is likely that a second purchase or more was made in addition to the one or more purchases documented in the submission. It is important, therefore, for manufacturers to accumulate data on their own refund programs so that they can eventually develop reasonably accurate projections.

THE ORGANIZED REFUNDERS

In the early 1970s, a new phenomenon burst on the American scene—the organized refunders, the coupon-redemption queens, and literally hundreds of swap clubs. In his guide to coupons and refunds, Martin Sloan, a syndicated columnist and leader of the new consumer group movement writes:

> Today, when most shoppers walk into the supermarket, they find inflation staring them in the face and they feel as if they don't have a friend. But you do have friends in the supermarket. As you walk down the aisles you have thousands of friends. Every manufacturer wants to be your friend—by saving you money. This year [1980] manufacturers will make more than 7,000 refund offers. Just pick up any national brand box, bottle, or can, and the chances are you can get a refund on it.[2]

Manufacturers do make refund offers in the anticipation and with the intent that they be used. Their usage is expected to be according to the terms of the offer, proper and fair. Unfortunately, abuse of these offers by some consumers is on the rise, which causes considerable concern among manufacturers about this type of incentive. Manufacturers are especially concerned by the attitude shown by some persons toward both refund offers and the manufacturers.

A recent article published in the *Pope County Tribune* news-paper, under the byline of Jeanne Olsen, quotes from a workshop conducted by Vickie Dosdall under the sponsorship of the West Central Communities Action agency:

> Refunding is apparently getting to be a big thing throughout the United States—you might ask how can these companies afford to do refunding. It's all a big tax write-off for them.[3]

Such attitudes on the part of leading refunders and the public agencies that encourage them are being communicated widely to consumers and translated into actions that flout the intent of the refund offer and the goodwill of the manufacturer. Again quoting from Olson's report on Dosdall's workshop:

> "Some offers will require a refunder to write down the UPC number, the first line of the ingredients panel, or some other part of the label if the container cannot be peeled off or cut apart. Then they'll ask for the cash register receipt with the purchase price circled. For that reason," she said, "she also keeps a file of cash register receipts. They don't know how much you paid for that item," she said. "It might have been on sale, and prices vary from store to store. Just find a comparable price, circle it, and use that receipt. You don't have to go out and buy that item again just to get the receipt." On offers that are limited to one per family, she gets around the restriction by having one sent to herself at a simple Cyrus address and another sent to her husband at the more complicated route and box number address. She also has them sent to friends and relatives who will save them for her.[4]

Obviously, manufacturers are facing a major educational challenge if consumers are to deal with refunds fairly and understand the nature and significance of such offers in the marketplace. Most consumers are honest and careful in their handling and submission of refund requests. Unfortunately, the number of those who stray either by omission or by commission is apparently growing.

As an assist to this educational push, the PMAA has released a *Consumer Quick Checklist*[5] to guide consumers in proper com-pliance with the terms of refund offers and encouraging the media publicity.

The Promotion Marketing Association of America, a national trade association representing many companies who sponsor consumer refund promotions, offers the following suggestions to assist consumers in the effective participation in mail-in offers.

Consumer Quick-Check-List

Before you invest your time and postage expense, be sure you . . .

☐ Include the official refund certificate. These are usually required and cannot be reproduced in any form.

☐ Check to see if this offer has geographic limitations or an expiration date.

☐ Print clearly your name, (apartment number), address, city, state and zip code to insure delivery.

☐ Include the proper proof(s)-of-purchase. These vary widely and many include box tops, box bottoms, special seals, U.P.C. symbol, labels, etc. Never use substitutes or facsimiles because it may disqualify the offer.
Also, some offers require cash register tapes. Check details of the offer carefully.

☐ Include proof(s)-of-purchase from the correct product, size, flavor, variety, etc.

☐ Enclose all of the materials in an envelope of sufficient size and strength to insure delivery. Make sure you indicate your return address on the envelope.

☐ Print clearly the exact offer name, box number and address on the envelope.

☐ Include sufficient postage on your envelope to insure delivery.

☐ Do not mail more than one request per envelope. Combining requests will result in processing delays or rejection.

Other Tips

☐ Be sure to allow sufficient time for delivery, usually 6-8 weeks. We suggest you keep records of what, when and where you sent for a mail-in refund. If you need to inquire about your refund request be sure to provide complete information.

☐ Print clearly, always include zip code, do not substitute proofs or copy certificates.

☐ Do not request mail-in certificates unless they are advertised as being available. Then limit requests to one certificate per envelope as most manufacturers will usually not honor multiple certificate requests. Many offers are limited to one per family, group, organization, address, etc. Many manufacturers use modern computers to check for duplicate requests. Following instructions will save you time and money and make your refund activities more rewarding.

☐ Except where authorized by the manufacturer, multiple requests on behalf of organizations may not be honored. Check before you mail and waste postage. Where offer is limited to "one per family" extra requests and the proofs may not be returned to you.

☐ Remember that mishandling of offers by consumers may be fraud. To keep our free American economy growing, don't contribute to mishandling of offers.

PR1882—rev.

PMAA's checklist for refunders.

224

Refunder
Check
List

pmaa
PROMOTION MARKETING
ASSOCIATION OF AMERICA

420 Lexington Avenue
Suite 2031
New York, N.Y. 10170
(212) 867-3990

Prepared by

pmaa

Promotion Marketing
Association of America

PMAA's checklist for refunders (continued).

CASH GIVEAWAYS

Cash giveaways provide shoppers with immediate monetary rewards that can be earned through specific actions in the marketplace. Manufacturers must publicize such programs in advance in order to effectively induce the type of behavior and action qualifying a consumer for the cash reward. In such giveaway promotions, manufacturers' representatives—often acting as mystery shoppers—monitor the qualifications of individual customers and make the awards on the spot when qualifications are met.

Customer screening can be conducted in homes, in street traffic, or in stores, depending on the objectives of the promotion. Usage of a new product and its availability in the purchaser's home can be encouraged and rewarded by means of a well-advertised "shiny new dollar coin" or a "fresh five-dollar bill" promotion, whereby monitors call on individual homes at random and make the award on being shown proof of product.

Awareness of product performance superiority points can be enhanced by talking to people in traffic and rewarding them on the spot if they mention any such points without prompting, which indicates top-of-mind knowledge. Advertising the promotion is equally essential, for the objective of inducing potential customers to become familiar with the product and the areas in which its performance is superior. As in the case of in-home cash giveaway programs, selection of individuals for interviewing is generally random.

Although they are limited to specific retail outlets, in-store cash giveaways follow a similar rationale. Purchasers of the product are immediately rewarded by a monitor who checks a bag or basket after it has cleared the check-out station. A variant of the standard money award is the immediate reimbursement of half or all of the money paid by the qualified shopper (that is, one who has bought the product) based on the shopper's cash-register slip. Obviously, no more than one award could be made in the store during one time period. The monitor may however return later. To enlist store management support and cooperation, a like award is sometimes made to the store manager. Here, too, prior advertising is critical if the program is to meet its objective.

On occasion, thematic approaches are used with cash giveaway programs, thereby giving them specific advertising "hooks" on which to peg the type of action desired from consumers. This kind of promotion may involve special costumes for the monitors and specially designed and decorated vans or cars, with each of these factors further enhancing the visibility, ergo the awareness, created by the promotion. Since such programs are very complex and can have only limited impact in the marketplace, their use has become marginal.

NOTES

1. "Guidelines for More Effective Refunding," *NCH Reporter*, November 3, 1981, pp. 10–12.

2. Martin Sloane, *1980 Guide to Coupons and Refunds* (New York: Bantam Books, 1980), p. 1.

3. Jeanne Olson, "Clipping Coupons Pays Off," *Pope County Tribune*, Glenwood, MN, 3/25/82.

4. Olson, "Clipping Coupons."

5. *Refunding Checklist*, (New York: Promotion Marketing Association of America, 1982).

SEVEN

Trade Promotions

Promotions directed to ultimate consumers are by nature highly visible—indeed their success depends on visibility to generate a substantial response. By contrast, promotional efforts directed to the trade are much less visible, less obvious to the general public. Trade promotions seldom, if ever, make use of major media, thus are seldom seen by ultimate consumers.

Nevertheless, the amounts spent on trade promotions of various kinds are huge and growing. Promotional expenditures against the trade cross many different types of programs, which tend to obscure the size of the total amount spent on trade promotion—in 1982, more than $2 billion—which is predicted to grow annually by 10 to 15% throughout the 1980s.

Some of the reasons for the spiraling spending on trade promotion were outlined by A.O. Witteman of H.J. Heinz Company at an Association of National Advertisers (ANA) Workshop.[1]

1. Trade promotional dollars are increasingly important to a company on several counts:

   a. Promotional cases—that is, cases of merchandise sold on the basis of promotional deals—make up an increasing portion of a brand's total volume.

   b. Promotional expenditures, unlike most others, including general overheads and raw materials, are discretionary and therefore controlled by management on a year-to-year basis. Consequently, effective promotions generate incremental profits that can be reinvested in still more efficient promotions.

    c. An increasing number of trade factors feel it is important to pass on some of the promotional money they receive to ultimate consumers, thus helping to accelerate consumer take-out.

    d. As competition becomes increasingly fierce, manufacturers will use more promotional dollars to match a competitor's activity and maintain market share.

2. Trade promotions are becoming a more acceptable way of building business as manufacturers come to see the success in this strategy and allot more money for such efforts.

3. Monitoring of trade promotions is on the increase, as more and more companies set up measurement systems, either internally or with outside specialists.

4. New-product and line-extension activities have created a need for more trade promotions as more manufacturers increasingly rely on new distribution and new placement allowances to gain position on the retail shelf.

5. Economic conditions favor the use of trade promotions. Trade-promotion dollars passed on to consumers through retail-price featuring generate positive buying responses, especially in a slow economy when shoppers tend to be more careful with their money.

6. Promotional dollars are increasingly important to the trade. Given the low net margins now common in the trade, promotional income can be highly critical to a retailer, as well as to others in the channel, as regards pricing and profit structure.

7. Trade pressure for additional promotional programs is increasing, especially in the food industry.

Witteman identifies four major trends, which together are putting heavy monetary pressure on grocery retailers:

A slow-down in real growth

Significant internal economic problems

A shift from at home eating to fast foods

Aggressive competition—witness the recent practice of redeeming manufacturer coupons at twice or three times face value

The introduction and growth of generics have apparently further aggravated the narrowness of trade profits. As long as these elements, or some of them, continue to influence the viability and well-being of the middlepersons in distribution channels, manufacturers will be under increased pressure to provide additional promotional support and allowances.

OBJECTIVES OF TRADE PROMOTIONS

The literature on trade promotion provides extensive lists on the specific objectives manufacturers seek to achieve with such promotions. Overall, trade promotions are designed to provide the *push* factor in the push–pull progression in the marketing process. Clearly, the trade must provide enough product in appropriate assortments on the retail floor if consumer take-out, the *pull* factor, is to be brought to optimum fruition. To accommodate and to some extent encourage increased and accelerated consumer takeout of the product, the manufacturer, working through trade channels, will seek

To exercise good stock management at retail, increasing the distribution of line and individual items and preventing out-of-stock conditions for both.

To obtain trade support through special featuring events—providing mentions of, and consumer price incentives in best-food-day ads and display activities—and generally increased pipelining to the retail floor during such events.

To inform and sensitize all retail personnel, down to the aisle clerks, about the need to recognize and support proper and sufficient stocking of the product.

To offset competitive drives for new and old products.

To support renewed listing and broad distribution of seasonal merchandise such as a sun-screen line or powdered drinks.

At times, one particular objective may pose the more immediate challenge; long-term, all the objectives are important and must be included in the overall brand strategy (with the exception of the relisting of "seasonals," which may or may not be applicable, depending on product mix).

PLANNING THE TRADE PROMOTION

Careful planning is particularly critical in trade promotions, because of the lead time required to position the events in the trade's own promotional calendars and the growing promotional "noise level" as promotions proliferate: "At the last meeting of the Association of National Advertisers," writes Ernest Obermeyer, vice president and publisher of *Supermarket News*, "John Young, Scott Paper's director of promotion, reported that 'Chain and wholesale buyers review 400–700 promotions per week on grocery products alone.' He then posed the question, 'What do you expect from someone reviewing 400–700 offers per week?' We believe the answer is self-evident— not much.... Even if that level were cut in half, which is not likely to happen soon, it would still be difficult for any single promotion to stand above the crowd."[2]

The bottom-line, single consideration that overshadows all others, is the extent to which a promotion will specifically benefit the trade factors involved, both in financial terms and the degree to which it can enhance their service to their customers. Assuming that the basic objectives for the trade promotion have already been defined, consideration must be given to planning and launching the promotion:

1. Formulation of the trade promotion and its component elements and their integration into a presentation format, capable of standing "above the crowd."

2. Determination of the proper launch, focusing on optimal conditions for both timing and duration. "Open to buys," for example, are more flexible at certain times of the year; trying to generate retail-floor displays for year-round products between Thanksgiving and Christmas has little chance of success among all the seasonal merchandise.

3. Careful review of the money available for the promotion versus the money needed to make it work. In other words, an undercapitalized trade promotion will fall flat and may even cause long-term damage to the brand.

TYPES OF TRADE PROMOTIONS

By and large, trade promotions rely on a broad range of monetary allowances. Some are given as incentives to the trade to stock up on the products offered by the manufacturer; others reward specific performance levels of trade factors.

Stocking Allowances

Consumer-packaged-goods manufacturers generally agree on the single problem that plagues them most: out-of-stocks at retail. In an attempt to obtain a measure of stock management at retail, manufacturers have set up systems of payments designed to increase the stocking of their products at warehouse levels and through to the retail floor.

Quantity Discounts. A manufacturer may offer quantity discounts to the trade to increase the level of purchases of its products. The discount may be calculated on the number of units of products bought or on the dollar volume. Discounts may apply to a one-time purchase or to multiple purchases over time. Mostly, such discounts are taken off invoice as earned, although on occasion—particularly if calculations are based on cumulative purchases—they take the form of a special payment, a payback as it were, by the manufacturer.

Such promotions are particularly powerful in the case of seasonal

products—for instance, cough and cold remedies—where the larger
the sell-in at the beginning of the season, the better the manufacturer's chance of preventing out-of-stocks while at the same time
ensuring a preferential home at retail.

Quantity-discount promotions are also indicated in conjunction
with trade-loading drives to increase pipelining at retail in anticipation of another consumer-oriented effort, for instance, a major
advertising campaign. One variant of quantity discounts is the *free-
goods allowance* given an account, whether wholesaler or retailer,
based on the purchase of a specified volume or assortment. Such
offers—2 free cases with 10 and 13 for the price of 12—appeal to
middlemen, who can profit from selling at full revenue merchandise
they received a no cost. To the manufacturer, free-goods allowances
have the added appeal of generating promotional values calculated
on the retail value of the merchandise, although the manufacturer's
financial burden is based on the cost of goods alone.

Case Allowances. Case allowances were originally meant as
extra incentives for the trade to buy increased quantities of a
manufacturer's product. Case allowances are now a mostly routinized offer, without which many sales people feel unable to make a
sale to the trade altogether. Since virtually all manufacturers offer
case allowances, the trade can pick and choose among competitive
products and normally prefer the products that have better markup
potential. Case allowances are not usually tied to quantity purchases
and thus do not entail a specific performance on the part of the
trade, but they nevertheless constitute a major promotional cost for
the manufacturer. In favor of case allowances are their simplicity
and flexibility. Lately, at least some major corporations have started
to review their case-allowance policies, with an eye toward finding
the most effective uses of promotional money.

New Distribution Allowances. Some manufacturers offer special allowances to compensate the trade for the expense of listing a
new product. Such an allowance can give the new product
additional clout as the manufacturer attempts to obtain for it broad
distribution, quickly. In reality, these allowances are just another

way to sweeten the deal and induce the trade to allocate space for the new product on the shelf. A variant of the new distribution allowance is the *new-item placement allowance,* which usually refers to line extensions rather than to new products.

Dating. Dating is strictly a monetary incentive, often used in the launching of new products. In effect, the trade is given additional time to pay invoices for the product—30, 60, or 90 days beyond normal due dates. The trade is allowed "to work" on the manufacturer's money, thus lessening the risk involved in taking on a new product whose consumer takeout rate is uncertain.

Special Performance Allowances

Certain trade-promotional allowances are offered in exchange for specific promotional tasks.

Display Allowances. It is an axiom that the more visible, the larger the quantities, and the better the product location in terms of store traffic, the faster the consumer takeout the product will enjoy. Since most products normally carried by an account have assigned places on the shelf, obtaining extra space on the floor, even for a short period of time, becomes the target of specific promotional efforts. Manufacturers usually seek to induce retailers to make such space temporarily available by paying them a special allowance. Since display space is at a premium—particularly when seasonals are crowding the retail floor—early presentations to the trade are necessary to obtain a place on an account's promotional calendar.
Display activity can be secured in several ways:

1. *Cut-Case Displays.* In the most common way to obtain displays on the retail floor, case tops are cut off, thereby exposing the individual units (cans, boxes) to pricing action. After the merchandise is priced, the cases are usually stacked in islands on the retail floor or on gondolas at the end of aisles. When they are placed in interior aisles, they must not hide the products on the shelves or block traffic in the aisle. The displays are usually spotlighted by riser cards

provided by the manufacturers and sometimes put up by their sales organizations or by simple store price-feature cards. Often, manufacturers help a retailer with the construction of a cut-case display by shipping in a display with the appropriate riser cards and other materials in slip-case cartons.

2. *Dump Displays.*   As the term implies, dump displays are open bins or baskets, on the floor or in the form of shelf extenders, which usually contain featured merchandise highlighted by a large and prominently displayed price tag. Some retailers, particularly those discounting health and beauty aids (HBA), set up permanent bin fixtures, often with three or four tiers, that feature salable samples of many products, including some that are competitive with each other. A variant of the dump display is the shopping-cart display, usually reserved for discontinued items or damaged merchandise priced for quick sale.

3. *Prepacked Displays.*   Displays prepacked by manufacturers can be permanent in nature or designed for short use only.

    a. *Permanent display* fixtures are designed to provide a distinctive, away from the shelf home for the products they carry. While considered a long-term proposition in ensuring the continuity of distribution, they do provide marginal promotional values by setting up the products separately, which allows the customer to focus on them specifically. Such displays are usually used for regularly stocked merchandise, with an emphasis on products susceptible to impulse buying.

    b. *In-and-out displays* are usually constructed of corrugated cardboard and are meant to be discarded after the merchandise they contain is sold. If buying is slow, the merchandise may be removed to a shelf or elsewhere in the store to make room for a more active product. Most in-and-out displays remain on the retail floor for a week or two; few make it beyond two weeks. Generally, the displays are tied to other trade and consumer promotional efforts, and they are particularly popular for introducing new products and line extensions.

Count and Recount.   *Count and recount* refers to special payments made to retailers in order to encourage accelerated pipelining of a product from warehouse to retail floor. Merchandise too often is bought by a key account—on a routine or deal basis—and then remains in the warehouse while out-of-stocks develop for the same merchandise on the retail shelf. This situation is particularly painful during the introduction of a new product, when retail distribution may significantly lag behind account authorizations or when successful consumer takeout may generate stock gaps on the shelf: The quicker the takeout velocity, the faster the incidence of out-of-stocks—precisely at the time when introductory advertising activity is at its zenith.

Count-and-recount promotions call for the manufacturer's representative to count and recount stock at retail and pay a special per-unit allowance for merchandise moved out to consumers between the two counts, usually a week apart. The promotion is designed to elicit high levels of stocking during the initial count, hence a high level of initial warehouse withdrawals. Count-and-recount promotions are not particularly popular, since they are hard to control and require a substantial amount of personal sales effort.

Goodwill Promotions

Much of the trade's promotional activity is meant to financially benefit the middleman accounts. Some trade promotions, however, are specifically designed to motivate goodwill and favorable attitudes toward a manufacturer's products on the part of individuals working in various trade channels. For the most part, goodwill promotions are personal incentives of various familiar types.

1. *Contests/Sweepstakes.*   Both trade oriented contests and sweepstakes are structured promotional programs, often focused thematically on an overall "event" designed to allow most persons in the affected channel to win cash, merchandise, or travel prizes.

Conditions for participation must be clearly stated in terms of entry, prizes, quotas, point systems, and any other qualifications. The difference between contests and sweepstakes rests in how prizes are given out. A contest participant receives a specified prize on reaching specific goals; in the case of sweepstakes, participants receive entry blanks and if specific criteria are met, have the opportunity of winning a prize in a drawing. Sweepstakes prizes are usually more expensive, and fewer prizes are awarded than in contests.

2. *Premiums.* At times manufacturers pack a premium directed to the dealer with a prepacked display as an inducement for specific merchandising support. The dealer, usually the store manager, may choose to keep the premium for personal use or use it for promotional purposes with store customers.

A variant of such premium programs is the *merchandise catalog*, from which dealers may select merchandise at a reduced price, based on points earned from specific performance levels defined by the terms of the program. A number of companies, such as S&H, known by consumers for its consumer-oriented Green Stamps, are active in the management of merchandise catalog efforts on behalf of manufacturer clients.

Another variant is the *coupon program*, whereby coupons endorsed with orders received from the manufacturer running such a promotion, can be redeemed for merchandise in a way similar to consumers redeeming trading stamps. Catalogs are also used in this type of promotion, but usually no additional payments are required.

Regular premium programs are usually run on a one-time basis. On the other hand, merchandise catalog and coupon programs requiring accumulated performance points span a much longer time period and in some cases are actually continuous promotions.

3. *PM Payments.* PM, push money, payments are made directly by manufacturers to specific retail personnel based on the units of merchandise sold by such personnel to consumers. PM promotions are common in the sale of upscale cosmetics in department stores, mass merchandisers, and large drug stores and are also used by many manufacturers of high-ticket items. PM payments are separate and in addition to any other type of compensation the individual clerk receives from the retail store.

4. *Mystery-Shopper Programs.* Mystery-shopper programs reward personnel in trade channels primarily for point-of-purchase results that benefited from personnel efforts. Checkers, acting and presenting themselves as regular shoppers, monitor stock levels, display activities, the familiarity of personnel with the promoted product or products as well as their readiness to mention the product to shoppers. The checkers dispense rewards on the spot to personnel who meet the criteria. Rewards range from "crisp" $5 bills to certificates for merchandise to chances to participate in travel sweepstakes. Rewards can also be earned by people not on the retail floor, for instance, broker retail representatives.

NOTES

1. A.O. Witteman, "Trends in Testing, Tracking and Evaluating Trade Promotions" (Paper presented at ANA Workshop, New York, 1978).
2. Ernest Obermeyer, "Combating the Promotional Noise Level," *Supermarket News Executive Update*, December 1982, p. 1.

PART THREE

MANAGEMENT OF THE PROMOTIONAL PROGRAM

EIGHT

Researching the Effectiveness of the Promotional Program

The need to know is as critical in the area of promotion as it is in any other marketing area. All marketing activities require corporate commitments of resources, and it has become increasingly important for the high levels in management to be able to judge the efficiency with which these resources are expended in order to set priorities for their allocation among the various marketing areas within the corporation.

Allocation decisions require valid information. Yet despite the growing amount of money spent on promotional activities of all kinds, the decision-making process committing expenditures for promotion often proceed without sufficient regard for or understanding of their potential outcome, In working toward the achievement of specific promotional objectives, one must know—to the extent possible and using available measurement techniques— which promotional tools are most likely to deliver the desired results and, after a program is executed, whether the results were obtained as planned. Further, since promotional strategies, as all strategies, are more than a series of tactics joined end to end, promotion measurements must be viewed, weighed, and positioned as part of the overall marketing strategy for the product or line involved.

243

An earlier chapter detailed the tremendous growth already taking place in promotional expenditures, with the indications that this growth will continue, perhaps exponentially, for years to come. Estimates of $60 billion by 1985 are certainly within the range discussed at most professional gatherings and in the trade press. Even with such explosive growth in promotional activities, the promotional area remains underresearched.

Roger Strang's report at the 1977 Association of National Advertisers (ANA) Promotional Testing/Evaluation workshop covered 55 leading corporations.[1] Strang reported that 20% of these corporations did not budget money for promotional research and evaluation and that the average expenditure of the companies who did was limited to about 1% of sales. Since that report, only marginal improvement can be detected in these figures. Also, since Strang's research was limited to a handful of major companies, it is likely that promotional research among all corporations marketing products in the United States is even less prevalent.

Over the years, much of the resistance to testing as well as to the pretesting of sales promotions was based on several fallacies. At the same 1977 ANA workshop, it was noted that "consumer sales promotions are not tested or pretested with the same intensity and serious consideration given a new product, an advertising campaign, or a marketing plan," and the author then critically discussed some of these fallacies.[2]

Fallacy 1.   There Isn't Any Time to Test

No one questions the fact that consumer sales promotions usually run on a very tight schedule. However, there is always time to test a promotion. Many tools are available to pretest swiftly and inexpensively a single effort or even a multistep campaign. If the promotion does not lend itself to actual prototypes, one can always resort to concept testing. What must be kept in mind throughout is that, by itself, testing a promotion does not represent a panacea or a substitute for judgment. Testing is used to enhance the odds of success.

Fallacy 2. Pretesting Really Can't Help a Promotion Much

If one can test commercials to find the better concepts and executions among the many that are initially developed, one can also pretest various promotional concepts to select the one or more that will best appeal to consumers. Let's look at it in dollars and cents. If the budget for consumer sales promotions is $5 million per year (not an exaggerated amount today), an improvement in dollar effectiveness of only 10% would translate into a half-million-dollar advantage. Should $50,000 per year be spent on testing in order to generate a half-million-dollar increase in effectiveness? What about a 20% improvement? Or more? Of course, the promotion manager must be willing to develop and review alternative promotions. If only one consumer sales promotion idea is considered, the idea of testing is moot.

Fallacy 3. No One Pays Much Attention to Sales Promotion When Making Marketing Decisions

If marketing management is thought to overlook promotional concerns in making marketing mix decisions, then, indeed, why bother with sales promotion? In fact, such thinking is dying out as promotional expenditures continue to increase at a much faster rate than expenditures on advertising.

Fallacy 4. You Can't Be Really Creative in Sales Promotion. For the Most Part, the Same Proven Promotion Patterns Prevail—So, Why Test?

This fallacy is cherished by persons who say they don't know what creativity means, or who find it easier to repeat promotions which in the past found favor with management. Yet the claim of noncreativity is probably the greatest fallacy of all. Actually, consumer sales promotions allow for greater creativity than is possible with any other marketing tool. They are almost totally open-ended; their boundaries are set by creativity and the amount of money available. By contrast, advertising is limited by media print dimensions or broadcast time clocks, as well as by a forest of rules and regulations far more restrictive and numerous than those faced by promotional activities.

Fallacy 5. It's Such a Creative Area That It Can't Be Tested

The persons who say this are claiming to know it all and assured that their flawless judgment needs no confirmation. Undoubtedly, there are a few—but very few—tremendously creative people who can intuitively develop great national consumer promotions from offices high above the crowds. But even these promotional giants have their share of failures. The objective of consumer sales promotion must be viewed in its simplest terms: moving merchandise at point-of-purchase. Promotional activities are aimed at influencing customer behavior in the marketplace. When a specific stimulus is used to influence behavior, there are always ways of measuring the effectiveness of that stimulus.

Fallacy 6. Market Researchers Are a Breed Apart; I Can Hardly Understand Them When They Talk—How in the World Can They Help Me?

Maybe some sales promotion people have problems dealing with market researchers, and undoubtedly some market researchers fail to understand that their function is to provide actionable information, not impenetrable treatises, to the various marketing functions. If objectives are carefully set and all the elements that need to be researched identified, there is no reason a company cannot educate its market researchers to generate the needed data, or otherwise, direct its data management to hire market researchers for that purpose. Pretesting a sales promotion campaign does not require a long, weighty research project with a great deal of money spent over a period of many months. This sort of research is generally put into large tomes that end up unused on library shelves. Sales promotion research must have immediate relevance. It should be able to give actionable answers quickly, whether it is carried out on a small- or large-scale.

INITIAL STEPS IN DEVELOPING THE RESEARCH PROTOCOL

Proper research requires proper planning. Poorly conceived investigations will usually yield faulty or at least unapplicable data, which either delay the decision-making process or, if time is short, significantly and needlessly increase the risks involved in the taking of actions based on such data. A carefully developed research protocol generally begins with these steps:

1. *Diagnostic Definition of the Promotion Situation.* This diagnosis involves a careful review of both existent and potential problems and opportunities. Such a review may consider specific targets, short-term versus long-term problems or opportunities, trade (distribution and support) and consumer (takeout, market share, and franchise building) considerations, overall shifts in consumer behavior toward or away from a product category, and competitive pressures. Basically then, this step is designed to determine conditions at a given point in time as a necessary foundation to setting up viable objectives leading to the execution of an actionable plan.

2. *Setting Measurable Objectives.* After the diagnostic review leads to the formulation of one or more optional plans of action, attention focuses on the determination of specific objectives to be achieved under these plans. These objectives must allow for measurable performance, both in the pretest stage to monitor the ability of a plan to reach objectives, and in postperformance evaluation.

3. *Determination of Specific Strategies.* Having identified objectives, the problem now is to formulate one or more strategies likely to serve the objective followed by the development of full-fledged plans of action. At this point, checks should be made that all

thinking is in line with overall marketing strategies and plans. Such plans may range from far-reaching, full-fledged promotional campaigns spanning years to limited-objective, single efforts requiring immediate and localized execution. For each plan, determination must be made of the financial parameters under which its performance will be judged successful.

4. *Selecting the Appropriate Research Design.* In measuring promotions, two types of research are primarily involved: *planning research,* or research that helps in developing the most appropriate promotional strategy among optional courses of action, and *evaluative research,* which enables the monitoring of performance of promotions during and after their execution. While planning research utilizes both quantitative and qualitative research tools and may be conducted under either simulated or real-life conditions, evaluative research—consisting of both concurrent and post measures—mostly depends on quantitative measurements obtained in the marketplace. *How much do we need to know?* Critical to any research program is the amount of knowledge required. Regardless of the comprehensiveness of the research protocol and the money spent to implement it, professional judgment is critical in any decision-making situation. Consequently, from the beginning, risk limits must be established as guidelines for implementing the recommendations generated by the research.

> The word "projectibility" is bandied around a lot. To some extent you pay for what you get. Are you likely to get 100% confidence on anything? You probably are not. So how much judgment and how many facts do you want to fit into your decision-making process? Let's ask it differently. How much risk are you willing to take? Are you willing to take the risk that you are 20% wrong and 80% right? Are you willing to take the risk that you are 40% wrong? Obviously, the more you want to reduce the level of risk, the more money you have to pay; the more extensive the research will become.

> If you talk about market testing the translation of a national plan, you can go to 20% or 25% of the country, spend a million dollars, and get relevant results with a level of confidence perhaps as high as 97%. However, do you need that much confidence? If you could obtain the data for only $50,000 and get only 80% confidence, would you be able to effectively work with it?

If it were possible, however desirable, to completely substitute facts for judgments, we could always ask the computer, get our answers, and not be in need of a sales promotion manager in the first place. It could all be done rather routinely. Further, one must guard against seeking information that is not immediately relevant to the decision at hand. It is only too easy to fall prey to the "nice-to-know" syndrome and collect reams of expensive data that end by gathering dust in corporate libraries until they are disposed of in the periodical house cleaning.[3]

Completing the Research Design

Various research tools are available, depending on the intelligence required, and are broadly classified in two groups—planning research and evaluative research.

Planning Research.   Under planning research, the task at hand is to provide decision makers with information that will allow them to develop and subsequently make the best possible selection among alternative promotions. Planning research tools include:

1.   *Focus group sessions* are primarily helpful in providing insights for targeting respondents' reactions to one or more promotional propositions. An excellent tool for helping in the conceptual development of alternative entries, focus group sessions are group meetings conducted by a trained moderator whose task is to generate "inter-reactions" among group members as they address themselves to the promotional stimuli introduced by the moderator. Given the small groups and limited-scale reach, focus group sessions cannot provide conclusive information. But in the hands of a good analyst, this research tool is very useful in spotlighting potential strengths and weaknesses quickly and on limited budgets, and it can provide good support for both planning and creative development.

2.   *Ballot tests* are a meaningful "action" technique to obtain a direct response on a specific number of optional offerings. Ballot tests are primarily used to test or screen consumer premium offers: Various offers are mailed to randomly selected panels of consumers. Return levels are then compared to select the optimum entry. It is desirable that at least one item of proven consumer appeal be

included in the test so that planning can include both relative and absolute terms of reference.

Ballot tests, particularly if large enough panels are used, are fairly indicative of relative potentials. Furthermore, they are generally inexpensive, can be quickly implemented, and provide simultaneous screenings of many items. However, they are very specific in terms of the information generated and can provide little or no insight about potential interactions with other elements in the marketing mix.

3. *Consumer surveys* potentially range from simple, centrally located, highly structured studies concerned with a limited number of factors to complex multifaceted studies seeking motivational direction through mostly open-ended interviews. Basic to all survey research is the survey methodology, which consists, simply, of asking questions by means of interviewing instruments. Surveys may be conducted in person, via the telephone, or by mail. They can be used to gather inputs on a variety of queries about attitudes and potential preferences among promotional ideas and programs. Costs range widely and depend on sample size and selection criteria, the amount of information required, the data collection method used, the extent to which the questionnaire is structured or open-ended, and the degree of data processing specified.

An important characteristic of this research tool is that survey research can provide meaningful measures of interaction with other elements in the marketing mix, in addition to readings on specific promotional ideas or programs. At the same time, responses that indicate how people "intend" to behave in the marketplace fall short of actual behavior in the marketplace. There is no real penalty involved in stating a wrong intention; there is a penalty for buying the wrong product.

4. *Controlled store tests* are in the realm of real-life testing. Observations of consumer behavior and actual purchase decisions in a controlled number of stores can generate considerable information on promotional alternatives. While they fall short of being regular market tests—they are usually conducted on too small a scale for direct projection to a large universe—they are nonetheless useful for obtaining relative readings on an array of coupons and coupon values, pricing differentials, off-label pricing, on-pack

promotions, take-one pads, refund and premium offers, and so on. Further, through careful selecting and matching of stores, controls can be implemented over trade conditions at retail, including shelf position, facings, and pricing. Equally important, by attending directly to the retail floor, these tests eliminate the salesforce performance variable. Controlled store tests take several forms, from simple to complex design, which fit into three groups: side-by-side tests, matched-store panel tests, and market tests.

a. *Side-by-side testing* is the least costly store test and is relatively easy to execute. It involves placing several promotional alternatives—for instance, an on-pack offer, a cents-off label offer, and a salable sample—side-by-side in a store, allowing the consumer to choose the alternative that is most desirable. This kind of testing is used primarily for quick tests of price, merchandise packs, and premium alternatives. Since it runs as a monopanel effort, it is advisable to include, for benchmark purposes, one offer of proven and measured appeal. On the negative side, this testing is subject to bias, since it tends to create some confusion in the mind of the consumer and gives the product being tested retail exposure in excess of its normally achievable levels.

b. *Matched-store panel tests* are more elaborate versions of controlled store tests. Only one offer confronts the consumer in a given panel, allowing him or her to react in a normal buying manner. Stratmar's PROMOTEST® studies are based on multiple panels of five to ten stores each, depending on the number of variables involved. Each panel receives a different test promotion. Stock levels of regular and promotional merchandise are well maintained to prevent out-of-stocks during the audited period. Stock is usually placed in a dump display. For tests with an established product, a two-week benchmark reading is developed for all panels before the promotional entries are brought in. Usually, for additional reference, one or two competing brands are also audited. Consumer takeout of the promotional offers are then determined by comparing the performance of several panels. Often, after the test period is completed, the movement of regular merchandise continues to be measured—the test merchandise has been removed—for several additional periods in order to determine residual effects of the promotion. Such aftermath testing may not be indicated if the product use cycle is protracted.

PROMOTEST originally was developed as a continuous system, on the rationale that benchmarks can be obtained in one product category while alternatives in another are tested. The result could be considerable savings in money and time. It was soon found, however, that few companies would elect a continuous process of developing and testing promotions.

c. *Market tests* are the expansion of store-panel tests to larger areas. The test protocol is also usually expanded beyond the test variables of promotional alternatives to include measurements of alternative marketing strategies. The elements of product, distribution, pricing, and advertising are kept constant in order to obtain reasonably bias-free measures of relative promotional effectiveness. Market testing is an expensive and time-consuming method, even though it does provide meaningful readings of interactions among various elements in the marketing mix as affected by promotional differentials.

Stratmar's MICROMARKET® research vehicle is designed to go halfway toward a full-fledged market test. Distribution is obtained for the test product in all food and drug outlets in selected small communities, usually on the metropolitan fringe. Product movement is constantly monitored and out-of-stock conditions avoided. Advertising and promotional programs, at levels translated from the national marketing plan, are also introduced. Random consumer audits via telephone are made at set periods to measure intent to purchase as well as repurchase plans among those who already bought the product. These audits further provide clearer dimensions of response to specific advertising and promotional stimuli, in addition to qualitative measures of product-in-use satisfaction and dissatisfaction. Clearly, MICRO-MARKET is more than a promotion testing vehicle. Nevertheless, it can be specifically adapted to such a purpose and can be used to test promotions on several products concurrently. Although conducted in markets too small to provide the same level of projectibility as large-scale market tests, such testing does offer actionable indications of feasibility and vitality at a fraction of the cost.

Evaluative Research.   Evaluative research broadly refers to the area of promotional research that concentrates on monitoring actual performance during and after a promotion in order to determine the promotion's effectiveness and to generate insights for improved future efforts. Meaningful monitoring presumes the existence of a set objective, extended over a certain time frame, and evaluators must be prepared to obtain and deal with data generated through a variety of media.

1.   Internal sources should be the first line in the reach for data. The cost and control factors of internal monitoring are generally easier to deal with, and a wealth of information on product shipments—both regular and promotional merchandise—, promotional allocations, levels of response to promotional efforts, and refund and redemption levels are readily available if the company's computer capabilities are fully exploited.

2.   Syndicated sources cover an increasingly broad range of information—from market-wide averages of product movement out of warehouse to the retail floor to consumer homes and from average levels of stocking and inventory assortments to specific measures of movement through specific trade factors. Other specialized syndicated services range from periodic visual checks of distribution to measurements integrating trade features, in-store displays, product movement, and shelf prices.

3.   Special trade studies are commissioned by most manufacturers at one time or another. These studies are special store checks designed to spotlight promotional and sales activities in specific areas, during specific time frames, and often only in selected trade

factors. Store audits differ from single-effort store checks in being more formal and by extending over longer periods of time with periodic readings.

4. Primary consumer research parallels research conducted at account and store levels and enlarges on the information obtained from the trade and on the retail floor. Account- and store-level research tells what is happening and where; consumer research tells why.

NOTES

1. Roger A. Strang, "Future Directions in Sales Promotion Research and Evaluation" (Paper presented at ANA Promotion Testing/Evaluation Workshop, 1977).

2. D. Ailloni-Charas, "The Practical Application of Research" (Paper presented at ANA Promotion Testing/Evaluation Workshop, New York, 1977).

3. Ailloni-Charas, "Research," pp. 1–2.

NINE

Organization of the Promotion Function

Since structure should follow strategy, the proper conduct of the promotional function requires an organizational and administrative framework that facilitates all aspects of promotion planning, execution, and control and integrates well within the overall corporate marketing structure.

THE EVOLUTION OF THE PROMOTIONAL FUNCTION

The recognition of promotional activities as an area deserving management concern has been slow in coming. Structurally, promotion has been viewed—if identified at all—either as a traffic function, primarily necessary to expedite the production of collateral materials, or as a purchasing function, mainly involved in the purchase of premiums. Within corporations, many different groups were charged with handling various aspects of the promotional function as adjuncts, and not very important, at that, to their other activities.

For the most part lacking central focus, promotional activities were poorly conceived, poorly planned, and only marginally effective. If promotional events nevertheless met with some success, it was owed more to the intuitive flair and capabilities of the decision maker involved rather than to a careful approach to opportunity and planning of resources. Unfortunately, the number of Barnums appearing on the promotional scene have been far and few between. Over the years, however, a number of factors played roles in pushing along the development of the promotional function as a separately managed marketing unit.

1. *Transition from a Supplier to a Buyer Market.* The same forces that fostered the marketing concept upon corporate America have also nurtured—as part of that concept—a growing awareness of the role of promotion in moving goods to consumers in an increasingly competitive climate.

2. *Emergence of the Advertising Agency as a Partner in Marketing Action.* Almost by default, advertising agencies have contributed to the definition and establishment of promotion departments in client companies. As advertising agencies won enhanced corporate perceptions of their expertise in the creation and effective dissemination of persuasive communications—critical influences on the development and maintenance of consumer franchises—advertising agencies also found themselves charged with providing promotional support. However, the income of advertising agencies mostly derives from media placements, as a percentage of media buys; promotional responsibilities merely saddled agencies with a "service" they were expected to provide clients essentially free, as part of the total account billings. While the creative and media placement slots on an account, particularly a large account, justify the best talent available, it is harder to make a similar talent assignment to a nonpaying "overhead" function. Although few will allude to agency motivation, it should not be surprising that the origin of many in-house promotion departments was due to the urging that client companies received from their advertising agencies.

3. *Increasingly Diverse and Complex Promotional Tools.* The growing variety and sophistication of promotional vehicles have caused many companies to acquire, internally, the expertise required to handle promotions selectively, effectively, efficiently, and in line with overall marketing objectives. Alternatively, some

companies assign the management of the promotional function to specialized sales-promotion agencies, which provide a promotion service akin to the advertising function served by advertising agencies.

4. *Increased Promotional Expenditures.* As indicated earlier, promotional budgets have steadily increased to the point where they generally exceed the money spent on advertising. High budgets have brought with them increased emphasis on accountability along with the consolidation of various promotional efforts, which had often been scattered throughout a company.

5. *Product Managers' Desires for Quick Returns.* The important role played by product managers in the establishment of separate promotion departments was suggested by Strang in a 1976 Harvard Business Review article.[1] Product managers were primarily concerned with the short-term aspect of product management success, judged by a manager's ability to deliver quick results. Promotion activities that generate accelerated results are finding increasing favor with product managers. Whether short-term hypes are consistent with long-term corporate strategies and what degree of involvement with promotional activities product managers should have are discussed later. Sufficient for this discussion is that such demands for promotional support eventually led to the establishment of separately managed promotion functions.

ORGANIZATIONAL TRENDS: 1978 ANA REPORT

Three generally similar surveys conducted by the ANA in 1957, 1973, and 1978 trace some of the organizational changes that have occurred in the promotion function in the post–World War II period. By and large, as indicated by Bill Lembeck, who was responsible for the 1978 study,[2] these surveys have provided information on organizational structure, the identification of responsibility for various promotion functions, promotion evaluation, and attempts to estimate the promotion dollars spent against both consumers and trade. While these surveys were confined to

ANA members, their findings are reasonably indicative of promotional realities at large.

Organization of the Promotion Function

According to the 1978 ANA study, in approximately a third of the companies responding, the promotion function was supervised by a marketing services department:

Marketing services department	32.1%
Advertising department	28.9
Corporate management	8.8
Product management	5.7
Sales department	4.4
Other	9.4
No answer	13.8

It is estimated that the marketing services department share advanced to over 50% by 1982. However, these figures do not fully represent the increased involvement of product managers in promotions. Neither do they indicate the other functions, apart from promotion, that are served by the marketing services department—for instance, marketing research.

The assignment of primary responsibility for promotional functions is charted below in a comparison of product management and promotion departments:

Promotional Function	Primary Responsibility	
Setting promotion objectives	Product management	66%
	Promotion department	29
Strategy development	Product management	54
	Promotion department	40
Tactical development	Product management	49
	Promotion department	33

Clearly, the closer promotion gets to planning and decision making, the greater the direct involvement and authority exercised by product management.

Further insight is provided by the allocation of budget responsibilities for promotional activities among the various departments:

Department	Setting-Up Promotional Budgets (%)	Control of Promotional Expenditures (%)
Product management	53.5	30.2
Advertising	32.7	37.1
Promotion	20.1	34.6
Sales	15.1	8.2
Other	12.7	12.5

Product management, which looms large in setting promotion objectives, is also charged in most cases with setting-up of the promotional budgets. Advertising management also plays an important role—indeed a dominant one—in financial determination and controls over promotional expenditures in about a third of the companies in this segment of the 1978 survey. The prominent position of advertising largely reflects the historical fact that promotional activities originally represented an extension of advertising. In his study of promotion planners, Strang found that product managers felt they had considerable authority over goal setting and budgeting of promotional efforts, but senior management saw their role in this area as more constrained and primarily limited to the coordination of promotional activities for their brand or brands and contributing to goal-setting and allocation initiatives.[3] The latter responsibility, however, must be viewed as part of the overall planning function each product manager is expected to perform for the brand or brands managed.

Differences by Size of Company

As a company grows larger, so does the capability of its promotion department to assume primary responsibility for promotional activities.

Company Size	Promotion Department Percentage Responsibility for		
	Objectives	Strategy	Tactics
Small	18.2	23.6	29.1
Medium	17.6	35.3	37.3
Large	33.3	41.2	49.0

The same pattern of progression applies to the setting of promotional budgets and controlling of promotion expenditures. The larger the company, the greater the influence of the promotion department in this area.

Company Size	Promotion Department Percentage Responsibility for	
	Setting-Up Promotional Budgets	Control of Promotional Expenditures
Small	10.9	23.6
Medium	21.6	37.3
Large	29.4	45.1

Changing Patterns

The ANA survey indicated specific trends in shifts in primary responsibility for various specific promotional activities. Primary responsibility for both merchandise and money promotions have shifted away from advertising and sales departments to product management and promotion departments.

Department:	Advertising			Promotion			Sales			Product		
Promotion	1957	1973	1978	1957	1973	1978	1957	1973	1978	1957	1973	1978
Premiums	65	34	20	22	38	40	20	4	13	5	16	30
Sampling	46	26	4	14	28	22	39	15	7	11	26	29
Consumer contests	73	40	18	21	28	36	18	3	10	2	16	21
Store demonstrations	30	24	8	18	28	20	51	28	18	5	16	21
Direct mail to consumers	83	48	34	19	29	32	7	1	6	1	15	21
Couponing	69	31	12	17	30	28	23	7	6	4	25	31

Since 1978 the shift in all these areas has continued toward the promotion department.

Primary responsibility for activities involving the production of promotional materials has generally followed a similar trend, although the advertising department continues to show strength, particularly where visual aids are concerned, probably as a result of the more technical nature of the task involved.

Department:	Advertising			Promotion			Sales			Product		
Promotional Material	1957	1973	1978	1957	1973	1978	1957	1973	1978	1957	1973	1978
Point-of-purchase materials	72	39	32	28	35	38	10	3	11	4	15	25
Visual aids	76	39	45	15	21	18	13	3	7	2	14	18

Finally, primary responsibility for promotional activities involving the internal sales organization and the trade continues to show the relatively growing influence of the sales department.

Department:	Advertising			Promotion			Sales			Product		
Trade Promotion	1957	1973	1978	1957	1973	1978	1957	1973	1978	1957	1973	1978
Dealer contests	35	17	13	20	26	23	57	34	38	5	18	19
Sales presentation	63	35	38	14	19	20	6	—	33	3	5	23
Direct mail to trade	74	41	27	21	31	28	18	9	29	2	13	14
Sales contests	22	20	8	21	39	24	72	69	59	4	30	15

Still, these figures fail to reflect fully the continued ascendance of the promotion department, particularly in the consumer packaged goods area. Says Lembeck:

> In the package goods field we broke the questionnaire into four subsegments. On most questions it was broken down into the department responsible for planning, for design, for production or procurement, and for scheduling and control. In virtually every one of those areas the responsibility was either in the hands of product management or the promotion department. In very simplistic terms, planning was almost exclusively the product manager's responsibility, while the promotion department had the responsibility for design, production, procurement, schedule and control.[4]

In the final analysis, continuity over the long haul is critical in the conduct of the promotion function and such continuity cannot be achieved by product managers, whose outlook is short-term.

Integration of the Promotion Function

Today, the promotion function has come into its own, at least in most of the larger companies. While usually viewed as a staff function, promotion tends nevertheless to be integrated in the marketing structure of a company and to be mutually accessible vis-à-vis other unit components in product management, sales, or market research.

The Place of the Promotion Department in the Marketing Organization. Essentially a headquarters function, promotion departments increasingly report to the top marketing functionary, that is, to the director or vice president of marketing. Under such an organizational plan, the manager of the promotion function is on par with managers of the other marketing functions and thus participates on equal footing in the planning and execution of marketing plans as they relate to promotional efforts. Where such an organizational plan has been adopted, promotional thinking and decision-making have been upgraded from mostly junior and clerical levels to higher professional levels. Apart from bringing much needed professionalism to the promotion function, corporate promotion departments have also enabled companies to implement corporate promotion calendars and thus optimize the performance of all promotional efforts. Slotting the promotions required by the various brand groups along the continuum of one single corporate or divisional calendar has a number of salutary effects:

1. Balancing the "load" carried by salespeople who have to present the promotional plans to their accounts and obtain trade support.

2. Balancing-out production schedules, so that promotional plans include enough tolerance to permit some shifting without causing noticeable hardship to any one brand.

3. Increasing the instances of corporate group promotions, whereby several brands cooperate in one promotional program with attendant savings in effort and costs. The use of group promotions has been spreading rapidly in the last few years. A group promotion usually has a central thematic format, which allows such a promotion to be widely advertised and publicized. Obviously, only companies with a large number of product lines can routinely implement group promotions to advantage. Sometimes, group promotions have been coordinated between two or more companies, but these promotions do not enjoy similar effort and cost advantages.

Internal Organization of the Promotion Department.   A promotion department may choose among a number of organizational charts. The department may include product promotion managers, whose duties are primarily the strategic planning and monitoring of promotional programs for their brands, and functional specialists, whose tasks are the efficient managing and applying of specific promotional tools in the service of brand-promotion objectives. The group of functional specialists include:

Premium specialists, whose task is to select, purchase, ensure delivery, and arrange for the fulfillment of premiums.

Couponing and refunding specialists who are assigned to the execution of couponing and refunding programs, the proper redemption of coupons, and the management of day-to-day relationships with redemption and fulfillment houses. The same specialists may also have primary responsibility for the management of an in-house redemption or fulfillment center.

Sampling specialists, who are charged with executing and coordinating all sampling programs—by mail, door-to-door, or in hand. Their duties include negotiations with outside contractors, securing samples through specified production runs and any special packaging that is required, arranging for shipping and at times for local warehousing, and monitoring delivery proofs.

Production specialists, mostly printing experts, who manage the preparation and production of all collateral materials needed for the various promotional programs as well as the design and production of all point-of-purchase signs and displays. In many companies, this production function is performed outside the promotion department by a corporate design and production group. In such case, a production coordinator in the promotion department may nevertheless oversee and expedite the work.

Analytical staff, whose function is to evaluate the performance of promotional programs in order to develop guidelines for future programs. This function is often performed by the market research department, although a specific researcher, either from market research or promotion, should be assigned to this area over the long haul in order to maintain long-term analytical continuity. This type of analysis can also be contracted currently from independent research firms.

Computer specialists—the wave of the future—who are responsible for programming and processing the vast amount of data generated by promotional programs. The advent of computers has resulted in tighter payout calculations and guidelines for better budgeting of estimated expenditures and accruals. As with certain production and market research tasks, actual computer-related tasks may be performed by a central data-processing department. In such case, a coordinator from the promotion department should be responsible for the proper interface of the two departments.

Since the promotion function is still emerging, the five steps suggested by Pearson and Wilson are helpful in making the product management system work better as applied to the promotion department.[5]

1. *Clearly delineate the limits of the promotion department's role and responsibility for the management of promotions.* Limits are particularly critical when the company adopts a corporate promotional calendar system.

2. *Build a strategy-development-and-review process to provide an agreed-to framework for promotion department operations.* As indicated earlier, the development of promotional programs requires strategic planning integral with overall marketing strategy. The strategy development for a brand—including a review of performance in line with objectives—must include proper inputs from the promotion department.

3. *Take into account areas of potential conflict between promotion managers*—those assigned to work with a specified brand or brand groups—*and promotional functional specialists when defining their respective roles.*

4. *Set up a formal process that forces to the top all conflict-of-interest situations among the various promotion managers and promotional functional specialists.* The management of the promotion department is called on, as part of the process, to arbitrate conflicts and make binding decisions.

5. *Establish a system for measuring results that is consistent with the promotion department's responsibilities.* Since the promotion department works in tandem with other marketing groups in bringing about the type of marketing action desired, a level of mutual dependency exists whereby one group's performance or lack of it directly affects the performance of the other groups. For example, if the salesforce cannot generate sufficient on-shelf distribution for a product, the effectiveness of the promotional program to move the product off-shelf into consumer homes is obviously reduced. In this case, measuring promotion by its performance in increasing consumer takeout of this product

does not conform with the promotion department's authority to control performance.

Strang's recommendations for improving promotion management are mostly process oriented.[6]

a. *Analyze Spending.* Such analysis should be regarded, diagnostically, as the first step to more efficient planning and control and should cover all expenses, including opportunity costs caused by revenue loss from temporary price reductions.

b. *Establish Objectives.* Management, Strang says, needs to clearly define the role of promotion in achieving its marketing objectives: "Is it tactical, strategic, or both? Will it be defensive or used for market expansion? What is its relationship to other elements of the marketing mix, especially advertising?"[7]

c. *Select Appropriate Techniques.* One technique or some number in combination may best achieve the specific objective.

d. *Pretest, Pretest, Pretest.* The selection of technique and specific vehicle can be greatly enhanced by pretesting. In fact, failing to pretest may be far more costly in the long run than the cost of research.

e. *Evaluate in Depth.* Planning research and pretesting must be followed up by evaluative research designed to monitor and judge results.

f. *Focus on the Long-Term.* Promotion planning must have a long-term perspective.

g. *Encourage Research.* Experimental research in the general field of promotion will lead to better promotional vehicles and tests of the relation of promotion to advertising and other marketing vehicles.

Staffing the Promotion Department. Except for a handful of university courses, there is little formal education in the field of promotion at college level. Whatever passes for a study of sales promotion is usually contained in one or two lectures in an advertising, basic marketing, or marketing management course.

Professional and trade organizations such as the Promotion Marketing Association of America (PMAA) and the Association of National Advertisers (ANA) have partially filled this need with seminars and conferences. Such presentations, however, are directed to practitioners already in place and are supported by companies which send their employees to them for further honing of skills. Seminars do little to attract new talent to promotion's professional ranks. Although most people coming into the promotion field cross over from brand management, sales, market research, and advertising, no particular pattern exists.

An unfortunate practice of some companies, now mostly in the past, was to steer to promotion any employee they wanted to keep but whom they found less than satisfactory in other marketing functions. That relegation process appears, by and large, to be over. Many of the major manufacturers now boast first-rate promotional departments, and they often recruit from college graduates, who then enroll in well-structured in-house training programs.

The need for promotion professionals will undoubtedly increase manyfold in the next decade or so, after the sharp rise of the last few years. As indicated by Louis J. Haugh in his trade column in 1982: "Because of the growth in promotion, the total number of jobs in the category is believed to have risen substantially over the last five years both with companies and among various service organizations in promotion."[8] Salary levels have also increased, as indicated by the following chart on salary levels of client and agency sales-promotion careers prepared by Edgar M. Joyce, president of Lauer-Joyce, a White Plains, NY recruiter, and printed in Haugh's column:

Client		Agency	
Title	Salary Range ($ Thousand)	Title	Salary Range ($ Thousand)
Promotion assistant	17–22	Assistant account exec*	20–22
Assistant manager	23–27	Account exec	28–32
Associate manager/ manager	30–46	Account superior	40–45
Director of promotion	55+	Management supervisor	55+

*One year experience required

About staff qualifications, Haugh adds:

> In discussing qualifications with industry executives two important attributes are almost always mentioned as key to success. First the candidates must be entrepreneurial and possess a self-starting drive that combines the understanding of risk-taking with the ability to implement. The other is the ability to communicate and present ideas and recommendations effectively.[6]

Managing Promotions without a Promotion Department. Enough companies, particularly small ones, operate in the promotional field without the benefit of an in-house promotion department. Also, in some companies many promotions still are conducted outside their promotion department. In such cases, the responsibility for planning, executing, and monitoring promotions usually falls to the respective brand manager and group. In cases handled by product teams, usually the most junior member of the team is charged with reviewing promotional options and then making specific recommendations for one course of action or another. Therein lies a major weakness. Given the limited practical experience of most junior associates, it is hardly surprising that much that is new in the field of promotion is screened out before it reaches higher levels in marketing management, while the tendency to continue repeating past programs is reinforced. Junior personnel who want to advance generally believe that playing it safe is the better course.

Small companies can compensate for a lack of promotional depth by consulting with a sales promotion agency for help in the conceptualization and planning of promotional events and hiring a supplier company to help in their execution. The firm's advertising agency may also be called on to help. Both supplier companies and advertising agencies also work with companies that have internal promotion departments.

THE PROMOTIONAL BUDGET

Although specific authorizations can be granted from an ad hoc promotional fund, such authorizations should not become a routine procedure whereby promotional programs are executed on a "panic-to-panic" basis. Expenditures for promotional programs should be part of the overall marketing budget—preplanned elements of marketing strategy or contingency allocations for tactical-response purposes. Further, budgeting promotional efforts as part of the overall marketing strategy sets the stage for evaluating the performance of these efforts and making them accountable in terms of bottom-line results relative to objectives. Promotional expenditures can be budgeted by various methods.

1. *Percentage-of-Sale Method.*   More often than not, marketing plans provide for promotional funds for the duration of the plan, as a percentage of budgeted sales—essentially a P/S ratio of total promotional expenditures allowable under the plan. These amounts are adjusted, quarter by quarter or more frequently, as sales figures come in. Usually, it is much easier for management to reduce allocated funds if sales fall below budget than to increase them if sales expectations are exceeded.

The popularity of this approach to promotional budgeting rests in its simplicity. While the objectives satisfied here are the overall objectives of the marketing plan, this form of budgeting does not always detail the specific ways in which the money is to be spent or the specific programs that are to be executed under the plan. These concerns must be tackled subsequently. So, while approval of the promotional budget is obtained at the onset as part of the total marketing budget, specific submissions for programs and actual expenditures are subject to individual authorizations as the marketing plan unfolds.

Sometimes, promotional plans are put together piece by piece, pyramid fashion, until the total amount of money needed to implement all the programs to meet a given sales objective is determined. That total amount may or may not meet the P/S level approvable under the plan, in which case it must be negotiated back and forth until an acceptable compromise is reached.

2. *Allocation-per-Unit Method.*   This budget approach is similar to the percentage-of-sales method, except that the base is in terms of unit sales rather than dollar-volume sales. It is not as simple to use, because the budget is naturally expressed in dollars while the

base is stated in units. It is also harder to reflect factory price fluctuations, which tend to come more frequently during inflationary periods. On the other hand, it is possible to establish several optional levels of promotional expenditures based on alternative product runs in response to variances in demand.

3. *Objective-and-Task Method.* Promotional efforts may be planned both offensively and defensively in order to achieve specific objectives beyond the overall enhancement of a product or brand. In this method, identified tasks are specifically costed out and, generally, authorized either as part of the overall budget or as supplementary allocations. For example, additional trade allowances may be required to forestall delisting in certain major accounts, or additional efforts may be needed to accelerate consumer conversions to an acceptable level.

4. *Percentage-of-Incremental-Sales Method.* The emphasis in this method rests squarely on obtaining incremental sales that may justify promotional expenditures above accepted strategic norms. Under this method, a company may be willing to spend disproportionate amounts of money as a percentage of incremental sales due to promotion. In the paper-goods category, for example, profitibility is closely related to the level of utilization of factory capacity. The higher the utilization, the more profitable the whole product run becomes. For such a manufacturer, it makes sense virtually to give away, through promotional devices, the marginal amount of product needed to lift utilization to higher levels—let us say from 88% to 92%—in order to achieve lower cost-per-unit savings across the board.

5. *Matching the Competition.* Competition is an uncontrollable factor in the marketing equation, but a company must nevertheless be ready to respond quickly to competitive efforts that may endanger one's position in the marketplace. Particularly dangerous is the competitor that fields a hard-hitting promotional program with potential implications for one's short- and long-term positions.

Double-couponing offers, whereby supermarkets allow customers double the discount offered by a manufacturer coupon, became widespread as a way of matching a competitive threat from other trade factors. So did the adoption of trading-stamp plans in earlier years. Competitive promotional thrusts and counterthrusts among manufacturers do not generally lead to the type of continuity trap presented by double couponing and trading stamps. Nevertheless, marketing people must be able to move quickly to deflect competitive pressures. For this reason, contingency funds must be budgeted to allow flexibility of unforeseen promotional action, when and if required. The emphasis in matching the competition is not on how the expenditure fits into the promotional and marketing budget. Rather, the decision centers on how much it will take to defend one's turf and what the opportunity cost will be if one chooses not to respond or to respond at a more modest level.

6. *Investment Spending.* Promotional expenditures in support of new-product introduction are usually included in the heavied-up, front-end investment budget, which is designed to get the product, or service, off the starting block. Promotional objectives here, as well as the objectives of the introductory marketing plan, call for the adoption of the new product and its growth into a viable entry within a given time period. Failure to achieve a payout of this investment within a reasonable time may be indicative of the inability of the new product to reach an acceptable sales/profit level.

Cost Comparisons of Alternative Promotional Programs

Alternative promotional programs can be compared on the basis of common cost denominators. A specific denominator must be selected, then, the unit cost of achieving the denominator must be identified for each of the programs under consideration. The most usual denominator is the cost per purchase or the cost per new buyer. The latter is of particular consequence, since the new buyer is likely to generate a number of "turns" beyond those required to achieve a payout.

Let us take an actual illustration. A specialized hand lotion enjoys a 5% share of the category and the product class itself is used in 50% of households. The promotion manager must recommend one of three sampling approaches designed to increase unit sales and to expand trial/purchase of the brand: door-to-door, by mail in a solo effort, or in-store.

The door-to-door effort consists of 144-sample packing cartons of

TABLE 1. Comparison of Costs for Different Sampling Methods: Gross Costs per Unit Sale and Unit New Buyer

Cost Items	Distribution Costs for 1,000 Samples		
	Door-to-Door	Solo Direct-Mail Program	In-Store Demonstration
Distribution (in thousands)	$240	$109	$220[a]
Samples[b]	100	100	11
Coupons[c]	10	10	10
List costs	—	25	—
Mailers	—	50	—
Packing/shipping	2	2	2
Collaterals	—	—	2
Total costs	$352	$296	$245
Estimated unit sales[d]	90	60	120[e]
Estimated new buyers[f]	65	35	70
Gross cost/sale	3.91	4.93	2.04
Gross cost/new buyers	5.41	8.45	3.50

[a]It is estimated that a distribution of 500/day is feasible in A+ supermarkets and drug stores and in mass merchandisers to category users (50% of all contacts); the in-store program is based on two days per store.

[b]Cost of regular samples is estimated at 10¢/sample. Retail value of tester is assumed to be $3. Given a 40% trade markup and a 70% gross profit, product costs for the 20 units to be used per 1,000 samples are estimated at $11 (figures are rounded up).

[c]Since the liability for coupon redemption is a constant regardless of method used and depends on the cents-off value of the coupons, the cost figure used here is for production only.

[d]While the in-store sampling effort is assumed to reach only category users—others would not be interested and would thus screen themselves out of the program—only 50% of those receiving a nonselective sample by mail or on their doorknob could potentially be users of the brand. The illustration does not take into consideration the pass-along of received but unused samples, the potential use of specialized—and costly—mailing lists or the application of statistical tools—for instance, regression analysis—to the generation of better and hence more productive routes for the door-to-door programs.

[e]This is an estimate of *immediate* sales only. Experience suggests that an equal amount of units will be sold on the average during the 4 weeks after the initial distribution as a direct result of the program.

[f]All sales over 5% are deemed to have been made to new buyers.

272

the product itself, properly and tightly packaged to maintain product integrity and prevent access by little children and a bag to hold the product and coupon and allow it to be hung on doorknobs (the method under consideration is "ring-and-leave"). The sample to be distributed by mail in a solo effort is packed in a mailer for a total weight under two ounces. The in-store program calls for demonstrators to use 50-sample product testers. Each potential customer "experiences" the product by having it sprayed on the back of a hand. Table 1 illustrates the comparative cost figures that help determine which sampling method should be chosen. The specific figures are for illustration purposes only.

Note that in this illustration we assumed that 18% of the category users will make a purchase as a result of receiving a sample door-to-door, while 12% of the category users will do so after receiving a sample in the mail or trying the product during an in-store demonstration.

The figures in Table 1 permit the following comparisons:

Promotion Type	Cost/Sale	Cost/New Buyer
Door-to-door	$3.91	$5.41
Solo direct mail	4.93	8.45
In-store demonstration	2.04	3.50

A further refinement is calculations based on net costs—that is, costs of a program less the gross profit generated by that program. This is shown in Table 2, using the same illustration.

On the basis of these figures in both calculations, the in-store program is indicated over the other two methods. However, costs alone are not sufficient for a final decision. Other important factors affect cost and should therefore be considered:

Which method provides for longer-term sales leverage?

Which program can best be implemented with salesforce capabilities?

Which program provides for deeper, or broader, or better-targeted reach?

TABLE 2.   Comparison of Costs for Different Sampling Methods:
Net Costs per Unit Sale and Unit New Buyer

Cost Items	Distribution Costs for 1,000 Samples		
	Door-to-Door	Solo Direct-Mail Program	In-Store Demonstration
Total costs (in thousands)	$352	$296	$245
Estimated unit/sales per thousand/distribution	90	60	120
Total retail[a]	270	180	360
Total wholesale $(60%)	162	108	216
Gross profit (70%)	113	76	151
Net cost of programs[b]	239	220	94
Net cost/sale	2.65	3.66	.78
Net cost/new buyer	3.67	6.28	1.34

[a]The retail price per unit is $3.

[b]Net figures do not take into account the number of units that would be sold if no promotional program were run; however, the net cost/buyer figure includes, by definition, an adjustment for regular usage/purchase. (Except for unit costs figures are rounded.)

Which program can best be contracted out?

Which program can be carried out most securely with least concern for potential abuse or fraud?

Payout Calculations

Payout considerations represent yet another dimension by which promotional programs are evaluated in the budgetary framework of the marketing plan while providing a way to evaluate and select among various promotional alternatives. To develop the proper payout calculations, both the amount of factory dollars potentially to be generated by the promotion and the gross profit obtained per unit of the product must be known. Further, the conversion figures of new triers to regular usage and the product usage/purchase cycle must be ascertained. Let us take the same illustration used earlier and apply payout calculations to each of the promotional alterna-

TABLE 3. Payout Calculations for Three Different Sampling Methods

Cost Items	Door-to-Door	Solo Direct-Mail Program	In-Store Demonstration
Net cost of program (in thousands of $)	$238.60	$220.40	$ 93.80
Estimated new buyers	65	35	70
Gross profit/unit sold	$ 1.26	$ 1.26	$ 1.26
Number of new buyers converted (50%)	32.5	17.5	35
Gross profit generated every 4 weeks	$ 40.95	$ 22.05	$ 44.10
Number of turns to payout	5.8	9.9	2.1

tives. For the purpose of this example, 50% of new buyers convert to regular usage, and the product usage/purchase cycle averages four weeks.

For comparing the above alternatives, payout periods range from approximately 9 to 40 weeks. Given different criteria for different products other modes of sampling may prove more dollar efficient.

Regardless, it is important to recognize that all promotional efforts, not only alternative sampling vehicles, can be cross-evaluated in terms of relative efficiency per unit of result obtainable, be it sales, new buyers, or payout periods.

NOTES

1. Roger A. Strang, *Sales Promotion—Fast Growth, Faulty Management,"* *Harvard Business Review*, July–August, 1976, pp. 115–124.
2. William Lembeck, "Promotion Management Update '78: Results of the ANA Survey," in *ANA Trends Promotion Workshop Update '78* (New York: ANA, 1978).
3. Roger A. Strang, *The Changing Roles of Promotion Planners* (Cambridge, MA: Marketing Science Institute, 1978).
4. Lembeck, "Promotion Management Update '78," p. 7.

5. Andrall E. Pearson and Thomas W. Wilson, Jr., *Making Your Marketing Organization Work* (New York: ANA, 1967), p. 13.

6. Roger A. Strang, "Sales Promotion."

7. Ibid., p. 121.

8. Louis J. Haugh, "The Undiscovered Profession," *Advertising Age*, August 16, 1982, p. M42.

Author Index

Subject Index

DATE DUE

AUG 3 0 1984		
APR 2 3 1986		
JUN 1 0 1987		
MAR 29 '88		
DEC 4 '89		
MAY 1 7 '90		
OCT 2 4 '90		
DEC 1 7 '90		
APR 2 12 1992 1991		
APR 2 2 1992		
MAY 2 2 1995		

GAYLORD   PRINTED IN U.S.A.